Action Theory for
Public Administration

Longman Professional Studies in
Public Administration
Editorial Advisor: Dennis L. Dresang

Action Theory
for Public
Administration

Michael M. Harmon
George Washington University

Longman

New York & London

ACTION THEORY FOR PUBLIC ADMINISTRATION

Longman Inc., 19 West 44th Street, New York, N.Y. 10036
Associated companies, branches, and representatives
throughout the world.

Developmental Editor: Irving E. Rockwood
Editorial and Design Supervisor: Diane Perlmuth
Manufacturing and Production Supervisor: Robin B. Besofsky
Composition: Book Composition Services, Inc.
Printing and Binding: Fairfield Graphics

Library of Congress Cataloging in Publication Data

Harmon, Michael M   1941–
    Action theory for public administration.

    (Professional studies)
    Includes index.
    1. Public administration.   2.   Social sciences.
3.   Act (Philosophy) I.   Title.   II.   Series: Pro-
fessional studies (New York)
JF1411.H36   350   80-27026
ISBN 0-582-28254-3
ISBN 0-582-28255-1 (pbk.)

Manufactured in the United States of America
9 8 7 6 5 4 3 2 1

Acknowledgments

Excerpts on pages 49–50, 51, 62, 178–79, and 179–80 from "Action Theory in Practice: Toward Theory without Conspiracy" by Bayard L. Catron and Michael M. Harmon, paper presented at the Annual Meeting of the American Society for Public Administration, Phoenix, Arizona, April, 1978. Reprinted by permission of Bayard L. Catron.

Excerpts on pages 88–91 from *A Theory of Justice* by John Rawls. Copyright © 1971 by Harvard University Press. Reprinted by permission of the publisher.

Excerpt on page 117 from "Beyond the Fringe, '64," Capitol Records, 1964, and M.C.A. Records Limited.

Excerpts on pages 132–33 and 136 from *The Social Construction of Reality* by Peter L. Berger and Thomas Luckmann. Copyright © 1966 by Peter L. Berger and Thomas Luckmann. Reprinted by permission of Doubleday & Company, Inc.

Excerpts on pages 175 and 176–77 from "Public Administration and the Challenge to Reason" by L. Vaughn Blankenship in *Public Administration in a Time of Turbulence* edited by Dwight Waldo (Chandler). Copyright © 1971 by Harper & Row, Publishers, Inc. Reprinted by permission of the publisher.

Excerpts on pages 182–83 from "Toward Public Administration Rather Than an Administration of Politics: Strategies for Accountable Disaggregation to Achieve Human Scale and Efficacy, and Live within the Natural Limits of Intelligence and other Scarce Resources" by Robert P. Biller in *Agenda for Public Administration* edited by Ross Clayton and William B. Storm. Copyright © 1979 by University of Southern California Press. Reprinted by permission of the author.

v

Contents

Foreword

For almost a quarter of a century, administrative theory discussions have presented little more profound than doubts about the value of the dichotomy between politics and administration. Those who theorized were at their best when explaining what public administration was not. What they offered descriptively and prescriptively had fatal flaws and serious limitations. In a bold, refreshing, and challenging way, Michael Harmon has broken from this pattern.

Harmon takes head-on two vexatious problems in public administration: the need to relate theories to practice and the need to integrate values into what many regard as a science. Harmon's action theory begins with the most basic experience of public administrators, namely the face-to-face encounter that requires a decision, a reaction, or a plan. This is not just a theory that applies to senior level policy makers. This applies as well to what have become known as street-level bureaucrats. Harmon encourages us to understand the meaning behind the actions administrators take in these encounters. To gain such an understanding of ourselves and others, Harmon provides a conceptual framework for viewing the relationships between an individual's values, knowledge, and psychological capacities to take action and risks. This framework also includes the interaction between individuals and their environments. Harmon's action theory is comprehensive without being confusing, and it is practical without being pedestrian.

Harmon's previous published works have been concerned with social justice, equity, and the actions of administrators. This concern is also central in this book. What we are presented with is not only a guide for considering values in policymaking, but also a framework for exercising discretion in policy implementation. A key argument is that the configuration of values involved in the face-to-face encounters should take precedence over more general or aggregate choices. This is carefully argued, fully cognizant of the conflict between this prescription and the mandates of traditional thought in public administration.

This book is particularly timely and relevant. Although it addresses issues that cross the boundaries of historical periods, Harmon's work appears at a time when his optimism for choice, creativity, and social justice in even the most rigid circumstances is important. It is now commonplace to observe that we are in a period where the scope of government activity will shrink. A retrenchment in government resources has begun. The politics of scarcity and cutting is likely to be mean and desperate. Self-interest and survival are likely to be the most prevalent concerns. In this setting, the hope and the challenge presented by Michael Harmon, based on an assessment of reality and not just on a set of preferred goals, is invaluable both to public administrators and educators of public administrators.

Dennis L. Dresang
University of Wisconsin-Madison

Preface

One of the more pleasing aspects of my study of public administration was the realization, beginning in 1963, that the field afforded some unexpected intellectual opportunities. They were unexpected in view of my previous and largely uninformed impression that public administration was a predominantly technical and impersonal activity. Not only did I soon find this was not the case, but I also sensed that one of the reasons for the existence of those opportunities was the field's ambivalence—and, to an extent, its naiveté—about the role of theory. Unlike the more established social science disciplines, in which the theoretical battle lines were sharply drawn, the relative absense of theoretical sophistication and coherence in public administration seemed to induce a receptivity to novel perspectives that was largely absent in other disciplines. To be sure, there was something called "administrative orthodoxy"; but only a few people took it seriously—except as an implied invitation that it be replaced by something better.

The lack of theoretical orthodoxy in public administration is probably attributable less to its relatively recent intellectual origins than to its continuing concern with problems of administrative practice. The diversity of practical problems in administration has had the happy consequence of making theoretical orthodoxy in the study of public administration an unaffordable luxury. This is not to say that theory is irrelevant to the field. But it does suggest that theory should be grounded in an appreciation of practical affairs so as to encourage critical self-appraisal of administrative practice—by academics and practitioners alike. This capacity for self-appraisal helps clarify the fact that administrative practice is far more than a technical or instrumental activity.

The purpose of *Action Theory for Public Administration* is to provide a context for the critical appraisal of public administration theory and practice. It is a context based on a particular point of view—here referred to variously as the Action paradigm, action theory, and the action frame of reference—informed mainly by interpretive sociology, phenomenology, symbolic interactionism, and other so-called antipositivist schools of thought in the literature of social science. The book undertakes the task of elaborating a theoretical approach to the field of public administration, based on a radical departure from the theoretical viewpoints that traditionally have been dominant in the field. The intended audience for the book includes both academics concerned about public administration as a self-aware field of study and practicing administrators who wish to reflect upon the moral-ethical aspects of their professional activities. Both audiences are equally important, especially in view of a central theme that permeates the book, namely, that the gap between administrative theory and administrative practice is a theoretical as well as a practical problem.

The early chapters present a fairly simplified synthesis of the action approach and related orientations in social thought that are already rather fully developed in other disciplines. The expectation that the book may make an original contribution lies primarily in its application of the action frame of reference to a novel reassessment of some issues traditionally regarded as important to public administration. These issues include administrative discretion and responsibility, decision rules and organization structure, and styles of administrative behavior. Finally, it is my hope that the book will stimulate an appreciation of the importance of theory to practical affairs of administration, both as a guide to informed action and as a device to enable critical reflection.

At various stages of the preparation of the manuscript, a number of colleagues, students, friends, and relatives gave generously of their time in offering helpful suggestions and criticisms. In the many instances in which I followed their advice, the manuscript was greatly improved. In those instances in which I ignored their advice, I fear that I have done so at my peril. In any event, I gratefully acknowledge my appreciation to Bayard L. Catron, Veronica Elliott, Bruce L. Gates, Robert T. Golembiewski, Carolyn Harmon, M. Judd Harmon, Jerry Harvey, Richard T. Mayer, Astrid E. Merget, Victoria Ann Singer, Susan J. Tolchin, Peter B. Vaill, Dwight Waldo, and Orion F. White, Jr.

Martha Glass and Suzanne Crane demonstrated remarkable patience, speed, and accuracy in typing the manuscript. I appreciate also the assistance of Dean Norma M. Loeser of the School of Government and Business Administration, George Washington University, who provided the funds for the typing. Finally, my thanks to G. Bruce Doern, director of the School of Public Administration, Carleton University, Ottawa, Canada, for both his financial and personal support during my sabbatical year, in which much of the book was written.

Michael M. Harmon

1

Introduction

In its formative years as a field of study and practice, American public administration was not only confident of its potential as a positive force for improving the administration of government but also certain of its political and moral legitimacy in performing that role. What is now called the Classical era, or paradigm, of public administration derived its theory of values from academic political science and, more generally, from constitutional democratic theory. Even before Woodrow Wilson,[1] the intellectual founder of American public administration, the role of administration in democratic government was clarified by John Stuart Mill,[2] who asserted the politically neutral character of administration and the accountability of administrators to elected heads of government. "Policy-administration dichotomy" was the term coined to describe the process by which political or "value" issues are decided by elected officials and implemented, efficiently and obediently, by professional appointees. The framework of accountability implied by the dichotomy was a logical extension of the theory of representative government: elected representatives are accountable to the public at large by means of the ballot box; administrators are accountable to the representatives by means of a hierarchical system of controls, rewards, and punishments. The belief of Classical public administration in its legitimacy as a professional and academic enterprise was the result of a largely unchallenged acceptance of the basic principles of representative government from which administrative values derived, as well as the fact that those values were quite simple and straightforward. However difficult they may be to attain in practice, the values of efficiency and obedience are fairly easy to comprehend, at least in the abstract.

The adherents to the Classical paradigm were confident about its promise to improve the efficiency and overall quality of administration because of the enchantment with science on the part of public administration and the society generally. In the *study* of administration, the scientific method offered the formula by which truths about the way organizations functioned could be discovered. The *practice* of administration, because of its isolation from the political process, could with the aid of science formulate the "one best way" of management.[3] These, at any rate, were the prevailing beliefs of administrative orthodoxy.

As governments grew larger and more complex (illustrated most dramatically in the United States by the advent of the New Deal), the euphoria of the Classical paradigm dissipated. The "breakdown" of the policy-administration dichotomy was widely proclaimed, resulting in growing skepticism about the adequacy of the principles of representative government as the sole normative basis for administration, as well us about the ability of science to comprehend, much less improve, administrative practice. This is not to say that the Classical orthodoxy was entirely abandoned. It persists, albeit in a weakened condition, while the search for fresh approaches continues. Although no consensus has formed around a new alternative, hard questions and issues are still being addressed. In their resolution rests the hope, at least for some, that new approaches to the theory and practice of public administration will be better suited to its radically altered political and social context.

Four sets of questions that bear on the reconstruction of American public administration deserve special consideration. While these questions are more often asked by academics than by professionals, they relate in important ways to the quality of administrative practice. The manner in which these questions are answered will provide important clues about the directions in which public administration theory and practice are headed. They are also the subjects of this book.

- Can academic public administration assist in improving administrative practice? Can the "gap" between theory and practice be closed?
- Should public administration as an intellectual endeavor be regarded as an academic discipline or a professional (applied) field? What are the benefits and other consequences associated with each of these alternatives?
- In view of the breakdown of the policy-administration dichotomy, and the consequent discretion required by administrators in making what are inevitably political or value decisions, does the field require a new theory of values? In the absence of clear goals and

standards, what does it mean for an administrator to act responsibly?

· Is the scientific method really useful in developing an accurate understanding of public organizations? Can scientific principles assist in improving administrative practice?

Instead of answering these questions fully in this introductory chapter (the eight chapters that follow will attempt to do that), I need only note here that each of the four sets of questions cannot usefully be addressed independently of the other three. They are all intricately interrelated and to address any one in isolation only results in propping up the Classical paradigm, which, by most contemporary accounts, is a futile exercise. The following comments illustrate how and why the questions are interrelated and provide a hint of the more elaborate argument that follows.

· To be genuinely helpful in improving administrative practice, theory must be conceptualized as theory *for* practice. Positivism, the dominant model of the scientific method on which most social science theory is based, is an inadequate model for practice theory. Thus, the so-called theory-practice gap in public administration is a *theoretical* as well as a practical problem.

· Public administration should be regarded *neither* as an academic discipline *nor* an applied field. Academic disciplines, as usually defined, are implicitly based on the positive science model, which is incapable of assisting, and in some ways detracts from, the improvement of practice. Because of their instrumental view of practice, applied fields necessarily deal inadequately, if at all, with fundamental moral-ethical concerns. The debate over academic discipline versus applied field, in short, is irrelevant and misleading.

· In view of the breakdown of the policy-administration dichotomy, administrative practice should be recognized as involving far more than the instrumental attainment of predefined ends. Administrative practice is a form of moral and committed action whose proper understanding and evaluation requires both a value theory and a theory of knowledge not readily inferred from the Classical paradigm.

· Not only is the positive science model of doubtful use in *improving* administrative practice, it is also incapable of *comprehending* practice scientifically in its most important sense: as a type of social action.

The basis for these assertions is embodied in a proposal for what will be termed an Action Theory paradigm for public administration. The purpose of the paradigm is to outline an intellectual approach to public administration that effectively integrates the social scientific concerns of the field with its long-standing commitment to improving administrative practice. This will be accomplished by articulating the essential features of a theory of knowledge and science (epistemology) quite different from that which underlies the current mainstream of social science and administrative thought. In addition, a theory of values will be presented that, while incorporating some of the Classical normative concerns of the field, is grounded in a view of human nature that derives its logic and support from intellectual vantage points far removed from traditional normative thinking in public administration.

In view of some justifiable criticisms of the natural science conception of paradigms (popularized by Kuhn [4]) as an appropriate metaphor for social science and practice, "paradigm" is redefined in chapter 2. The idea of paradigm, in substantially altered form, is a valuable device for clarifying interrelationships among epistemologies, value theories, modes of social action, and administrative practice. The redefinition of paradigm is the subject of the first of eighteen propositions that constitute the Action paradigm and the overall argument of the book.

THE PROPOSITIONS

1. In public administration, regarded both as a branch of social science and as a category of social practice, *paradigms* are appropriately conceived as theories of values and knowledge whose purposes are to improve administrative practice and integrate types of theory.

2. Beliefs about human nature are central to the development of theories in public administration as well as all other branches of social science. In order to provide the foundation for developing and integrating epistemology with descriptive and normative theory, these beliefs should be ontologically grounded rather than selected for reasons of convenience.

3. The primary unit of analysis in social theory should be the face-to-face situation (or encounter), which is preferred over the individual and more encompassing units of analysis such as the group, the nation-state, or the "system."

4. People are by nature active rather than passive, and social rather than atomistic. This means that people have a measure of autonomy in determining their actions, which are at the same time bound up in a social context. This social context is necessary not only for instrumental purposes but also because it defines people's status as humans.

5. People's "active-social" nature implies an epistemology (i.e., ground rules for determining the validity of knowledge), which

focuses on the study of subjective meanings that people attach to their own actions and the actions of others.

6. Description and explanation in social science should be primarily concerned with *action,* a concept that directs attention to the everyday meanings people give to their actions.

7. The concept of action provides the basis for challenging the adequacy of social science theory whose fundamental orientation is toward the observation and analysis of behavior.

8. The primary conceptual issues in the development of a theory of values for public administration are the relation of substance to process and of individual to collective values.

9. The primary value in the development or a normative theory for public administration is mutuality, which is the normative premise deriving from the face-to-face relation (encounter) between active-social selves.

10. Just as descriptive theory about larger collectivities is derivative of the encounter, so too should normative theory about those collectivities be derived from mutuality, the normative expression of the encounter. The idea of social justice is the logical extension of mutuality applied to social collectivities and should therefore be regarded as the normative premise underlying "aggregate" policy decisions made by and implemented through public organizations.

11. Although public administration shares certain assumptions with all other branches of social theory and is bound by common epistemological rules, its uniqueness stems from its primary practical and theoretical concern with the rules and processes used in making and legitimating decisions in public organizations. Decision rules and institutional processes associated with them are the primary ingredients of organization "structure." Five kinds of rules are or can be employed in public organizations: hierarchy (unilateral decision), bargaining or market rules, voting, contract, and consensus.

12. The selection of decision rules is the fundamental normative decision in determining the structure of public organizations. The effect of particular decision rules on the quality of the *processes* by which social meanings are negotiated and the compatibility of various rules with the normative theory of the Action paradigm are the primary criteria for the normative assessment of decision rules. The *consensus* rule logically satisfies these criteria better than the rules of hierarchy, bargaining, voting, and contract.

13. Administrative responsibility is the major concept ordinarily employed in the normative assessment of administrative ac-

tion. In the Classical public administration paradigm, responsibility implies various mixtures and three conceptually distinct meanings: accountability, causation, and moral obligation. Classical definitions of responsibility are subject to criticisms implied by aspects of the Action paradigm discussed previously: the active-social conception of the self, the normative preference for consensual and disaggregated decisions, and the critique of action conceived exclusivley in rational-instrumental terms.

14. Criticisms of classical responsiblity implied by the action approach suggest an alternative and normatively preferred meaning of responsible administrative action, namely, personal responsibility. Personal responsibility implies that actors are *agents* who must bear the moral brunt of their actions, rather than shift the blame or responsibility to other people or external standards of "correctness." While the concept of personal responsibility is derived from and supported by various elements of the action approach, classical meanings of responsibility are nonetheless necessary, but in a normatively subordinate position. The crucial "institutional" task is to manage effectively the tension between personal and classical notions of responsibility.

15. *Irresponsible* administrative action is rooted in the cognitive processes that lead people to deny or simply not comprehend personal responsibility for their actions. These processes constitute the problem of *reification,* that is, the tendency to view systems, institutions, roles, and other social artifacts as both existing and having legitimacy independent of the intersubjective processes people actually use in creating, sustaining, and transforming them.

16. Administrative action is explainable in terms of the relationship between situations or contexts as perceived by administrators and their predispositions both to initiate projects and to respond to claims and demands originating in their environments. An administrator's "style" is defined as an interrelated set of predispositions toward initiative and responsive action growing out of the administrator's emotional and cognitive development, values, knowledge, and experience.

17. Prominent role prescriptions (or "ideal-typical" styles) in the public administration literature may usefully be differentiated according to their orientations toward *initiative* and *responsive* action.

18. The preceding propositions constitute an outline for an Action Theory paradigm for public administration. The integration of its assumptive, explanatory, and normative elements satisfies

the criteria of paradigm status and adequacy noted in the first proposition. It provides a framework within which "applied" theory and administrative practices may be developed and critically evaluated.

A COMMENT ON THE SCOPE OF THE THEORY

A persistent problem in the development of general theories of public administration is to determine the boundaries that properly and realistically define the limits and scope of the field. While accusations of excessive breadth or narrowness of scope may in some instances reflect simply a peevish preoccupation with academic territoriality, in other instances such charges surface legitimate substantive issues and should be taken seriously.

It is likely that this volume will invite criticisms that its scope is both too broad *and* too narrow. That is, on the one hand, the thrust of the argument may be viewed as too "political" because it attempts to justify a position that, in the minds of some, confers an excessive amount of decisional discretion to public administrators; on the the other hand, the book may appear to ignore larger political, social, and economic inequalities that make futile any attempts to alter administrative institutions in socially consequential ways.

Concerns that the Action paradigm, as represented by the eighteen propositions, is too broadly political will not be addressed in this chapter; these concerns are explicitly dealt with in virtually every succeeding chapter. Criticisms of the opposite kind, that the scope of the book is too narrow, deserve immediate comment, inasmuch as answers to them are not as clearly implied in later chapters.

This book is generally limited to issues over which nonelective public officials might exert considerable influence—to some extent independently of (and sometimes in concert with) representatives of the political and economic spheres. The question, then, is whether the kinds of administrative changes implied in the book would be of trivial consequence without prior actions leading to a more equitable redistribution, on a massive scale, of political and economic resources. Can problems of alienation between social service recipients and service providers, for example, be ameliorated without first eliminating the larger social and economic inequalities that presumably gave rise to them?

Despite the patent legitimacy of widespread concern about these inequalities, their elimination is not an absolute precondition for meaningful administrative change (although their elimination would certainly help). Nor is the reduction of economic inequality, measured in terms of material things, a guaranteed solution to problems of social alienation and disaffection, which, after all, afflict both rich and poor alike, and advanced democratic-socialist countries as well as all others. Thus it is urged that the reader adopt a nonreductive view about the causes and cures of social ills and grant that the administration of government institutions is one place, among many, to begin or continue the quest for a just social order. Although particular theories and strategies for bringing about comprehensive social, political, and economic changes may sometimes seem to be logically compelling, they may be moot as a practical matter. In view of their relative scarcity, opportunities for social change should be seized upon when and where they appear, regardless of whether the actions taken in the light of those opportunities conform to a grand design. Organizations of government are among the most important of those opportunities currently available.

CHAPTER SUMMARIES

Chapter 2, "A Redefinition of 'Paradigm' for Public Administration" (proposition 1), criticizes the natural science conception of paradigm as an inadequate basis for understanding social science and social practice. An alternative meaning of paradigm is presented, which proposes that the primary purposes of *public administration* paradigms should be to clarify the relationships among various categories of social science theory and provide an epistemology and a theory of values relevant to the improvement of administrative practice.

Chapter 3, "Human Nature, Epistemology, and Social Science" (propositions 2 through 5), "grounds" public administration in social science theory. The "face-to-face encounter" is proposed as the basic unit of analysis in social theory. The encounter, in turn, provides the framework within which various conceptions of the "self" (human nature) and epistemologies (assumptions and rules governing scientific inquiry) are described and evaluated. An "active-social" conception of the self is proposed as the logically preferred view of human nature, followed by a recommendation for an "intersubjective" epistemology, which focuses on the everyday *meanings* and understandings that people give to their own actions and the actions of others. Epistemologies and views of human nature, even (and perhaps especially) when they are implicit, constitute the basic assumptions of all social theory. Invariably the assumptions profoundly influence the character of social theory and practice.

Chapter 4, "Action and Behavior" (propositions 6 and 7), begins by distinguishing between the ideas of behavior and action. *Behaviorist* social science assumes that what people do is explainable in terms of external stimuli or causal forces, thus minimizing if not excluding the significance of intrinsic motivational factors. The concept of *action* provides a satisfactory alternative to behaviorism by virtue of its (action's) compatibility with the active-social conception of the self. Action, an idea that directs attention to people's intentions and subjective meanings, provides the basis for a descriptive framework of administrative action consistent with the epistemology discussed in the previous chapter. The chapter concludes with a typology of administrative environments that is a corollary to the administrative action framework.

Chapter 5, "Normative Public Administration Theory: Mutuality, Justice, and Equity" (propositions 8, 9, and 10), explains the relationship of "assumptive" theory (the nature of the self and epistemology) to theories of values. The logical relationship of the encounter between active-social selves (or the "We-relation," as Schutz[5] calls it) to the norms of *mutuality* and *justice* is developed here. Alternative means for logically defending values are critically evaluated; and the relationship between other normative criteria commonly employed in public administration and alternative conceptions of the self are discussed. Other normative criteria are shown to be logically subordinate to the norms of mutuality and justice.

Chapter 6, "Decision Rules," is a development of propositions 11 and 12. The chapter starts with the premise that decision rules, because they are the key formal ingredients of organizational structure, are central to the analysis of decision making in public administration. The first part of the chapter describes five decision rules: hierarchy, the market, contract, voting, and consensus. The second section evaluates the five decision rules on the basis of their compatibility with the normative theory and epistemology of the Action paradigm. Although the consensus rule is shown to be normatively preferred, conditions are specified under which other rules are normatively acceptable. The chapter ends with the argument that epistemology is nothing more than organization theory (decision rules). Consensus, as a process, is the means by which social meanings are intersubjectively agreed upon and other rules, such as hierarchy, imply decisional processes that deny the intersubjective processes by which those agreements are reached.

Chapter 7, "Administrative Responsibility and the Problem of Reification" (propositions 13, 14, and 15), summarizes four definitions of responsibility, a concept traditionally employed in normative assessments of administrative action. The four meanings of responsibility—accountability, moral obligation, causation, and personal responsibility—are shown to be logically connected to the various decision rules previously discussed. Further, the plausibility of each meaning of responsibility derives directly from assumptions about the nature of the self. Of the four definitions, personal responsibility receives the most extensive discussion, owing to its relationship to consensual decision processes and the active-social view of the self. Personally *irresponsible* action is explainable in terms of the cognitive processes by which people deny or fail to comprehend their personal and shared responsibility for their actions. The concept to be used in exploring this problem is *reification*, the cognitive tendency to perceive social phenomena, such as institutions, roles, and principles, as if they were things.

Chapter 8, "Administrative Styles and Role Prescriptions" (propositions 16 and 17), discusses the generic idea of administrative "style." Based on the administrative action framework discussed in chapter 4, an administrative style is defined as a set of predispositions toward administrative action influenced by the administrator's values and general cognitive orientation. The second portion of the chapter presents a typology of "ideal-typical" administrative role prescriptions called the "Administrative Styles Grid." The various role prescriptions are evaluated against the major issues and arguments presented in the preceding chapters, including assumptions about the nature of the self, decision rules, and conceptions of administrative responsibility. A normatively preferred administrative role, called the "Proactive" style, is described, which is supported by the general argument of the book.

In chapter 9, "Action Theory and Administrative Practice" (proposition 18), the implications of the Action paradigm for the improvement of administrative practice are explored by demonstrating how the paradigm satisfies the criteria of paradigm adequacy outlined in chapter 2. The moral-ethical, as opposed to the strictly "instrumental," nature of administrative practice is reaffirmed, and suggestions are made for "non-conspiratorial" approaches to the development and use of theory for administrative practice.

NOTES

1. Woodrow Wilson, "The Study of Administration," *Political Science Quarterly*, June 1887. Wilson's classic essay was later republished in *PSQ* 66 (December 1941): 481–506.

2. John Stuart Mill, *Considerations on Representative Government*, intro. F. A. Hayek (Chicago: Regnery, 1962).

3. In an important volume edited by Luther Gulick and L. Urwick, the spirit of "scientism" popularized at the turn of the century by F. W. Taylor's "scientific management" was extended to public-sector administration. See *Papers on the Science of Administration* (New York: National Institute for Public Administration, 1937).

4. Thomas S. Kuhn, *The Structure of Scientific Revolutions* (2nd ed.; Chicago: University of Chicago Press, 1970).

5. Alfred Schutz, *Collected Papers*, ed. Arvid Brodersen (The Hague: Martinus Nijhoff, 1962), 1:150–203.

2

A Redefinition of "Paradigm" for Public Administration

Scientific theories about complex subject matter almost invariably claim to have, and often do have, an internal integrity whose origin is located in the theories' basic assumptions about knowledge, truth, fact, or nature. These assumptions are *pre*theoretical because, by themselves, they do not explain the subject matter in question; rather, they establish the *ground rules* for subsequent explanations. That is to say, the basic assumptions are the lenses through which the subject matter is seen and interpreted.

Internal integrity is a criterion of a theory's adequacy that holds for scientific investigations of both the natural and social worlds. Although usually regarded as a virtue, the internal integrity of individual theories is often an impediment to weighing the relative merits of two or more theories that purport to explain the same phenomenon. This is because the tightness and complexity of a theory often obscure what is basic assumptions are and shield the theory, especially its basic assumptions, from challenges by its detractors. Thus, advocates of opposing theoretical viewpoints frequently "talk past one another" by failing to recognize the basic assumptions of other, and often their own, theories.

When theoretical disagreements involve conflicts over basic assumptions, the debate may be characterized as a debate about, or between, *paradigms*. The notion of paradigm, initially developed by Thomas Kuhn as a device for explaining historical progress in the natural sciences, has also gained currency in social science disciplines.[1] In public administration, for example, Kuhn's account of the nature of scientific progress, *The Structure of Scientific Revolutions,* served to transform the quest for new theoretical approaches to the field into a search for a new paradigm. That the "Classical *othodoxy*" was relabeled the "Classical *paradigm*" attests to the power of the natural science metaphor in administrative and social science thinking, despite Kuhn's warnings of its limitations. Although he provided no single definition of paradigm, it is useful to summarize Kuhn's general meaning of the term inasmuch as it illustrates how public administration's "intellectual crisis" has been conceptualized in recent years.[2]

By paradigm Kuhn meant, among other things, a framework of basic assumptions—including standards for determining the validity of knowledge, rules of evidence and inference, and basic principles of cause and effect—shared by a scientific community.[3] These shared assumptions determine the correctness of particular methods of scientific inquiry and the admissibility of findings, as well as the questions or problems thought to be important for scientific investigation. In addition to their purely scientific functions, paradigms perform an important legitimating function in the social structures of scientific communities, in a manner akin to mythology and ideology in nonscientific communities.

A "crisis" occurs when crucial problems are found to be unsolvable or unexplainable by an established paradigm. "Normal science," the accumulation of knowledge through research and experimentation within a given paradigm, is disrupted while debate ensues about the fundamental adequacy of the old—now no longer shared—assumptions and beliefs. A "revolution" is consummated when a new paradigm emerges, and is accepted, that is capable of both resolving the problems or "anomalies" for which the old paradigm was inadequate and explaining what the old paradigm *could* explain. Paradigm struggles are political and often bitter because the stakes (the careers and reputations of the scientists) are high and the future direction, not just the methods, of scientific inquiry hangs in the balance.

Few signs are evident promising early closure or agreement among the current contenders for paradigm supremacy in public administration. In fact, it is doubtful, for reasons to be noted shortly, whether the idea of paradigm as depicted in descriptions of the natural sciences is fully appropriate as a metaphor for understanding theoretical debate in administration or, for that matter, social science generally. Both as a field of academic study and as a category of social practice, public administration is sufficiently different from the natural sciences that one is obliged to be judicious in inferring lessons from Kuhn's analysis, and in accepting some of his various meanings of paradigm, as applicable to public administration. In other instances, however, Kuhn's ideas may serve as a highly useful point of departure for assessing the internal integrity of theoretical approaches in the field. A definition of terms and the terrain of public administration, especially as it contrasts with natural science, is thus required.

· *Public administration is a category of social practice.* To the extent, then, that significant differences exist among the proper ways of understanding the actions of people, on the one hand, and the bahavior of physical objects, on the other, the meaning of paradigm as applied to the social world should reflect an appreciation of those differences. Practice, as opposed to behavior, implies some volition or intent on the part of the subjects being observed, which is absent in objects. This difference between theory appropriate for the social as opposed to the natural sciences is currently a crucial and "paradigmatic" issue *within* the social sciences, including public administration. By explicitly reconstituting the concept of paradigm in ways germane to *social* theory and practice it is possible to avoid the pitfalls of uncritically assuming the applicability of natural science assumptions and methodologies to public administration.

· In addition to being a category of social practice, *public administration as an academic field is also the self-conscious study of that practice.* For this reason, public administration paradigms involve both the practices of administrators and *"scientific* practice" (i.e., the systematic *study* of that practice). In his account of the progress of natural science, by contrast, Kuhn was concerned about scientific practice but not, understandably, about the practice of the objects or natural phenomena being studied.

· *As a category of social practice, public administration is more or less distinguishable from other such categories by virtue of its primary concern with social practices taken in, or through the auspices of, institutions charged with a public purpose or otherwise accountable to the "will of the state."* The idea of "publicness" implies that mechanisms of accountability or other means of obtaining public agreement exist, either in fact or in principle, for determining the efficacy or legitimacy of such practices. An additional characteristic of paradigms concerned with aspects of the social world, therefore, is that they include assumptions, beliefs, or principles about the moral legitimacy of their particular domains of practice.

· In view of these definitional statements, the question arises whether Kuhn's general meaning of paradigm is encompassing and flexible enough to include the study and practice of public administration and to illuminate important issues about the field. Irrespective of what Kuhn's intentions were regarding the scope of the applicability of his conclusions, it is evident that he used the idea of paradigm to convey a wide range of meanings. Masterman, for example, has identified twenty-one meanings of paradigm used in *The Structure of Scientific Revolutions,* several of which appear to be highly relevant to the theory and practice of administration.[4] At various points in Kuhn's book Masterman finds the following senses, among others, in which paradigm is used: "as a 'philosophy,' or constellation of questions" (p. 62 in Masterman); "as a source of [conceptual or instrumental] tools" (p. 63); "as an organizing principle which can govern perception" (p. 65); "as a general epistemological viewpoint" (p. 65); "as a new way of seeing" (p. 65).

Taken together, these meanings stress the importance of basic assumptions about inquiry that are no less characteristic of the social sciences and public administration than they are of the natural sciences. Moreover, an analysis of these assumptions, insofar as they influence the character and internal integrity of paradigms dealing with social practice, has more than simply intellectual or theoretical significance. Basic assumptions underlie not only science and theory; they are also imbedded in social practice and social institutions. As a result, they have important social consequences, the explication of which should be of some concern to those interested in a critical examination of the field of public administration.

PROPOSITION 1. *In public administration, regarded both as a branch of social science and as a category of social practice, paradigms are appropriately conceived as theories of values and knowledge whose purposes are the improvement of administrative practice and the integration of types of theory.*

Proposition 1 suggests that the idea of paradigm, with some refinement, may be useful in clarifying both the social-scientific and the moral-ethical nature of public administration. Paradigms may be helpful in clarifying, for example, the ways in which various kinds of theoretical and practical concerns are interrelated. Before discussing how these concerns may be illuminated by a revised conception of paradigm, however, some attention is given here to three objections that the advocacy of paradigms in public administration may invite.

First, assuming for the moment that the idea of paradigm is generally relevant to an understanding of theoretical progress and conflict in public administration, the *advocacy* of paradigms before the evidence is in, so to speak, may be argued to be inappropriate. At least as Kuhn described them, radically new beliefs and assumptions *emerge from* findings revealed by crucial experiments. They achieve what might be considered to be paradigm status only after research and experimentation are conducted—and often only gradually as the increasing weight of evidence lends support to them. For this reason, the before-the-fact advocacy of a particular paradigm may appear to be hubris, if not an outright contradiction in terms.

Clearly, certain liberties are taken in redefining the idea of paradigm if one proposes that they may be advocated "before the fact." Such a departure from Kuhn's interpretation may be warranted, however, in view of distinctions noted earlier between public administration and natural science. Public administration theory must encompass value issues and practical concerns highly dissimilar from those of the natural sciences. Value questions, especially, cannot be settled by ''the weight of evidence'' since empirical evidence presupposes agreement on the nature of the problem to be solved. Even among competing paradigms in the natural sciences, Kuhn notes that agreement on the nature of the problem is often difficult to attain.[5] In public administration, or indeed any social science, the difficulties in reaching agreement on problem definition are greatly compounded because what people *value* is the primary source of disagreement. While it is certainly true that values may, to an extent, be ''discovered'' or informed by the evidence of experience, the varied and highly subjective nature of that experience means that value issues such as those that bear on public policy questions cannot be settled on the basis of findings from a crucial social experiment. Assuming, for example, that agreement could be reached on methodological issues and findings related to research hypotheses in income maintenance studies, such agreement would by no means point automatically to policy solutions in the area of welfare reform. Such findings would be interpreted not only on the grounds of their methodological and scientific adequacy but also in terms of the value stances of policy makers and policy analysts. These value stances, moreover, are not only highly variable but are often not explicitly formulated in the minds of the actors.

The central position of values in public administration—construed here both as an area of social science and as a field of practice—suggests that competing paradigms in the field differ most fundamentally on questions and definitions of dominant values. These are mainly philosphical rather than empirical differences, which may, and in fact should, be addressed mainly in terms of philosophical arguments that are logically prior to the evaluation of empirical evidence. This is not to suggest that agreement on social science paradigms defined in this manner could subsequently reduce empirical and practical questions about administration to the level of puzzle solving. It does suggest, however, that the primary assumptions and beliefs of various approaches to the study and practice of public administration should be seen initially as a philosophical problem. Moreover, it also warrants the view that paradigms in the field may be seen as constellations of particular assumptions and beliefs about values. The advocacy and defense of paradigms so defined by and large precede and inform subsequent questions of an empirical and practical nature.

A second objection to the idea of paradigm is that, in proposing paradigms for public administration, their advocates promise more than they deliver. What is more, even if the promises were kept, the profession would be saddled with a rigid dogma incapable of responding to the enormous diversity of problems with which it is confronted. This two-pronged argument places paradigm advocates in a difficult position. A paradigm, according to Kuhn, is a set of assumptions, beliefs, and methods capable not only of resolving anomalies and problems for which a preceding or othodox paradigm was found wanting; it is also capable of explaining and comprehending at least some of those phenomena for which the earlier paradigm was adequate. This is obviously a tall order for any complex domain of inquiry, doubly so when the constituencies of public administration academia—practicing administrators and the public—define so diversely and unpredictably what that domain is.

The claim to paradigm status using virtually any of Kuhn's definitions is ambitious given the distinction he draws between "revolutionary" and "normal" science.[6] A revolution occurs when a new paradigm replaces an old one, a process that culminates in the triumph of not only a new world view and set of ground rules but a new cast(e) of rulers and minions. After the revolution, relative calm ensues with scientists setting about the mundane business of normal science, which consists of solving puzzles made apparent and presumably solvable by the new assumptions and rules.

Paradigm advocates in public administration are thus confronted with the understandable skepticism of others that the acceptance of a new paradigm could reduce subsequent administrative problems to mere puzzle solving. Moreover, the skeptics would probably be appalled if paradigms *could* perform this function. This skepticism is reminiscent of an episode told about a nationally prominent Ivy League professor who taught a graduate-level course in "scope and methods" of political science. Nearly halfway through the semester, a concerned and earnest student remarked that to that point the course had dealt entirely with "scope" (e.g., boundaries of the field, epistemology, historical development of the discipline) and asked when and if attention would be paid to the nitty-gritty methodological techniques the students could actually use in their future research. After pondering the question for a moment, the professor declared (reportedly with tongue in cheek), "We leave that to the *state* universities." The task of normal science, it seems, is akin to that of the "state universities," a task of dubious respectability and challenge to those who are asked to believe that someone else's paradigm has already answered the most interesting and fundamental questions.

Another difficulty for paradigm advocates is that the promise of their proposed alternatives is often remarkably modest, conventional, and undogmatic, especially considering the radical nature of paradigm change implied by Kuhn's account of the history of natural science. Critics of Ostrom's proposal for a "public choice" paradigm of public administration, for example, are more often critical of the conventional nature of his preferred assumptions than they are of any unitary and dogmatic theory of truly Kuhnian proportions implied by his analysis.[7] It is likely, however, that the critics' knives would be equally sharp had Ostrom's claims for public choice been more sweeping than they were. Paradigm advocates whose theories are measured against Kuhnian standards, it seems, are damned if they do and damned if they don't.

A third objection to the idea of paradigm is that public administration is more properly conceived as a profession than a science. Relatedly, the day-to-day concern with the practical problems of administration makes unnecessary and self-defeating explicit attempts to develop and defend theoretical or scientific paradigms. This argument appears to be supported indirectly by Kuhn's recognition that no single scientific paradigm can provide guidelines appropriate to the full range of inquiry in a given field. Similarly, given the vast range and diversity of values, questions, and world views in public administration, it is doubtful whether any paradigm could be sufficiently comprehensive either to encompass all the above or to reduce concrete problems of administration to mere puzzle solving.

As far as it goes, this argument is helpful in alerting us not to expect too much from paradigms, especially if they are intended to span an entire discipline. Indeed, it is one reason why Golembiewski[8] has proposed "mini-paradigms" for public administration, similar to Merton's[9] suggestion several years previously for the development of "middle-range" theory in sociology. What is unfortunately glossed over, however, is the crucial nature of the relationship between theory and practice. The implicit assumption seems to be that the current division between academics and practitioners—between theory and practice—may be closed by reducing the *scope* or *level* of theoretical concern. While one may be sympathetic to the view that practice theory should be situationally based, an important paradigmatic issue for public administration is the nature of the relation of theory to practice. The so-called theory-practice gap is fundamentally a theoretical as well as a practical problem seldom discussed in the public administration literature.[10] The task of eliminating the gap has less to do with the level and scope of the theory than with the distinctive nature of social theory in general and theory for practice in particular.

The comprehensiveness of any given paradigm is limited by the extent of agreement both on its basic theoretical assumptions and on the kinds of questions that its supporters believe to require answers. Given the contradictory nature of their basic assumptions, competing paradigms cannot be collapsed into an overarching paradigm since the assumptions of one of the paradigms must be either rejected or relegated to a subordinate and contingent status in the other. Because proponents of competing paradigms often disagree on the nature and/or relative importance of particular problems, however, even mutually intelligible debate about basic assumptions may be infrequent.

The idea of comprehensiveness may be given a different and more modest meaning for public administration paradigms in view of the normative and practical concerns which distinguish the field from natural science. Specifically, theory in public administration is typically concerned not only with description and explanation but also with normative questions such as "administrative responsibility" and the "public interest," and practical problems that confront administrators. By revising our generally accepted meaning of comprehensiveness, a requirement for a particular kind of comprehensiveness of *public administration* paradigms may be proposed. Specifically, a paradigm may be said to be comprehensive to the extent that it assists in comprehending the interrelationships among *categories* of theory, such as descriptive, explanatory, normative, and "practice" theories. (This is not to be confused with attempting to reconcile or integrate *competing* theoretical paradigms whose basic assumptions are mutually exclusive and contradictory.) Viewed in this way, comprehensiveness is a criterion for assessing the internal integrity of particular paradigms as represented by their capacity to integrate various kinds of theoretical concern.

INTERRELATIONSHIPS AMONG CATEGORIES OF THEORY

The eclectic and somewhat disjointed character of public administration theory is mainly attributable to the varied purposes that the field has intended theory to serve. In addition to requiring theories for the scientific purposes of explanation and prediction, public administration has also employed different kinds of theories, usually borrowed from political science and management science, in order to inform judgments about value questions and issues related to administrative practice. Although the kinds and purposes of public administration theory have been differentiated in a variety of ways, four categories suggested by Bailey are noted here because they are representative of some rather commonplace distinctions that appear in the public administration literature.[11] Bailey's four categories include descriptive-explanatory, normative, assumptive, and instrumental theory. The first category includes propositions and models abstracted from observations of reality that assist in explaining and, in some cases, predicting behavior in public organizations. Normative theory is concerned with the prescription of futures and with the assessment and application of standards by which moral-ethical judgments about administrative action may be made. Assumptive theory, for Bailey, involves "propositions which articulate root-assumptions about the nature of man and about the tractability of institutions."[12] Finally, instrumental theory derives from the first three categories by helping to provide answers to "how" and "when" questions in specific situations.[13]

The interrelationships among the various categories of theory warrant greater emphasis than Bailey gave them. While he sees instrumental theory as derivative of the first three, for example, Bailey makes no mention of the influence that values and norms (often hidden) have on the development of descriptive categories or of the fact that description and explanation, if sufficiently powerful, may subtly reinforce existing normative preferences.[14]

Interrelationships among the four categories of theory provide clues regarding the multiparadigm character of public administration. Those same interrelationships also provide a context for putting in bold relief some questions of general theoretical and practical interest to the field.

1. What, if any, should be the overarching values for public administration? Where do such values come from and are they amenable to reasoned discourse?

2. Is there a gap between theory and practice in public administration? If so, why does it exist and with respect to what kinds of substantive concerns is it most problematic? What implications does the "professional" character of public administration have for the role of theory?

3. How are descriptions and explanations of administrative issues, actions, and events influenced by unconscious value presuppositions? If this is a problem (which is itself eminently debatable), how can it be recognized and guarded against? If it is an asset, how can it be capitalized on?

Although all these questions deserve fuller treatment than they can be accorded here, discussion of them shall be limited to the reasons why each set of questions can be satisfactorily addressed only from the standpoint of the relationship between at least two, and usually among three, or even all four, categories of theory.

Democratic values and public administration. Since the demise of the Classical paradigm, academics have grappled in a variety of ways with the problem of reconstrucing a coherent value or normative theory for the field. In addition to reinterpreting constitutional democratic theory, the more sophisticated attempts have self-consciously examined the underlying assumptions about human nature and motivation that affect the development of value theory. One effort in this regard is Ostrom's theory of "democratic administration," which is grounded in the "methodological individualism" of public choice theory, that is, the assumption that individuals, the primary unit of analysis for public choice, are rationally motivated to maximize their individual interests.[15] An altogether different attempt is Winter's case for an "intentionalist" style in social science and public policy, which is grounded in a carefully articulated theory of the "self" (human nature) drawn from symbolic interactionism and phenomenology.[16] While neither Ostrom nor Winter's positions will be developed fully here, they are especially noteworthy for their attempt to identify the linkages between assumptive and normative theory.

Theory and practice.   Concern over the relevance, or lack of it, of theory to practice in public administration is commonly attributed, on the one hand, to the frequent insensitivity of theorists (who are often concerned mainly with generalized descriptions and explanations that cut across a fairly wide range of phenomena) to the unique and specific needs of professionals. Theorists, on the other hand, became frustrated with professionals whom they often see as dealing with management or policy concerns in an ad hoc and unreflective manner that militates against serious attempts to draw from theoretical and empirical findings. This usually boils down to admonitions that both sides should try harder, in the case of academics to be "more relevant" and for professionals to take a "broader-gauged view."

The theory-practice gap, however, is something more than a problem of good-faith efforts. Rather, we might productively inquire into the purposes and assumptions underlying descriptive-explanatory theory (a prominent domain of academic theorists) to see whether and in what kinds of instances such theory may or may not be instructive for administrative practice, that is, translatable into what Bailey calls instrumental theory. It is at least a plausible hypothesis that the theory-practice gap is fundamentally a *theoretical* problem having to do with the relationships among description, explanation, and action, rather than merely a symptom of ivory tower theorists and unreflective administrators.

Value presuppositions, description, and explanation.   A rigid distinction between the categories of explanatory and normative theory is tenable if one accepts as possible and desirable the logical-positivist distinction between value and fact. From this perspective, the intrusion of value assumptions upon factual explanation is something to guard against, a task calling for great rigor and care. Both the possibility and desirability of holding facts and values (description and normative judgment) separate has been seriously challenged, however, in many quarters. Louch, for example, contends that descriptions of human action are sterilized, if not meaningless, if they are stripped of evaluative terminology; and in a similar vein, that a superficially value-neutral word such as "intelligence" is nothing more than a symbol to characterize the cognitive abilities necessary to perform tasks which are *valued*.[17] While the relationship between values and facts is not especially problematic in natural science, it is a subject of lively debate still in philosphy and the social sciences. The liveliness of that debate is itself sufficient reason for exploring some of the ways in which normative and descriptive-explanatory theory are variously related.

PARADIGM REDEFINED

The complex interrelationships among the four categories of theory suggest some important reasons, as well as ground rules, for redefining the concept of paradigm for public administration.

1. Paradigms may be useful devices for clarifying the particular manner, in schools of thought and modes of practice, in which categories of theory are logically interrelated.
2. The "comprehensiveness" of a paradigm may be judged by the extent to which it is able to comprehend and successfully integrate assumptive, descriptive-explanatory, normative, and instrumental theory, irrespective of the size of the domain it presumes to encompass. Comprehensiveness thus is a criterion of adequacy that applies equally to "mini-paradigms" as well as to paradigms whose scope is intendedly very large.
3. In view of the field's historical commitment to the improvement of administrative practice, a public administration paradigm's adequacy is contingent on its potential application to practical administrative problems and contexts and its explication of the manner in which theory and practice are interrelated.
4. As a normative framework concerned with the improvement of administrative practice, a public administration paradigm may be evaluated on the explicitness and defensibility of its theory of values.
5. Since public administration is a subset of social action, its paradigms should be grounded in a general understanding of social theory and practice. That is, the term "public administration" is a category of social practice, adopted for convenience, to "bracket" particular concerns, but whose basic moral, practical, and theoretical purposes are derived from the purposes of philosophy, social practice, and social science.
6. Individual paradigms in public administration (for example, Classical, Public Choice, Action Theory) are "symbolic universes" constructed in order to organize related concepts, theories, and modes of practice. Comparisons between or among paradigms permits a more rigorous clarification of the differences between and implications of alternative theoretical approaches and modes of practice.

Before offering a redefinition of paradigm, it is necessary to specify what the term *does not,* and reasonably cannot, mean for public administration. First, the infinite variability of administrative issues and contexts makes it highly unlikely that public administration will have in the foreseeable future only one paradigm. The field will continue to be characterized by multiple paradigms, with advocates of each either vying with one another for supremacy or simply agreeing to disagree. This is not to say, however, that paradigm *advocacy* is not appropriate, so long as it is recognized as a normative endeavor.

Second, since the nature of social action is fundamentally different from that of physical objects, the assumption that causal laws can be discovered which can explain and predict human action is an unwarranted expectation for paradigms in social science.[18] Indeed, this is the reason why social science paradigms cannot, even hypothetically, reduce questions of administrative practice to the status of normal science as described by Kuhn. Paradigmatic debate is philosophical and epistemological debate rather than a debate over the relative predictive and explanatory prowess of one or another paradigm.

Finally, a general preference for one paradigm need not preclude a recognition of the usefulness of values, methodologies, and modes of practice commonly associated with other paradigms. A particular paradigm simply provides the context or ground rules within which alternative values and modes of practice may be evaluated, adjusted, or ranked.

The preceding discussion suggests the following definition of paradigm for public administration: *an interrelated theory of values and ground rules for the development of knowledge whose primary purposes are to describe, inform, and evaluate the practice of administration in public organizations.* The adequacy of a paradigm may be judged by

1. The defensibility of its theory of values
2. The extent to which it successfully integrates various kinds of theory
3. Its ability to assist in improving administrative practice in a manner consistent with its theory of values.

This definition, along with the three criteria of adequacy, does not bias paradigm development and evaluation in the direction of one paradigm or another. Moreover, it leaves open, within certain constraints, the particular manner in which paradigms may be either constructed or inferred from current theory and practice. By viewing comprehensiveness as a measure of integration rather than of scope, paradigm development and discussion may avoid both dogmatism and unfulfillable promises. Finally, the reconstituted concept of paradigm forces a consideration of normative (moral-ethical) concerns to center stage in public administration theory and practice.

NOTES

1. Thomas S. Kuhn, *The Structure of Scientific Revolutions* (2nd ed.; Chicago: University of Chicago Press, 1970).

2. Vincent Ostrom, *The Intellectual Crisis in American Public Administration* (University: University of Alabama Press, 1973).

3. Since Kuhn does not provide a single unambiguous definition of paradigm, the meaning of the term noted here is distilled from various statements in his book, especially in his chapter on "Revolutions as Changes of World View," in Kuhn, *Structure of Scientific Revolutions,* pp. 111–35

4. Margaret Masterman, "The Nature of a Paradigm," in Imre Lakatos and Alan Musgrave, eds., *Criticism and the Growth of Knowledge* (Cambridge, England: Cambridge University Press, 1970), pp. 59–89.

5. Kuhn, *Structure of Scientific Revolutions,* pp. 109–10.

6. Ibid., see especially chapters 2–4.

7. Ostrom, *Intellectual Crisis.*

8. Robert T. Golembiewski, *Public Administration as a Developing Discipline,* pt. 1 (New York: Marcel Dekker, 1977).

9. Robert K. Merton, *Social Theory and Social Structure* (Glencoe, Ill.: Free Press, 1949).

10. For a notable exception, see Orion F. White, "The Concept of Administrative Praxis," *Journal of Comparative Administration,* May 1973, pp. 55–86.

11. Stephen K. Bailey, "Objectives of the Theory of Public Administration," in *Theory and Practice of Public Administration,* ed. James C. Charlesworth (Philadelphia: *Annals of the American Academy of Political and Social Science,* October 1968), pp. 128–39.

12. Ibid., p. 133.

13. Chapter 9 will argue at some length that "instrumental" theory is too restrictive a term to grasp satisfactorily the relevant contributions of theory to practice. Practice, as conceived by the Action paradigm, is fundamentally a moral-ethical concern and is only instrumental in limited contexts.

14. J. Peter Euben, "Political Science and Political Silence," in *Power and Community,* ed. Philip Green and Sanford Levinson (New York: Pantheon, 1969), pp. 3–58.

15. Ostrom, *Intellectual Crisis.*

16. Gibson Winter, *Elements for a Social Ethic* (New York: Macmillan, 1966).

17. A. R. Louch, *Explanation and Social Action* (Berkeley: University of California Press, 1969), p. 54.

18. The subject of causality will receive more elaborate treatment in the critique of positivist social science in chapters 3 and 4.

3

Human Nature, Epistemology, and Social Science

If beliefs about human nature and epistemology are the starting points for the development of social science paradigms, the question naturally arises whether compelling reasons can be given for preferring one set of beliefs over others. Is a particular viewpoint about human nature, for example, simply a matter of faith or intuition, or is it amenable to logical argument? The answer to this question determines whether reasoned debate about social science paradigms can take place at all. Since value theories and modes of scientific explanation are derived from these basic beliefs, their logical defensibility determines whether a preference for one paradigm or another can be nonarbitrary.

This chapter outlines the book's basic theoretical assumptions and discusses several issues, pertaining to social science generally, that should be considered in order to provide adequate grounding of those assumptions. Prominent among the subjects to be addressed are beliefs about human nature and the ground rules for determining the validity of what passes for knowledge or facts (epistemology). Attention is also given to the units of analysis that not only inform empirical inquiry but influence as well reasoned preferences for particular beliefs about human nature and epistemologies over others. Although this chapter is intended to ground the action approach to public administration in the broader context of social science, its more important purpose is to set the stage for subsequent chapters, which elaborate some preferred approaches to the formulation of descriptive-explanatory and normative theory, and the implications of those approaches for administrative practice.[1]

PROPOSITION 2. *Beliefs about human nature are central to the development of theories in public administration, as well as all other branches of social science. In order to provide the foundation for developing and integrating epistemology with descriptive and normative theory, these beliefs should be ontologically grounded rather than selected for reasons of convenience.*

As a self-conscious field of study, public administration has been influenced by a wide variety of academic disciplines. While this probably explains, in part, both the vigor and growing influence of the field, it may also account for the absence of thoughtful discussion—much less, agreement—regarding the basic assumptions which do or should guide its inquiries. The lines of debate about basic assumptions and beliefs are typically more sharply drawn in the more established disciplines than in public administration, although anything approaching consensus about these beliefs in any discipline is certainly the exception rather than the rule.

To encourage such discussion in public administration is not with the expectation, or even hope, of conferring disciplinary status on the field. Substantial arguments (discussed in chapter 9) may be offered that such status would not serve the field's practical interests. Rather, the reasons for discussing basic beliefs and assumptions for public administration are twofold. First, the discussion establishes the possibility for more adequately grounding the field in social theory generally, a task that entails more than simply drawing indiscriminatingly from other disciplines for reasons of convenience. The discussion of basic beliefs and assumptions would permit a more thorough and critical understanding of both the possibilities and limitations inherent in public administration's interdisciplinary character.

The second reason for discussing basic assumptions and beliefs in public administration is to determine whether it is wise and/or possible to develop a coherent theory of values for the field. This book takes the view that it is both possible to develop such a value theory and that the field would benefit from having one. Such a theory need not be simplistic and dogmatic, nor need it presume to offer facile prescriptions to practicing administrators. Instead, it should offer the field a framework within which to assess, in a reasoned and self-reflective manner, the normative implications of administrative institutions and practice. Instead of absolving public administration of the requirement for value theory, the practical commitments of the field serve instead to highlight the field's need for one.

Perhaps more to the point, value theory is in a sense unavoidable inasmuch as value statements, while often artfully obscured by the terminology of contemporary social science, are always imbedded in everyday and scientific descriptions of the social world. They are also found in, and are derivable from, the assumptions and beliefs in which those descriptions are grounded. The self-conscious analysis of those beliefs assists not only in the logical presentation and defense of value theories but serves also in the *identification* of value considerations when they are hidden or implicit.

The search for a coherent theory for public administration will begin with a consideration of some of the means by which basic beliefs about human nature may be identified. Particular attention is given to the suitability of these means for reaching agreement on beliefs about human nature that satisfy the normative (valuational), as well as the descriptive, requirements of social science paradigms. The preference for ontologically grounded beliefs over both empirically based assertions and *a priori* normative assumptions should be evident from the following discussion.

Empirically based assertions about human nature are derived from empirical evidence about people's dominant motives for acting. The presumed advantage of such assertions is that they are grounded in the "real world," which reduces the risk of undue pessimism (sometimes attributed to Hobbes) or excessive optimism (commonly attributed to Rousseau) of purely metaphysical speculation.

Empirically based assertions, however, suffer from a number of logical difficulties, the first of which is that the relationship between the assertion and the supporting evidence often degenerates into a tautology. That is, one simply redundantly confirms the other; there is no possibility of independently confirming or disconfirming the empirical validity of the assertion.[2] For example, if, as the public choice approach suggests, people are rationally motivated to maximize their individual interests, then the question arises as to what are unambiguous indicators of self-interested behavior. The tendency to interpret *any* behavior as self-interested may reach extreme proportions, as the following paragraph illustrates:

> To demonstrate whether individuals always or usually act in their self-interest, the content of "self-interest" must be known. . . . Interests [according to public choice] are inferred from behavior. But consider an example. It may be postulated that people want more rather than less food. If dieting is observed it might be inferred they are maximizing their health. If they diet but do not eat nutritional food they are maximizing the trimness of their appearance. Alternatively, if they do not eat much but specialize in fattening, easy-to-fix food, they may be maximizing their time watching television. Because utility or self-interest is given no a priori specification, any behavior is assumed to maximize utility, which, as it turns out, only goes to show the people are utility maximizers. The empirical defense of the utility maximiza-

tion assumption is entirely circular; *no conceivable behavior can refute the assumption*.[3]

To overcome the problem of circularity, indicators would have to be self-evidently (or universally agreed to be) indicators *only* of self-interest and subject to no other reasonable interpretation. A further requirement would be either the creation of equally self-evident indicators depicting an *alternative* assumption, or set of assumptions, about human nature to that of self-interest, or clear criteria and measures of disproof of the self-interest assumption.

Let us further assume that the above problems have been solved; what then are we to make of the evidence accumulated? Suppose that 55 percent of the population behave in ways consistent with "self-interest" indicators and the remaining 45 percent with, say, "altruism" indicators. Does the majority rule in answering the question of human nature? If so, this ancient philosphical question could be resolved (and re-resolved as modes of behavior change) by commissioning the University of Michigan Survey Research Center or, indeed, the Gallup organization to make periodic investigations into the matter.

The absurdity of this suggestion, of course, derives from attempting to equate human *behavior* with human *nature*. By whatever definition, human nature is intended to be descriptive of qualities or characteristics that transcend individual differences among people. Even if, according to some empirical measure, everyone behaved similarly (e.g., pursued his or her self-interest), we still should be extremely cautious in making inferences about human nature from such evidence. There are numerous possible explanations of self-interested behavior other than its "naturalness," such as economic or institutional constraints of one sort or another.

The problem with using empirically based assertions about human nature as foundations for paradigm construction is that the concept of human nature (or the nature of the "self") is fundamentally a philosophical rather than an empirical concept. Empirical evidence at best simply helps clarify the degree to which the behavior of individuals or aggregates corresponds to a previously agreed upon philosophical conception of human nature. For this reason, empirically based assertions are incapable of providing the basis for a theory of values.

A priori normative assumptions are those that assert someone's intuitively plausible yet explicitly value-laden view of human nature (e.g., "man is basically good, rather than evil," "people are by nature perfectible"). While such assumptions clearly offer the basis for some sort of theory of values, the fact that they are intuitively based begs the question of why other people should also regard those assumptions as plausible. Since intuitive judgments vary from person to person, agreement about those assumptions is unlikely in the absence of standards of logic and an agreed upon mode of analysis that establishes the possibility for a reasoned consensus.

Ontologically grounded beliefs about human nature are intended to describe universal characteristics of people (i.e., characteristics that transcend individual differences). Ontology, which refers to the nature of being or existence, is not an empirical concept, nor does it imply that beliefs about human nature, for example, need be based simply on faith or intuition. Moreover, ontological statements are not value statements as such, although they form a basis from which values may be reasonably inferred. Ontological assumptions about human nature are derived from the primary unit of analysis or starting point of inquiry of a paradigm. Before offering reasons for preferring a particular set of beliefs about human nature, therefore, it is necessary to consider the reasons for preferring one primary unit of analysis over others. From that basis, a preferred ontological conception of human nature, the subject of proposition 4, may be plausibly demonstrated.

PROPOSITION 3. *The primary unit of analysis in social theory should be the face-to-face situation (or encounter), which is preferred over the individual and more encompassing units of analysis such as the group, the nation-state, or the "system."*

The initial issue to be resolved in deciding on a primary unit of analysis has to do with the level or size of the phenomenon the unit presumes to encompass. On the one hand, it may appear reasonable to start with an analysis of the *structural* dynamics of larger units such as the system, nation-state, or organization, from which inferences may then be made about the behavior of smaller units such as groups or individuals. On the other hand, the analysis may begin with a smaller unit, such as the individual or the face-to-face relationship, and work "upward," thus explaining more encompassing units as derivative of interrelationships among aggregates of the smaller units.[4]

The attractiveness of the structuralist position stems from its initial attention to the "big picture" of social life, which may provide the basis for explanations of the apparent complexity of interrelationships among system subunits. The complexity or even chaos of these systems may be comprehended more adequately by making some simplifying assumptions, for example, that systems, as "wholes," have needs such as survival, equilibrium, and so on.

Opponents of the structuralist view typically hold that the advantages accruing from it are more than offset by its limitations. One limitation salient to the present discussion is that the more encompassing the unit of analysis, the more abstract and remote it is from personal experience. The more remote the unit of analysis is from our experience, according to this view, the more skeptical we should be about the reliability of data derived through reference to that unit. Since larger units of analysis are necessarily symbolic artifacts used to depict phenomena beyond our immediate experience, greater caution is in order regarding our willingness to accept those artifacts as accurately depicting social reality.

The structuralist view is frequently accompanied by the tendency, especially among some systems theorists, to speak of systems metaphorically, as if they were something other than abstractions, that is, as if they were tangible things, organisms, or even people.[5] For example, the *a priori* assumption that social systems have a natural need for survival seems questionable inasmuch as we are asked to believe, in effect, that there is such a thing as a natural abstraction and, further, that abstractions, like people, may have needs.

Alternatives to the structuralist position begin with smaller units of analysis, such as the individual or the two-person encounter, which form the basic building blocks from which explanations of the behavior of larger social units are subsequently derived. Such approaches often evoke the rather immediate, and sometimes well-founded, criticism by the structuralists that they are reductionist; that is, using the individual or the encounter as the primary unit of analysis oversimplifies explanations of larger and more complex social phenomena by reducing their explanations to a single cause, motive, or variable. This criticism, in turn, is countered with the argument that reductionism is a sin that may be committed irrespective of the primary unit of analysis employed and that "holistic" explanations that appreciate motivational as well as structural factors may be developed by using smaller units of analysis as the starting point.

It is tempting to try to resolve the problem of units of analysis by simply stating that their selection should depend on the nature or level of the phenomenon one wishes to study. In other words, one should use pragmatic, situational tests in making judgments about the proper unit of analysis. While there are no doubt some practical merits to this suggestion, its consequence is that the ubiquitous problem of values remains unaddressed. Differing units of analysis result not only in differing descriptions but also in differing, often conflicting, theories of values. For example, structuralist approaches, especially in American organizational and sociological literature, typically imply a commitment to rather conservative values, such as system maintenance, stability, and order.[6] Such values stand in sharp contrast to, and indeed may be seen as violating, more individually based approaches in which primary value is placed on, for example, the maximization of individual interests, self-realization, or psychological "liberation" of one sort or another. Agreeing to disagree about primary units of analysis has the effect of agreeing to disagree about values as well. The result is an inability to engage in reasoned discussion about the priority of values or how to make informed judgments regarding tradeoffs among values associated with various units of analysis. The choice of one primary unit of analysis does not preclude an appreciation of values associated with another unit of analysis. That choice does, however, force a coming to grips with value questions that inevitably bear upon all levels of analysis and, therefore, transcend the full range of human experience.

The position of this book is that an analysis of values at the personal level of experience should take precedence over other values and that this commitment should be reflected in the choice of a primary unit of analysis. To grant agreement on this (still debatable) issue, however, leaves open at least two possible alternatives mentioned earlier, each implying value stances that differ radically from one another. The first is the individual—in particular, methodological individualism espoused by public choice theory—and the second is the face-to-face relationship (or encounter) common, for example, to interpretative sociology.

As the term suggests, "methodological individualism" is an assumption chosen mainly for methodological convenience and is not necessarily presumed to include beliefs about people's ontological status. The most common meaning of methodological individualism depicts the assumption that rational people will employ, to the extent that information and circumstances permit, strategies that maximize their individual interests.[7] Despite some knotty empirical problems of defining interest either too narrowly or too broadly, methodological individualism has often served as a powerful device for explaining behavior associated with the expression of people's known preferences, especially as those preferences may be expressed in the voting booth and the marketplace or discernible from demographic analysis.

As an assumption on which to base a more comprehensive social theory, however, methodological individualism's advantages are less evident on both explanatory and normative grounds. There is reason to question, for example, whether a thorough understanding of human experience is reducible to the maximization of interests, however broadly the idea of interest is defined. Similarly, a heavy emphasis on "preferences" may unduly confine our understanding of the complex array of motives and meanings associated with people's actions, some of which may have little or nothing to do with expressing preferences or pursuing interests. Finally, since social science is the study of various forms of *relationships* among people, it is reasonable to insist that the primary unit of analysis take into account the relational character of social action. For this reason, the individual cannot be used as the primary unit because to do so either takes for granted or leaves unresolved the question of the individual's moral nature or ontological status vis-à-vis other people. Without some resolution of this issue, we are left with little guidance in the development of a theory of values.

Three reasons are offered here for the face-to-face encounter as the beginning point of paradigm development. First, it avoids the structuralist liability of treating abstractions as if they were real things. Second, it provides a vehicle for inquiring systematically into the moral nature of the self. And third, the encounter depicts a level of analysis most directly related to our concrete experience and is therefore the most elemental—and, in a sense, real—unit of human interaction. That is, the face-to-face encounter is the prototypical case of social interaction from which all other cases are derived.[8] Unlike more remote forms of relationships (e.g., individual-group, intergroup, group-society), the encounter permits the presence of each person to be immediately apparent to the other. In addition, the encounter is more flexible than other forms of interaction inasmuch as it is less bound by stereotyping and other factors that may "depersonalize" interaction.

Because of its apparent simplicity, it may be objected that the encounter does not convey many of the complexities of human behavior as influenced by history and larger social collectivities. Variations of the encounter, however, far from excluding these factors, have been employed successfully as the primary units of analysis for a wide range of theories of history and society.[9] In addition, the encounter provides a framework within which the relationship of language, as we shall see in the discussion of proposition 4, to human nature may be assessed.

PROPOSITION 4. *People are by nature active rather than passive, and social rather than atomistic. This means that people have a measure of autonomy in determining their actions, which are at the same time bound up in a social context (i.e., the presence of others). This social context is necessary not only for instrumental purposes but also because it defines people's status as humans.*

PASSIVE VERSUS ACTIVE CONCEPTIONS OF THE SELF

Two prominent outlooks that characterize social and psychological thinking regarding the causes or sources of human behavior differ mainly in their beliefs about the extent to which people's behavior or actions are subject to control by others. They differ as well in the degree of their optimism regarding the social consequences of behavior that is not externally controlled.

The idea that people are essentially *passive* holds that human behavior is principally explainable in terms of external causes or forces, inherited drives or instincts, or some combination of the two. To the extent that external forces are seen as primarily important, the task of social science (mainly psychology) is to discover the laws that govern the effect of environment on behavior. The mode of scientific explanation assumed by the passive view, therefore, is virtually identical to that of the natural sciences. The passive view also holds that people are malleable in the sense of being rather easily susceptible to manipulation. Thus the discovery of those laws provides the knowledge that may inform the creation of the social apparatus to be used in controlling or directing behavior toward socially beneficial ends. Distrustful of the social consequences of uncontrolled behavior, proponents of the passive conception of the self see the development of the means of social control as not only possible but also necessary.[10] Their intellectual debt to Thomas Hobbes, therefore, is equal to that owed B. F. Skinner.

Although other criticisms of the passive view of the self will be made later in this chapter, one criticism is noted here concerning an apparent inconsistency in the view that laws determine human behavior, on the one hand, and that it is possible either to manipulate such laws toward some end or even to persuade people to obey them, on the other. Gibson Winter has stated the dilemma inherent in the passive view as follows:

> When the subject matter of social science is handled like the subject matter of physical science, knowledge of social laws becomes a knowledge of laws which control man's activity. Knowledge of society reveals man's enslavement to societal forces. Man ceases to be a "subject" and becomes an "object" of calculable forces external to him. Whereas physical science increases man's control of his situation, social science discloses man's bondage to his situation. Every attempt to exercise choice in shaping social life is rejected unless it reproduces the activities of laws alien to that choice. Man the scientist discovers himself to be the victim of science.[11]

The only apparent escape from the contradiction described by Winter is for social scientists to make the dubious presumption that, unlike the subjects of their studies, *they* are immune from the social laws they purport to describe.

As a contrast to the passive view of the self, the *active* view holds that behavior can be adequately understood only in terms of the subjective meanings people impute to what they see and do. People actively interpret environmental events and phenomena and, by doing so, determine the "forces" and events that have influence. Moreover, the direction of influence between people and their environments is reciprocal, thereby granting people a measure of autonomy in their thoughts and actions. In other words, the relationship between individual and environment is characterized by interdependence rather than (exclusively) dependence as implied by the passive conception.

Also characteristic of the active conception is the belief in an emergent quality of human action whose wellspring is located in the unconscious.[12] Advocates of the active view are also generally optimistic about the social consequences of actions motivated by the unconscious and are, correspondingly, skeptical about the possible effectiveness of mechanisms of social control derived from the discovery of psychological "laws." Insofar as such mechanisms seem to work, they may be explainable in terms of the regrettable tendency of people sometimes to deny the more basic aspects of their nature.

While perhaps congenial in spirit, the active conception shares only a superficial resemblance to earlier, heavily rationalistic, conceptions of free will characteristic, for example, of the Englightenment period. To say that people are active is not to say that they are wholly masters of their fate. The active view of the self implies a somewhat less heroic and less autonomous view of human nature, which grants that people participate in the creation of the social world and are responsible for it by virtue of their abilities to reflect upon the meaning of their participation.

With varying degrees of explicitness, the passive/active distinction is evident, although not necessarily central in all cases, in contending schools of thought within numerous social science areas. Controversy about the passive vs. active view of the self is evident, for example, in psychology (reinforcement learning, behaviorism, and Freudian psychology vs. cognitive-developmental, humanistic, and symbolic interactionist theories), epistemology (logical positivism vs. phenomenology), statistical theory (classical vs. Bayesian),[13] and empirical political theory (democratic pluralism vs. what Bachrach has called the "self-development" conception of democratic theory).[14]

The major difficulty in resolving the differences between the passive and active conceptions is finding a suitable common ground on which the argument may take place. That is, the terms of the argument should not exclude, *a priori,* one position or the other from serious consideration. Finding that common ground, however, is no easy task, as evidenced by a tendency on both sides to frame the issue improperly. For example, the differences between the passive and active conceptions should not be seen as resolvable by empirical evidence since such evidence *presupposes* agreement about theoretical assumptions. Since proponents of the passive and active conceptions sharply disagree about theoretical assumptions, empirical evidence accumulated in the absence of such agreement leads each side redundantly to confirm its own assumptions.

A second mistake, especially common to advocates of the active conception, is to state the case loosely on moral-philosophical grounds. Rogers and other psychologists whose theories of personality have a highly "philosophical" flavor are critical of the passive conception for its denial of (what is to them) evidence of people's capacity to make autonomous moral choices.[15] Their position is subject to the retort that talk about free will is a lot of wishful thinking and that people's moral possibilities are necessarily circumscribed by aspects of their nature that must be empirically verified or logically demonstrated. Psychologists whose theoretical orientations presuppose a passive conception of the self offer formidable arguments to the effect that what passes for active or autonomous behavior is actually the result of complex processes of conditioning over which people have no real control.

The problem, it appears, is first to identify the crux of the disagreement between the passive and active views and, second, to employ a method and unit of analysis within which both conceptions of the self may be evaluated, bearing in mind that the analysis must avoid the liabilities of the kinds of argument noted above. Earlier it was noted that the major difference between the passive and active conceptions derives from differing views as to the causes or sources of behavior. The two conceptions are divided *not* over the question of *where* those causes originate but over the legitimacy of the concept of *causation* itself. The question is whether there is good reason to believe that behavior is reducible to explanations of relationships among independent factors that are causally related to one another.

Adherents to the passive view, which answers this question in the affirmative, must satisfactorily explain the *origin* of the cause if they wish to show that evidence supporting their hypotheses is not simply tautological. Moreover, while granting that the idea of causation satisfactorily explains events in the physical world and the behavior of lower forms of animal life, advocates of the passive view are obliged to demonstrate that *human* behavior may be explained by fundamentally similar concepts. Behaviorists, however, may object to this requirement by asserting that the burden of evidence rests with proponents of the opposing view, who must demonstrate sufficient reasons to believe that human behavior is fundamentally *different* from that of other animals.

Those who hold the active conception, which believes that causal explanations are unsatisfactory, (1) must show why they are insufficient for explaining at least some aspects of human behavior and (2) are obliged to explain the sources of (active) behavior in terms other than causal relationships. The active conception of the self does not preclude the belief that *some* human behavior is explainable in causal terms, nor does it necessarily dismiss as nonsensical the belief that genetic predispositions play an important role in explaining what people do. The active conception does hold, however, that people's capacity for self-reflection, enabled by language, must be included as a significant part of a comprehensive explanatory scheme of human activity. This self-reflective capacity, according to the active view, means that scientists should be extremely circumspect in making causal inferences from empirical data since noncausal explanations might also be employed in the analysis of the same data. Seen in this light, the passive and active conceptions of the self are not polar opposites. Rather, the active view *encompasses* aspects of the passive view but also includes the belief that people's creative and reflective capacities are not merely illusory. Thus, human experience is trivialized, if not negated altogether, by reducing it exclusively to causal explanations.

From the standpoint of the face-to-face encounter as the unit of analysis, the passive view suggests that the encounter, in its simplest form, consists of two elements: the *cause* (in the form of a stimulus generated by one person to another) and the *effect* (the response of the second person to that stimulus). Behaviorism and other psychological theories that implicitly assume a passive conception offer highly elaborate explications of the cause-effect sequence. For example, a person's response to a stimulus will be influenced by prior conditioning, including, of course, previous encounters. However, this qualification does not vitiate the behaviorist model's central assumption of cause and effect.

Two limitations of the cause-effect idea in explaining human interaction deserve mention. The first is that if one person's behavior is caused by (is a response to) a stimulus generated by another person, the other person's behavior (the stimulus) must itself logically be the effect of some prior stimulus. This assumption of inifinite regress raises the question of where the *first* cause (the ultimate origin of the stimulus) came from. The question is unanswerable by behaviorist theories, except by resorting to explanations of physical determinism or divine intervention.

A second limitation of causal explanations of human behavior is their apparent inability to grasp adequately the role of language in influencing thought processes and mediating human interaction. "First-person reports" must necessarily be regarded as autonomous acts inasmuch as their content is so complex and variable that they cannot be checked against external stimuli or events.[16]

The more fundamental argument against the passive view, however, which is also the basis for the active conception, is the existence of language itself. The plausibility of the active self is based on the ability of people to conceive of phenomena in symbolic terms (words) and to understand what they see and feel through the construction of sentences. The act of symbolization itself—by which people comprehend the world through words—is unexplainable by behaviorist theory and thus makes necessary a theory of the self fundamentally different from theories of behavior of the lower forms of animal life.[17] The act of "naming" (conceiving of phenomena by means of symbols) is a process that is generically different from those explainable in terms of energy exchanges, cause and effect, stimulus and response. The naming of objects and phenomena, that is, the process by which people attach meaning to them, permits people to *reflect* upon, temporarily to stand apart from, immediate events. This reflective capability, which is made possible through language, means that people, unlike other forms of animal life that may react to signs, are not compelled to respond to events or stimuli; rather, they have the capacity to make choices about whether, and what kind of, action or response is called for.

Closely related to language and hence to the active conception of the self is the idea of *intentionality*. Intentionality replaces the concept of causation that underlies the passive view and provides the basis for the position that reality is "constructed," rather than existing independent of people's conceptualization of it.[18] For purposes of explaining the nature of human action, the active (or intentionalist) view holds that people act from the basis of rules of their own devising, rather than being driven solely by forces beyond their control. Further, their actions are mediated by the subjective meanings that they attach both to past experiences and explorations leading to future experience.

ATOMISTIC VERSUS SOCIAL CONCEPTIONS OF THE SELF

The question whether people are basically atomistic or social beings is fundamental to the issue of the individual's relationship to others and hence to society. While this issue has roots in classical philosophy, its contemporary formulation can be traced to social contract theory (which supports the atomistic conception) and the more recent "social behaviorist" theory of George Herbert Mead (which supports the social conception).[19]

With the exception of behaviorist psychology, most atomistic theories implicitly assume an active rather than a passive conception of the self. These so-called voluntarist theories, which are most common in social sciences other than psychology, derive their major premises from social contract theory.[20] Voluntarism assumes, first, that the individual, the primary unit of analysis, is sovereign and is capable of actively making rational choices in furtherance of his or her self-interest. Second, social relationships are primarily for utilitarian purposes and have, at least theoretically, no bearing on the existence of the self, which is assumed to exist prior to and independent of those relationships. Thus, the coincidence of one person's interests with those of others is problematic, rather than fundamental to his or her moral existence. Lastly, the basic purposes of social organization for the voluntarists is the maintenance of order and the maximization of the sum of individual interests. The atomistic (voluntarist) concept of the self underlies such diverse schools of thought in social science as classical economic theory, utilitarian political philosophy, democratic pluralism, public choice theory, and "rational" organization theory.[21]

One of the first comprehensive attacks on the atomistic conception of the self was launched in the early part of the present century by George Herbert Mead, a social psychologist and pragmatic philosopher at the University of Chicago. Mead, whose theory was commonly referred to as "social behaviorism," began by reversing the assumption of social contract theory that society can be explained by assuming the prior existence of selves. The "self" is a product of social interaction in which a person not only behaves in response to others but, through "role taking," incorporates in his or her own behavior the behavior of others. Human behavior involves the *interpretation* of events or phenomena and the *sharing* of those interpretations with others. "Human society rests upon a basis of *consensus,* i.e., the sharing of meanings in the form of common understandings and expectations." [22] Thus, the ongoing consensus that holds society together is important beyond utilitarian considerations; rather, consensus is the mechanism that makes possible the realization of both individual identities and the social fabric.

A brief summary of Mead's theory of the self is generally sufficient to establish a plausible basis for a social, as opposed to an atomistic, conception of the self. Some contemporary criticisms of Mead's framework, however, suggest some ways in which it can be altered in order to take account of the self's active (or creative), as well as social, nature. A revision of his theory, which supports the active-social conception, provides the underlying assumptions for a descriptive framework of administrative action presented in chapter 4.

Mead's theory of the self was a response to what he regarded as serious inadequacies of behaviorist psychology, whose major exponent in Mead's time was John Watson. That Mead's theory was often referred to as "social behaviorism" is indicative of his inability, according to some of his later critics, to overcome totally the deterministic biases of behaviorism. His major departure from conventional behaviorism was his rejection of the stimulus-response interpretation of human behavior. While Mead agreed with the behaviorists that the *beginning* point in the study of psychology is behavior, he departed from them by arguing that the *reasons* for behavior could be adquately explained only in terms of the subjective meanings that people attach to it. By focusing on the meaning that people attach to experience, he laid the groundwork for a psychology that viewed people as participants in the creation of the social world, a world that was, in turn, the source for the development of their individual identities.

While he was successful in demonstrating the inadequacies of stimulus-response explanations of behavior, Mead has been criticized for being unable to escape the determinism that had plagued other behaviorist psychologies. [23] He went only part of the way from a passive to an active conception of the self, even though the general framework of his theory permitted a more complete transition. Mead replaced mechanistic theories of social determination with a more radical, but still deterministic, theory based on his concept of the social self.

The reason for judging Mead a determinist has to do with his failure to account for the *source* of the first of three elements in his model describing the internal processes of social interaction that lead to the development of the self. Unlike the behaviorists, who were largely unconcerned with these internal processes, Mead said that the development of the self can be best explained by attempting to understand ways in which people both interpret the gestures of others and seek to comprehend the meaning of the other's responses to them. Specifically, the face-to-face situation involves, first, the initiation by the self of a *gesture* to the other; second, a *response* to that gesture by the other; and third, the *interpretation* of the response to the gesture by means of the self's taking the role of the other (i.e., the internal participation in the perspective of the other). The self develops through sharing in and adopting the concerns, values, and so forth, of the other. The "socialization" of the self is explained by the concept of the "generalized other," an amalgam of the values and mores of society.[24]

Mead's concept of a self "created" by society suggests that the main criterion for successful psychological development is the extent to which the individual's values conform with those of the society at large. The notions of creativity and deviance are glossed over, giving the impression that they have little to do with, or are even at odds with, healthy development. While Mead did acknowledge the individual's participation in the creation of societal norms and often stressed the importance of individual creativity, these factors are inadequately accounted for in his theory.

The flaw in Mead's account is that while the second and third elements of his model—the response to the gesture and interpretation of the response—support the idea of a *social* self (which he called the "me"), *the source of the gesture* (the "I") is not adequately explained. This is an important limitation because an explanation of the source of the gesture is necessary in order to determine whether, in addition to being social, the self is active or passive. The "I" through whom the gesture originates cannot be presupposed without collapsing the "I" into the "me." And without a satisfactory explanation of the source of the gesture, there is no reason to believe in the existence of an independent "I," or active self.[25]

An effort to resolve the problem of social determinism in Mead's theory of the self has been made by Gibson Winter. Winter finds the solution to Mead's unsolved puzzle in the phenomenology of Alfred Schutz, specifically, in Schutz's version of the face-to-face encounter he called the "We-relation." [26] The fundamental sociality of Mead's concept of the self is affirmed by Schutz, but in such a way that the initiation of the gesture is satisfactorily explained. Schutz said that in the face-to-face situation, awareness of the other logically precedes awareness of the self; an awareness of the self occurs only afterward through reflection. In describing the encounter, he states,

> . . . each of us can experience the Other's thoughts and acts in the vivid present whereas either can grasp his own only as a past by way of reflection. I know more of the Other and he knows more of me than either of us knows of his own stream of consciousness. This present, common to both of us, is the pure sphere of the "We." And if we accept this definition, we can agree . . . that the sphere of the "We" is pregiven to the sphere of the Self. . . . We participate without an act of reflection in the vivid simultaneity of the "We," whereas the "I" appears only after the reflective turning. . . .[27]

Schutz further suggested that knowledge of the social world is created intersubjectively through a mutual participation in each other's consciousness. By stipulating that there are sufficient commonalities in everyone's thought processes, it is possible for people mutually to share in each other's stream of consciousness, which Schutz called "the general thesis of the alter ego's existence." [28] The first step of Mead's model—the unexplained source of the gesture—is replaced by a mutual sharing in the stream of consciousness of the other. The basic sociality of the self is thus the logical beginning point of Schutz's model, in contrast to Mead's in which sociality is asserted to be the outcome of a process whose first step is assumed rather than explained.

The *active* conception of the self makes plausible the notion of *intentionality* wherein people's perceptions necessarily include the subjective meanings that they impute to what they see. One is never merely conscious; rather, one is always conscious of *something*, which is to say that consciousness is always intentional (or "intentive").[29] In and of itself, however, intentionality gives no answer to whether the self is more appropriately viewed as atomistic or social.

Walker Percy has offered a provocative analysis of consciousness that supports the social conception of the self.[30] His argument, inspired by the work of Mead's contemporary and fellow pragmatist Charles Saunders Peirce, asserts that (intentional) consciousness is the linchpin between language and society. It is insufficient merely to say that a person is conscious *of* something. Rather, she or he is conscious of it as *being something,* that is, having a name or symbol that is understood by another person. Without the other person, language, and hence man, would be impossible.

> Besides the symbol, the conception, and the thing, there are two other terms which are quite as essential in the act of symbolization. There is the "I," the consciousness which is confronted by the thing and which generates the symbol by which the conception is articulated. But there is also the "you." *Symbolization is of its very essence an intersubjectivity.* If there were only one person in the world; symbolization could not conceivably occur (but signification could); for my discovery of water as something derives from your telling me so, that this is water for you too. The act of symbolization is an affirmation: yes, this is water! My excitement derives from the discovery that it is there for you and me and that it is the same thing for you and me. Every act of symbolization thereafter, whether it be language, art, science, or even thought, must occur either in the presence of a real you or an ideal you for whom the symbol is intended as meaningful. *Symbolization presupposes a triad of existents: I, the object, you.* [31]

The conclusion to be drawn is that if language defines the nature of the self, and if language (symbolization) is by its nature intersubjective, then the self can rightly be viewed only as social. Intersubjectivity, *ergo* sociality. By means of this argument, the relationship between language and man is clearly drawn, and in such a way that the concept of the "We-relation" is clarified, but not substantively altered.

The "We-relation" provides the basis for a concept of the self that accounts for human freedom and creativity, as well as for sociality. From the standpoint of the "We-relation," sociality is not synonymous with determination; interdependence rather than dependence characterizes the self's relationship to society. One of people's essential tendencies is toward the unification of self and society, which necessarily presupposes the existence of "a self which can set itself apart from its world while at the same time being open toward that world." [32]

SUMMARY CRITIQUE OF THE FOUR CONCEPTIONS OF THE SELF

The general conclusion to be derived from the analysis of the passive/active and atomistic/social dimensions is that, in addition to concepts of the "social" self, there also exists in the person an "active" or "creative" self that provides the basis for a more balanced view of the relationship of the self to society. The passive/active and atomistic/social dimensions suggest four possible combinations depicting distinct conceptions of the self. Figure 3.1 summarizes these combinations and also notes the relationship implied by each conception to society.

The "We-relation," which provides the theoretical foundation of the active-social conception, is in addition the basis from which the major weaknesses of the other three conceptions may be summarized.

FIGURE 3.1 Conceptions of Self in Terms of Relation to Society

Passive-Social	*Active-Social*
(Mead: Social Behaviorism): Dependent	(Schutz: Intentionalist): Interdependent
Passive-Atomistic	*Active-Atomistic*
(Behaviorist/ Stimulus-Response): Dependent	(Voluntarist): Independent

1. *Passive-Atomistic* **(Behaviorist)** *Conception.* (*a*) Does not explain the sources of stimuli that "cause" behavior; (*b*) presupposes the logical existence of the self prior to and independent from social interaction in contradiction of the logic of the "We-

relation''; and (*c*) does not adequately account for people's active or creative nature, especially its social implications.

2. *Passive-Social* (**Mead's Social Behaviorist**) *Conception*. (*a*) Same as 1*a*, since the *first step* in Mead's model presupposes the existence of the self prior to social interaction; (*b*) resulting sociality of the self reduces the self to a reflection of societal mores and values, which excludes the possibility of an active self.

3. *Active-Atomistic* (**Voluntarist**) *Conception*. (*a*) Same as 1*b*, that is, the existence of the self is assumed to be independent of society; and (*b*) ''active'' or creative behavior would be assumed to stem from supposedly self-evident criteria of self-interest in which social relationships could be explained only in utilitarian or instrumental terms.

PROPOSITION 5. *People's "active-social" nature implies an epistemology, that is, ground rules for determining the validity of knowledge, which focuses on the study of subjective meanings that people attach to their own actions and the actions of others.*

An epistemology is a set of rules and assumptions used to determine what is to be regarded as valid knowledge or fact. Two general orientations, commonly referred to as ''objectivism'' and ''subjectivism,'' characterize much of the current debate about epistemology in both the natural and social sciences. The objectivist, or positivist, orientation holds that reality, physical or social, exists independent of the (scientific) observer and that laws are discoverable that govern the behavior of objects and people. Ideally, what the observer sees is unbiased, that is, not influenced by judgments; and behavioral laws are true irrespective of time or context.

The subjectivist orientation, which derives in large part from phenomenology, holds that facts are simply the products of explicit or implicit agreements among people. While subjectivists do not deny the facticity of physical objects, they argue that *perceiving* involves a transaction between the perceiver (the subject) and the perceived (the object). Moreover, facts or knowledge that we assume to be objective in an everyday sense are simply what we have agreed (usually without much difficulty or even being aware of it) to treat *as if* they were objectively true. This is known as the process of ''objectivation.''[33]

The limitations of the objectivist frame of reference for social science are most clearly evident when one considers that the phenomena social scientists describe are almost invariably intangible (e.g., roles, institutions, relationships, personalities), giving rise quite understandably to disagreements as to the true character of the phenomena. The correctness of a perception for the objectivist is determined by appeal to an external or objective standard of truth typically embodied in the scientific method. The objectivity of the external standard, however, is highly suspect for the same reasons that Thomas Hobbes was suspicious of the doctrine of divine right.[34] Kings may indeed speak to God, but they are also obliged to offer proof of their conversations. So too are the objectivists obliged to offer proof of what they purport to be social facts.

The easiest and most convincing case against the objectivists is simply to note that disagreement continues to exist about social facts, making it necessary to rely on agreements between and among people based on their subjective understanding of the phenomena in question.[35] From the standpoint of a subjectivist epistemology, however, the reliance on subjective agreement among people about social meaning is *not* a second-best expedient in lieu of available objective standards of proof. To the subjectivist, such standards cannot possibly exist in any unequivocal sense because the social facts the scientist attempts to understand have no existence other than as artifacts of shared agreements among people. Applied to the social world, the subjectivist epistemology based on shared understanding among scientists is essentially the same as the process by which the social world is created and maintained in the first place. Seen in this light, social science entails a *self-reflective* and necessarily subjective understanding of those social phenomena *taken for granted* and subjectively understood by lay people.

The two key concepts of the subjective epistemology, intentionality and intersubjectivity, logically derive from the previous section in this chapter that dealt with the active-social nature of the self. The notion that the self is, in important respects, active rather than exclusively passive explains as much about perceiving as it does other aspects of human action. The active (intentional) nature of perceiving means that the consciousness of the actor is intended toward the object (or other person) and that the particular character of a person's intentionality is mediated by his or her prior subjective experiences.

The social nature of the self, as suggested earlier, bears on the concept of intersubjectivity, that is, the idea that knowledge of any kind is a *social* product, a result of either tacit or explicit agreement among people. Even seemingly autonomous acts of perception require the use of language, which itself is possible only in a social context.

EPISTEMOLOGY AND ORGANIZATION THEORY

Chapter 2 stressed the importance of the logical connections among kinds of theory within individual paradigms. This has just been illustrated by showing how epistemology is influenced by assumptions about human nature. Thayer develops a similar line of argument by demonstrating the relationship between epistemology and organization theory. For Thayer, epistemology *is* organization theory. "An epistemology, or theory of knowledge, cannot be anything but a specified decision-making process for the legitimation of truth in the community involved with any given subject matter; thus any epistemology is an organization theory, and *vice versa.*" [36] The major questions for organization theory have to do with who makes these decisions, who obeys them, and what structures exist for their legitimation. Although the notion of objective truth is a fiction, it is nonetheless an important one and depends for its maintenance in specific instances on the power or authority of some people to impose the fiction on others. Organizationally, this is accomplished through superior/subordinate relationships: hierarchy. Hierarchy, in other words, is the organizational equivalent of an objectivist epistemology, one that incorrectly assumes the existence of known or discoverable truths.

Two other epistemological views and accompanying organizational decision rules are possible. One is *intra*subjectivity, in which individuals subjectively create meaning or knowledge independent of one another. From the standpoint of the social conception of the self, such autonomous creation of knowledge is in a strict sense impossible inasmuch as the creation of meaning and knowledge requires the use of language, which is by its nature a social and therefore *inter*subjective system of symbols. Nonetheless, rough approximations of *intra*subjectivity imply the absence of social or collective decision rules about knowledge creation that organizationally (or, in this case, nonorganizationally) is tantamount to anarchy and epistemologically the equivalent of solipsism.

The second, and for Thayer the preferred, alternative epistemology is *inter*subjectivity, which stresses that in addition to its fundamentally subjective character, knowledge is also necessarily a *social* product resulting from *shared* meanings and perceptions.[37] The organizational arrangement (or decision rule) that most fully acknowledges the intersubjective nature of social knowledge is "structured nonhierarchy" (i.e., organizational arrangements devoid of superior/subordinate relationships), and the process that logically accompanies it is consensus. Consensus is an active and a social process in which scientists and lay people alike create both scientific and everyday knowledge as well as social institutions such as organizations.

To be sure, the "real world" is not always, nor even very often, characterized by the absence of superior/subordinate relationships. As Giddens has noted, "The production of an 'orderly' or 'accountable' social world cannot merely be understood as collaborative work carried out by *peers:* meanings that are made to count express asymmetries of power." [38] Power asymmetries, however, are maintained organizationally, in Thayer's terms, through hierarchy and are to that extent normatively unacceptable and epistemologically wrong. The identical nature of his normative argument against hierarchy generally and his case against an objectivist epistemology supports the position developed in chapter 2 that epistemology is first and foremost a normative issue. Assumptive theory (epistemology) and normative theory, therefore, are not only related but are more likely one and the same.

An illustration of the normative implications of the objectivist/ subjectivist controversy has to do with the manner in which each side treats the distinction between "values" and "facts." For the objectivists, the difference is very clear. Facts exist independently from the perceiver (scientist); his or her task is to discover what they *are,* although even an objectivist might readily concede this or that "value" (e.g., love of truth, the desire to cure cancer) as a motive for seeking to discover certain facts. Irrespective of such motives, however, facts are facts and the purposes to which they are put, that is, their "value" implications, are wholly another matter. This separation makes plausible a number of long-standing dichotomies familiar to public administration, namely the distinctions between politics and administration, planning and acting, policy formulation and implementation. While objectivists grant that in a practical sense the distinction between facts and values is often clouded, the conceptual difference still holds, providing a plausible basis for a normative system of accountability of administrators to political superiors.

The intersubjective epistemological view radically disputes the conceptual distinction between fact and value and, by extension, the other dichotomies that derive from it. The basis for challenging the distinction is twofold, the first of which is Louch's[39] position that appraisal of human action is necessarily a moral activity. That is, it involves description of behavior in terms of the purposes of actors, calling into question the moral intent and consequences of that behavior. Description of action without regard to its moral nature would be utterly trivial, if possible at all. Thus action is always moral both from the standpoint of the motives of actors as well as from the moral categories of appraisal employed by observer/ scientists, who are necessarily moral actors themselves. The meaning of "moral" is employed here not in the sense of the correctness of the action but in the procedural sense as stated by Louch:

> . . . insufficient attention is paid to the possibility that rational action, and morality itself, might be defined or characterized in terms of procedures as against the consequences that match or fail to match particular moral standards. On the procedural view, a man whose actions are guided by his assessments, and his understanding of his own and other's actions by the grounds he finds for those actions in the situation of the actor, is looking at behavior morally.[40]

The second, and closely related intersubjectivist challenge to the fact/value dichotomy derives from the previously discussed concept of intentionality. The idea that perception involves an active and transactional process between the subject (observer) and object suggests that what we see and how we see it is in large measure influenced by usually unconscious value presuppositions. This idea is crucial in understanding the creation and maintenance of social institutions, which are, after all, the historical products of intersubjective agreements among people, even though these agreements are often unconscious and only infrequently characterized by equal influence among people in the process. The creation of relationships and institutions is necessarily a moral act; and the modes of appraisal and analysis of them by social scientists and lay people not only involve the imposition of moral categories but such descriptions may also unintendedly serve to maintain the institutions described. Thus, presumably value/free

> . . . descriptions may, through political education, become a series of self-fulfilling prophecies; that ''the social scientist actually helps make his objects of study what they are,'' so that his studies of manufactured material redundantly confirm his science. The failure to appreciate such possibilities and the dependence on the fact-value opposition is linked to the use of the phrase ''in the real world.''[41]

When it refers to aspects of the social world, the term ''in the real world'' is seldom simply a neutral description. Since the social world is real only by virtue of the actions that make it real, the real world is also one for which the people in it are morally responsible for creating, sustaining, and transforming it. The ''real world,'' however, tends to obscure the moral nature of people's actions by giving the false impression that the current world is the inevitable product of destiny or fate and that its legitimacy is therefore beyond serious question. Thus, the ''real world'' subtly fuses description with an implied suggestion of moral acceptance.

The active-social nature of the self, the face-to-face encounter as the primary unit of analysis, and the intersubjectivist epistemology constitute the key ingredients of the assumptive theory of the Action paradigm. Little attention has been given thus far, however, to the concept of action itself inasmuch as an adequate appreciation of it presupposes a grounding in the material just presented. In the next chapter, the concepts of ''behavior'' and ''action'' are distinguished, permitting a fuller elaboration of the idea of action. The discussion is introduced by considering the problem of theory as conspiracy.

NOTES

1. Stephen K. Bailey, ''Objectives of the Theory of Public Administration,'' in *Theory and Practice of Public Administration*, ed. James C. Charlesworth

(Philadelphia: American Academy of Political and Social Science, October 1968), pp. 128–39.

2. Robert T. Golembiewski, "A Critique of 'Democratic Administration' and Its Supporting Ideation," *American Political Science Review* 71 (December 1977): 1488–1507.

3. Michael Harder, "An Analysis of Public Choice Theory" (unpublished paper, Department of Public Administration, The George Washington University, Washington, D.C., April 1977), pp. 23–24.

4. For an argument favoring the latter view, see Richard VrMeer, "Phenomenology in the Radical Reconstruction of the Study of Public Administration: An Overview" (paper prepared for the Southwest Political Science Association Conference, March 1970).

5. This is the thrust of David Silverman's criticism of both structural-functionalist and systems organization theory. See *The Theory of Organizations* (New York: Basic Books, 1971), chaps. 2 and 3.

6. Gibson Burrell and Gareth Morgan, *Sociological Paradigms and Organizational Analysis* (London: Heinemann, 1979).

7. Vincent Ostrom, *The Intellectual Crisis in American Public Administration* (University: The University of Alabama Press, 1973), pp. 50–52.

8. For a more extensive discussion of the encounter as the primary unit of analysis in social theory, see Peter L. Berger and Thomas Luckmann, *The Social Construction of Reality* (Garden City, N.Y.: Anchor Books, 1967), pp. 28–34.

9. Constructs similar to the face-to-face situation are found, for example, in the works of Martin Buber, George Herbert Mead, Alfred Schutz, Max Weber, and Gibson Winter, among others.

10. For an especially grim analysis of the manipulative uses made of behavior modification techniques by contemporary management theory and practice, see William G. Scott and David K. Hart, *Organizational America: Can Individual Freedom Survive Within the Security It Promises?* (Boston: Houghton Mifflin, 1979), chaps. 4–6.

11. Gibson Winter, *Elements for a Social Ethic: the Role of Social Science in Public Policy* (New York: Macmillan, 1966), pp. 9–10.

12. This position, inspired largely by the writings of Carl Jung, has been developed quite extensively by Orion F. White, Jr., in "The Concept of Administrative Praxis," *Journal of Comparative Administration*, May, 1973, pp. 55–86.

13. Bruce Gates, "Some Implications of Statistical Analysis for Normative Theory in Public Administration," in *Organization Theory and the New Public Administration*, ed. Carl J. Bellone (Boston: Allyn and Bacon, 1980), pp. 80–105.

14. Peter Bachrach, *The Theory of Democratic Elitism: A Critique* (Boston: Little, Brown, 1970).

15. Carl Rogers, "Toward a Science of the Person," in *Behaviorism and Phenomenology: Contrasting Bases for Modern Psychology*, ed. T. D. Wann (Chicago: University of Chicago Press, 1964), pp. 109–33.

16. Norman Malcolm, "Behaviorism as a Philosophy of Psychology," in Wann, *Behaviorism and Phenomenology*, pp. 144–55.

17. The argument developed in this chapter concerning the relationship between language and human nature is based largely on Walker Percy's *The Message in the Bottle: How Queer Man Is, How Queer Language Is, and What One*

Has to Do with the Other (New York: Farrar, Straus and Giroux, 1975).

18. Berger and Luckmann, who develop this thesis extensively, derive their argument in large part from the phenomenology of Alfred Schutz. A central theme in Schutz's writings, as well as those of Edmund Husserl and other phenomenologists, is that consciousness is always intentional.

19. Charles W. Morris, ed., *Works of George Herbert Mead*, vol. 1, *Mind Self, and Society from the Standpoint of a Social Behaviorist* (Chicago: University of Chicago Press, 1934).

20. Jerome G. Manis and Bernard N. Meltzer, *Symbolic Interaction* (Boston: Allyn and Bacon, 1972), p. 9.

21. An exposition of the atomistic conception of the self in the public choice literature can be found in chapter 2 of James M. Buchanan and Gordon Tullock, *The Calculus of Consent: Logical Foundations of Constitutional Democracy* (Ann Arbor: University of Michigan Press, 1964), pp. 11–15.

22. Manis and Meltzer, *Symbolic Interaction*, p. 8.

23. Winter, *Elements for a Social Ethic*.

24. Ibid., p. 21.

25. Ibid., pp. 23–25.

26. Alfred Schutz, *Collected Papers*, vol. 1, ed. Arvid Brodersen (The Hague: Martinus Nijhoff, 1962).

27. Ibid., p. 174.

28. Ibid.

29. The word "intentive," suggested to me by Bayard Catron, may be less confusing than "intentional," which can often convey to the lay reader a meaning identical to "deliberate." For a further elaboration of the relationship between consciousness and action, see chapter 3 of Catron's "Theoretical Aspects of Social Action: Reason, Ethics, and Public Policy" (Ph. D. dissertation, University of California, Berkeley, 1975), pp. 64–106.

30. Percy, *Message in the Bottle*.

31. Ibid., p. 281. For Percy's discussion of language and consciousness, see chapter 8, "Toward a Triadic Structure of Meaning," pp. 159–88.

32. Winter, *Elements for a Social Ethic*, p. 104.

33. For a discussion of the process of objectivation, see Berger and Luckmann, *Social Construction of Reality*, pp. 47–128.

34. Thomas Hobbes, *Leviathan*, intro. A. D. Lindsay (New York: Dutton, 1914), chap. 32.

35. White, "Concept of Administrative Praxis."

36. Frederick C. Thayer, "Epistemology as Organization Theory," in Bellone, *Organization Theory*, pp. 113–39.

37. The idea of intersubjectivity is used by objectivists as well as subjectivists, but different meanings are given to the term by each side. For the objectivists, intersubjectivity (usually used as an adjective, e.g., "intersubjective validation," "intersubjective transmissibility") is typically employed as a methodological hedge, or error-correction device, against inaccurate observations by individual researchers. For the subjectivists, intersubjectivity is the basis for the epistemological stance underlying their descriptions of how the social world is created, maintained, and transformed.

38. Anthony Giddens, *New Rules of Sociological Method: A Positive*

Critique of Interpretive Sociologies (New York: Basic Books, 1976), p. 53.

39. A. R. Louch, *Explanation and Social Action* (Berkeley: University of California Press, 1969).

40. Ibid., p. 51.

41. J. Peter Euben, "Political Science and Political Silence," in *Power and Community: Dissenting Essays in Political Science,* ed. Philip Green and Sanford Levinson (New York: Pantheon, 1969), p. 17.

4

Action and Behavior

THEORY AS CONSPIRACY

When Bernard Shaw said that all professions are conspiracies against the laity, social science theory had not yet evolved to a state of sufficient elaboration and complexity to qualify for professional, and therefore conspiratorial, status. It now has. By conspiracy is meant the inclination of those with specialized knowledge to enhance their power to manipulate, control, or confuse their clients. Just as physicians have been increasingly forced to answer their patients' prickly questions and otherwise cooperate with them in matters of diagnosis and treatment, social scientists might well consider, in a similar spirit, some nonconspiratorial ground rules in developing theory that takes account of the meanings and concerns of the subjects being studied. These ground rules have to do not only with ethical matters, such as protection of the rights of research subjects, but bear directly on the epistemological and descriptive adequacy of the theory itself. Before outlining some rules for nonconspiratorial theorizing, however, some additional specification is required of what is meant by conspiratorial theory. In the case of administrative theory in particular, evidence of conspiracy is found in

1. the tendency of adminstrative theory to employ unwarranted *a priori* assumptions about the "true" nature of organizations and of the people who work in them or are affected by them;

2. the frequent covert introduction of normative judgments disguised either as facts or "neutral" methodological assumptions; and
3. the relative neglect of the political and moral nature of administrative practice.[1]

Among the theoretical assumptions and beliefs discussed earlier that seem to qualify as conspiratorial include the methodological individualism of public choice theory. In this chapter, the criticisms offered of both behaviorism and functionalism are largely derived from the three criteria of conspiratorial theory listed above. Taken together, the three criteria illustrate once again the interrelationships among categories of theory. *Assumptions* influence *descriptions,* which in turn determine the manner in which *normative* questions are dealt with, resulting in a tendency to construe issues of administrative *practice* in purely instrumental terms.

An illustration of the conspiracy of theory is provided through a brief summary of the systems approach to organizational theory. Although the systems approach is highly abbreviated and simplified here, the criticisms implied by the conspiracy criteria are fairly representative of the kinds of criticisms currently made by opponents of the systems view.

Systems theories, which are usually based on either mechanistic or organismic metaphors, typically assume that an organization is comprised of interdependent parts which, taken as a whole, are governed by certain needs that must be satisfied in order to assure the organization's survival. Moreover, survival is made possible by "inputs" from the environment on which the organization is contingent. Thus, action taken by the organization on the basis of its assessment of observed environmental contingencies can be seen as a natural outgrowth of its need to survive.

The *a priori* assumption that organizations, as systems, have survival needs conforms to the first criterion of conspiratorial theory for the reason that organizations are abstractions, and abstractions cannot have needs (although people may). If the "organization's need for survival" is simply intended as a shorthand expression to reflect the intersubjective agreement among the organization's members that they wish to survive collectively as an organization, then the statement that this is somehow a *universal* need is arbitrary. The problem here is the confusion of frequently observed motives with causal laws expressed in the form of universal needs.

The covert introduction of normative judgments by the systems approach is evident if one recognizes that organization members, as agents, are free to define their "needs" in practically any way they wish, including the possible decision to disband as an organizational entity. These decisions are, among other things, moral choices in which no outcome preconceived by the theorist should be regarded as more natural than any other. Organizational survival, properly understood as a normative issue, is highly problematic in the same sense as Camus' statement that the only relevant philosophical question for mankind is suicide. By reducing moral questions to organismic analogies, systems theory perpetuates a conspiracy that either obscures normative issues altogether or reinforces a conservative bias toward the status quo.

The final criterion of conspirational theory, that is, the tendency to ignore the moral and political character of administrative practice, is evident in an important school of management thought—contingency theory [2]—derived from the systems perspective. Contingency management interprets practical questions of administration as being limited almost exclusively to the instrumental attainment of predefined organizational goals. Even such humanistic concerns as self-realization and personal growth, which *are* addressed by some contingency theorists, are "contingent" on their compatibility with goal attainment. Thus, normative questions about the political legitimacy either of organizational ends or of rights and needs of individual members are excluded as important concerns of administrative practice.

While more will be said in this and subsequent chapters about theory building, and especially about the relationship of theory to practice, some ground rules are suggested here that may permit the development of nonconspiratorial and therefore useful social theory.

1. Theory must not violate the domain which it purports to describe, explain, or otherwise address.
2. When social theory is about social practice, its political and moral content must be explicitly recognized.
3. Theory must be recognized as rising from social practice, although theory influences practice.
4. The social theorist should understand himself to be a social actor, and not purely an observer—and this understanding must be reflected in the theory itself.
5. The theoretical interest in generalization and law-like behavior must not negate the uniqueness and discretion of individual actors.[3]

The impediments to eliminating conspiratorial theorizing are more formidable than they may initially appear inasmuch as the conspiracy is so firmly imbedded in particular modes of describing *what* people do and explaining *why* they do it. The possibilities for nonconspiratorial theory and description, therefore, are initially addressed here by looking at a long-standing disagreement in social science regarding the relative desirability of particular approaches to describing and explaining human activity.

Two words, which in everyday parlance are typically used interchangeably, depict that disagreement: *action* and *behavior*. The debate over the merits of action and behaviorist approaches is closely tied to the distinction made previously between the active and passive conceptions of the self. Chapter 3 noted that the active and passive conceptions are not mutually exclusive, but that the active view of the self *subsumes* the passive conception—while the reverse does not hold true. That is, the passive view, as usually construed, forecloses the possibility of an active self. The same relationship holds between the concepts of action and behavior. The idea of action suggests that descriptions of human activity should include attention to behavior but that behavior of any important social consequence should also be understood as action bound up in the meanings of the actors. Thus, descriptions of behavior alone are not necessarily wrong; they are simply insufficient—or, to borrow Guerreiro-Ramos' word, "naive." [4] Such descriptions are naive in the sense that they uncritically accept conclusions drawn from sensory observations without reflecting about the basic assumptions that underlie those observations.

The following section of this chapter expands on proposition 6, by exploring the idea of action and clarifying its relation to the earlier discussion of the nature of the self and epistemology. Proposition 7 is critical of behaviorism and its attendant assumptions. Additionally, the varying meanings and purposes of description, explanation, and prediction, which differ radically between the action and behaviorist approaches, are compared, culminating in the presentation of a descriptive framework for administrative action and a typology of administrative environments.

PROPOSITION 6. *Description and explanation in social science should be primarily concerned with action, a concept that directs attention to the everyday meanings people give to their actions.*

The idea of action as it has evolved up to now draws upon a remarkably diverse array of historical and contemporary sources beginning with Aristotle's notion of *praxis*, through more recent Kantian and Marxist traditions. In the present century, the major sources of influence on the action approach include the fields of symbolic interactionism,[5] pragmatism,[6] philosophy,[7] interpretive sociology,[8] the sociology of knowledge,[9] critical theory,[10] and phenomenology.[11]

Perhaps the most important influence on nearly all of the more recent contributors to the action approach is a name familiar to any beginning student of public administration: Max Weber. This may seem surprising, at first glance, in view of the centrality of Weber's articulation of the "rational-bureaucratic" model of organization to the Classical public administration paradigm. Yet Weber, who was by no means a normative advocate of bureaucracy, left an indelible mark on European sociology, influencing a wide range of contemporary movements. Prominent among these is modern phenomenology, which has drawn substantially from Weber's concept of social action.

In action is included all human behavior when and insofar as the acting individual attaches a subjective meaning to it. . . . Action is social insofar as, by virtue of the subjective meaning attached to it by the acting individual(s), it takes account of the behavior of others and is thereby oriented in its course.[12]

Although Weber was not a phenomenologist, he and Edmund Husserl,[13] the founder of modern phenomenology, were the major sources of influence on Alfred Schutz, whose writings provided the basis for the active-social conception of the self. Most of Schutz's work, begun in Germany in the 1930s and completed in the United States in the late 1950s, can be seen as an effort to develop Weber's sociology, especially his theory of action, within the phenomenological tradition begun by Husserl.

Schutz's writings are particularly noteworthy for their attempt to depict, in a nonreductive fashion, the richness, complexity, and nuance of human experience. Recognizing that the domain of human action is infinitely varied, Schutz is careful to avoid the tendency either to circumscribe the range and kinds of actions that deserve investigation or to impose *a priori* explanations on those actions. His approach to understanding action is mentioned here by virtue of its contrast with the tendency of much of organization theory to limit its analysis of organizations to action concerned exclusively with the calculation of means in the attainment of ends. Even our beliefs about what it means to be *rational* have been impoverished by reducing the word to a synonym for instrumental calculation.[14]

This complaint is not primarily intended to suggest that greater attention be paid to the role of "feelings," which, in any event, are often trivialized by bestowing on them the label of "nonrational" or denuded through the use of theoretical categories that tend to sterilize rather than enrich our understanding. Rather, the concern here is that a fuller grasp of organizational life must also include a consideration of meanings and actions involved both in the *formulation* and in the *absence* of organizational ends, as well as action directed toward their attainment. This, in turn, requires attention to how organizational actors make sense of their world, decide what is worth doing, and reflect on the meanings of their own and others' actions.

Among Schutz's major contributions bearing on the argument of this book are his ideas of intentionality and intersubjectivity (discussed in the preceding chapter), the "project," human "agency," and motives. Schutz viewed people as agents (active selves) whose actions are understandable in terms of projects.

The distinguishing characteristic of action is precisely that it is determined by a project which precedes it in time. Action then is behavior in accordance with a plan of projected behavior; and the project is neither more nor less than the action itself conceived and decided upon in the future perfect tense. Thus the project is the primary and fundamental meaning of the action.[15]

In other words, description of action is impossible without including statements about the meanings and purposes associated with it by the actor. None of this, of course, is plausible unless one grants that people are agents acting on the basis of *motives*, rather than "behavers" reacting to causal forces or stimuli.

In discussing the subject of motives, Schutz seeks to clarify the relationship between past experience and future actions.[16] "In-order-to" motives, he says, are statements *by actors* about why, with what aims or purposes, they undertake actions. Further, "In-order-to" motives are the motives behind projects and are always in the future tense, even when looked upon retrospectively (e.g., "I shall open (I opened) my umbrella in order to keep from getting wet"). "Because" motives, on the other hand, are *past tense* explanations made by the actor of the conditions or past experiences that predisposed him or her to act in a certain way (e.g., "I opened my umbrella because that is what I have learned to do to keep from getting wet when it rains"). It is important to note, however, that Schutz stopped short of equating the "because" motive with "cause" in the behaviorist sense inasmuch as actors, as agents, may choose to disregard prior conditioning or experience (e.g., "To hell with the umbrella; I'd like to get rained on today").

To be sure, both classes of motives are intertwined and often confused with one another. We sometimes act unaware of our motives (of either kind); we may be hypocritical and self-serving in our public statements of them; and we often "discover" our motives only upon reflection subsequent to acting. All these qualifications to the rudimentary presentation of the two classes of motives are reminders that "motivated" action is not always, nor perhaps even most often, rational and self-aware.

At social, or aggregate, levels of analysis (e.g., organizations, cultures, societies, or nation-states), the action frame of reference emphasizes that such collectivities are the historical products or "constructions" resulting from shared (intersubjective) meanings and actions of their members, both past and present. Anthony Giddens, following closely in the tradition of Berger and Luckmann [17] and Schutz, has formulated some "new rules" of sociological method that summarize the general thrust of the action orientation as it bears on descriptions of social collectivities.

Sociology is not concerned with the "pre-given" universe of objects, but with one which is constituted or produced by the active doings of subjects. Human beings transform nature socially, and by "humanizing" it they transform themselves; but they do not, of course, produce the natural world, which is constituted as an object-world independently of their existence. . . .

The production and reproduction of society thus has to be treated as a skilled performance on the part of its members, not as merely a mechanical series of processes.[18]

Giddens goes on to say that "human agency is bounded," that is, social institutions form the context that simultaneously *constrains* and *enables* human agency.[19] The role of the sociologist (and, by extension, social scientists generally) is to explicate and interpret the social world as constituted within the structures of meaning of the social actors themselves.[20]

PROPOSITION 7. *The concept of action provides the basis for challenging the adequacy of social science theory whose fundamental orientation is toward the observation and analysis of behavior.*

A hint of the behaviorists' antipathy toward the action and related orientations is often revealed in the pejorative terms employed in their criticisms. "Today a social scientist who uses human purpose as an organizing entity will likely be accused of 'vitalism,' 'anthropomorphic subjectivism,' and 'normative thinking,' only a few of the epithets in the [behaviorists'] arsenal."[21] The most influential modern behaviorist, B. F. Skinner, disapprovingly refers to psychologies predicated on such notions as consciousness, intentionality, motive, and purpose as "mentalist." While he does not exclude the possible existence of consciousness by granting that ". . . a small part of the universe is enclosed within the human skin,"[22] Skinner insists that such mental processes "are ruled out of scientific consideration."[23]

There is reason to question the basis on which Skinner rules out of scientific consideration these "mentalist" approaches. Despite his claim that behaviorism has philosophical status, his rejection of approaches concerned with subjective experience appears to be based more on grounds of methodological convenience than on the absence of a philosophical foundation. Moreover, Skinner's critics are quick to point out that his thory of operant reinforcement, which explains behavior in stimulus-response terms, lacks firm theoretical grounding by virtue of its naive acceptance of a causal model borrowed from the natural sciences. It is instructive to note that in *About Behaviorism,*[24] his systematic attempt to answer his critics (mainly of *Beyond Freedom and Dignity*[25]), Skinner begins by stating that the task of psychology, not only behaviorism, is to explain the causes of human behavior. If one accepts this definition of the problem, Skinner's task is a relatively easy one because he *assumes* what is most problematic: the conditions under which causal explanations are logically admissible. The kinds of actions Schutz describes by means of "because" motives, Skinner assumes to be unambiguous evidence of the validity of causal explanations similar to those of natural science.

On the surface, Schutz's and Skinner's accounts seem equally plausible; the only means for resolving the difference between the two is to assess the epistemological limitations of the idea of causality, rather than simply its methodological convenience. This is an issue Skinner does not address, an especially troubling omission in view of the first sentence in his introduction to *About Behaviorism:* "Behaviorism is not the science of human behavior; it is the philosophy of that science." [26] The danger inherent in Skinner's confusion of the methodological with the philosophical has been addressed by Catron.

> For the "methodological behaviorist" [namely Skinner], the problem of explaining action is, purely and simply, a methodological one. . . .
>   This methodological commitment, however, . . . tends to become ensconced as an ideology, and frequently takes the form simply of reducing action to behavior, and declaring what ever might be left over as mystical or at any event nonscientific. [27]

At stake here is the philosophy underlying behaviorism, a form of positivism that (1) stipulates that the only admissible knowledge is that which is accessible through the senses and (2) includes "a faith that the methods and logical structure of science, as epitomized in classical physics, can be applied to the study of social phenomena." [28] Positivist theory, whether behaviorist psychology or social science theories about larger social units, is tenable only insofar as one is willing to accept *a priori* causal explanations.

CAUSATION, MEANING, AND VALUES

The nature of the disagreement about causal explanations bears upon our understanding of, and indeed our willingness to accept as important, the notions of meaning and motive. The controversy surrounding the idea of causation is relevant not only to the tension between the passive and active conceptions of the self, discussed in chapter 3, but also to disagreements concerning the degree to which modes of scientific explanation of the natural world are appropriate to an understanding of the social world.

Some common ground for agreement does exist among the contending viewpoints with respect to causation as an idea which could, in theory, explain human activity and social relationships. Schutz, for example, concedes to Nagel that the *logic* of causal explanations used in the natural sciences also pertains in social science and that it is possible to conceive of "an ideally refined behaviorism" [29] based on that logic. (Even the notion of meanings, one assumes, might be explainable in terms of "causal" connections among neurological synapses, the discovery and theoretical explication of which are, to be sure, currently far beyond reach.) But Schutz is quick to remind Nagel of his own stipulations that the actual development of a comprehensive social theory along these lines may be a "fancy," that the theory would be highly abstract, and that its "concepts will have to be apparently remote from the familiar and obvious traits found in any one society."[30]

Schutz's quarrel with the use of the natural science metaphor, then, is not with its assumption of causality as such, nor that the idea of causality logically precludes attention to meanings and motives. Rather, he is critical, as is Nagel, of the tendency of behaviorism, and positivist theory generally, to make naive assumptions about causal relations in descriptions of the social world by virtue of their disregard for the meanings of actors. He is also critical of their tendency to impose *a priori* explanatory theories on observations of behavior such that those theories are not subject to falsification.

For Schutz, the goal of social science is to develop systematic knowledge of social reality, which he defines as "the sum total of objects and occurrences within the social cultural world as experienced by the common-sense thinking of men living their daily lives among their fellow-men. . . ."[31] The foundation of the theories about social reality must explain, rather than simply take for granted, intersubjectivity, processes of social interaction, and language. These concepts are at the root of the differences between the natural and the social sciences. As Schutz explains:

> It is up to the natural scientist and to him alone to define, in accordance with the procedural rules of his science, his observational field, and to determine the facts, data, and events within it which are relevant for his problem or scientific purpose at hand. Neither are those facts and events pre-selected, nor is the observational field pre-interpreted. The world of nature, as explored by the natural scientist, does not "mean" anything to molecules, atoms, and electrons. . . . The thought objects constructed by the social scientist [by contrast], in order to grasp this social reality, have to be founded upon the thought objects constructed by the common-sense thinking of men, living their daily life within their social world. Thus, the constructs of the social sciences are, so to speak, constructs of the second degree, that is, constructs of the constructs made by the actors on the social scene, whose behavior the social scientist has to observe and to explain in accordance with the procedural rules of his science.[32]

The second-order character of these constructs restricts the manner in which causal (or determinate) relations among social units may be inferred, but it does not foreclose them altogether. Objectively verifiable social theories are possible, Schutz says, through the development of "objective ideal typical constructs."[33] These constructs, for example, include typical kinds of actions that are explainable in terms of common motives and meanings understandable to the particular actors by means of their "common-sense interpretation of every-day life." [34] These constructs, moreover, are empirically observable, although Schutz adds that empirical observation should not be restricted to the *sensory* observation of objects and behaviors. [35]

Schutz realizes, of course, that the richness and diversity of social life is not always reducible to ideal-typical constructs, quite apart from the formidable methodological problems involved in their validation. Individuals, at most, only partially conform to others' expectations, including those of social scientists. The powers of thought and reflection, while they make possible a *shared* social existence, also enable the *diversity* of human experience and make plausible the idea of the individual's existential freedom. This reminder, in fact, helps account for the skepticism with which those who are sympathetic to Schutz's perspective regard so-called functionalist social theory.

To some extent inspired by the metaphor of the biological organism, functionalist anthropology and sociology seek to explain the survival, maintenance, integrity, and, to some extent, the processes involved in changing social and cultural systems. They do so through primary attention to the functions of and interrelationships among the parts of those systems. One classic, although not altogether representative, statement of the functionalist perspective is that of Malinowski who said that functionalism

> . . . aims at the explanation of anthropological facts at all levels of development by their function, by the part which they play within the integral system of culture, by the manner in which they are related to each other within the system, and by the manner in which this system is related to the physical surroundings. . . . The functional view of culture insists therefore upon the principle that in every type of civilization, every custom, material object, idea and belief fulfills some vital function, has some task to accomplish, represents an indispensable part within a working whole. [36]

It should be stressed that many contemporary functionalists have been sensitive to the criticisms leveled against Malinowski's perspective and have attempted to alter their theories accordingly. His statement is nevertheless useful because some of the more obvious limitations of it underscore the kinds of criticisms that functionalist analyses tend to invite. The criticisms have to do with both the explanatory and the normative adequacy of functionalist approaches.

The plausibility of Malinowski's view as the basis for explaining the behavior of social systems depends on whether one is willing to agree at the outset that *every* custom, object, idea, and so forth performs a *vital* system function. Note that this implies the *a priori* assumption of determinate relationships of a *particular kind,* that is, relationships that contribute to the system as "a working whole." The possibility that some parts do *not* contribute is excluded *before* analysis begins, which means that evidence suggesting the contrary necessarily requires either a rein-terpretation of it to fit the theory or simply further research. An alternative way of handling discrepancies between the theory and the evidence is to label nonconforming system units as "dysfunctional." The term "dysfunctional" almost inevitably implies a pejorative normative meaning, given the functionalists' overall concern with system requirements for survival. This, then, leads to the charge that functionalism typically imports an implicit bias in favor of conservative, that is, system-maintaining, values. Critics of the functionalist view, therefore, have been often vociferous in condemning it as tautological, on the one hand, and for declining to make explicit and defend its value position, on the other.

Despite these nagging problems, the idea of the biological (or organismic) metaphor may still be useful as a descriptive framework so long as the determinate nature of the relationships among system parts is not assumed in advance. Social life, after all, is made possible by social relationships, which are explicable through attention to the structures of meaning of social actors, as many functionalists will readily agree. But, as Schutz reminds us, the determinate nature of those relationships in the social world can be grasped only partially—through the highly abstract device of the ideal-typical construct.

These qualifications aside, one further warning is suggested here having to do with the value premises implicit in an extreme functionalist view. Granting for the moment that the study of biological organisms and social systems might share a common descriptive metaphor, problems emerge when one uncritically accepts the value premises implied by an organism's "need for survival" as extending to the normative evaluation of social systems. In the former case, the "value" of the survival of biological organisms may usually be taken for granted (making normative discussion superfluous), so that we may quickly proceed to an empirical investigation of the means by which they do so. Moreover, unless the organism in question is a person, it will have no opinion regarding the merits of its own survival; nor will the organism's various organs or parts, those of people included, be concerned about the extent of their particular contributions to the life of the organism.

In the analysis of the social world, however, the treatment of persons, if only by implication, as the functional equivalent of lungs or kidneys tends to obscure the realization that values are virtually always problematic in social life. They are problematic to such concerns, for example, as the survival of social systems, the desirability of changing or maintaining particular configurations of political power and the social order, or the continued existence of one organization or another. Moreover, such value questions cannot seriously be addressed in other than personal, human terms. Unlike biological organisms, which are tangible, the idea of a "social system" is an abstraction that is remote from the ways in which people typically experience the social world. *A priori* constructs along functionalist lines run the risk of disregarding the common-sense experience of social actors and, by extension, may also do violence to the things those actors value.

THE PROPER ROLE OF "BEHAVIOR" IN SOCIAL SCIENCE

Harré and Secord have snidely observed that behaviorism does have its place: in departments of physiology.[37] To study behavior in the social sciences, however, does not necessarily make one a behaviorist (or positivist), if the relationship of behavior to action is carefully observed. In a rough sense, behavior is related to action in the same way that an "objective (or *objectivated,* strictly speaking) reality" is related to inter-subjective meaning. Behavior, as well as the idea of objective reality, is a partial idea that is subordinate to the more encompassing notion of action, which includes a consideration of commonly understandable meanings and motives of social actors. The study of human behavior may be productive when little doubt exists about the actual or likely subjective meaning of the behavior to the actors being observed. Behavior, then, may in many cases be an adequate surrogate in lieu of the "real thing"—that is, accounts by the actors themselves of their motives or purposes. From an epistemological standpoint, data derived from *observations* of behavior are always second-best expedients, but are acceptable especially when one has reason to distrust the reliability of the actors' accounts. In some cases, for example, people may lie, forget, be confused, or be out of touch with their own purposes. While this may often be the case, it is nonetheless important to recognize particular misgivings about the reliability of the actors' accounts as a methodological, rather than a theoretical or epistemological, problem.

A related issue concerning the admissibility of actors' statements about meanings and motives has to do with the manner in which they are interpreted by the social scientist. Many non-Skinnerian positivists readily accept, both in principle and in practice, the admissibility of such statements, but proceed to confine the interpretation of them to the *a priori* models they (those social scientists) are already predisposed to accept as true. In other words, the data—the statements of actors—are manipulated to fit the theory.

An obvious practical reason for using behavioral measures is simply convenience. Since behavioral observation is ordinarily less time-consuming than depth interviewing, the former may appear to be preferable when little doubt exists among researchers about the motives behind the behavior. For example, if it is assumed that people are admitted to hospitals because they are in need of medical attention, a quick survey of hospital admission records (to count or measure behavior) is apparently more practical than interviewing singly all those patients admitted in order to determine whether their motive was in fact the receipt of medical care. The slightly lower reliability (i.e., the correspondence between the behavior and the motive presumed by the researcher) of the "behavioral data" is accepted in view of the time saved by not interviewing all the patients. The convenience of behavioral measures increases, of course, when research populations are large and aggregated, as is often the case in research efforts pertaining to public organizations and their clients.

A great deal of caution is in order, however, with respect to the readiness with which typical motives are assumed to represent accurately particular behaviors. Just as actors' statements about meanings and motives cannot always be accepted at face value, neither can it always be assumed that the behavior of actors will be adequately depicted by the theorist's preconceived categories of meaning. The reasons why people are admitted to hospitals, for example, range from the obvious to the bizarre and are influenced by a host of people other than the patient, including family members, friends, physicians, and others.

Action theory can make no legitimate claim that its interpretations of actors' statements are correct. Rather, the "objectivity" that action theorists aspire to results from their reluctance to prejudge actors' meanings and motives in terms of their relation to observable behaviors.

BEHAVIORISM AND ACTION THEORY: CONFLICTING REQUIREMENTS

Both the positivist model of science on which behaviorism is based, as well as the action orientation, share some important and familiar requirements for judging the adequacy of social science theory: (1) the accuracy of the *descriptions* based on the theory, (2) the adequacy of *explanations* of and *generalizations* about why individuals and collectivities behave or act as they do, and (3) the *predictive* accuracy of the theory regarding future action or behavior. Although to some extent all these requirements hold for both approaches, each is interpreted differently. The major difference between the two approaches is based on disagreements concerning causal models.

Description. In the positivist orientation, descriptions are based on categories or taxonomies that reflect the theorist's preconceived judgments about the kind of behavior that are most deserving of study and occasionally about the likely social meanings associated with that behavior, either to the actors themselves or to people who are or may be affected by the behavior. For the action theorist, categories of behavior and meaning that provide the basis for organizing descriptive data typically emerge out of the theorist-researcher's synthesis of subjects' responses to highly open-ended, nonleading questions, for example, "How do you see this situation?" "What would you like to do (or get) that you are not doing (getting) now?" Although all theorists are required to make judgments about the significance of data, the discussion here suggests the wisdom of suspending those judgments for a longer period of time and appreciating the data in terms of categories of meaning inferred from the subjects' own accounts.

Explanation. Explanations are post hoc answers to why people do what they do. Although shades of gray exist between the polar extremes of positivism and action theory, the former, in its more extreme forms, seeks to discover lawlike explanations of behavior. At least in theory, laws are discoverable that may explain behavior with great certainty, although in practice this may be difficult. Such difficulties for the positivist, however, tend to be seen as evidence either of the wrongness or insufficiency of particular hypotheses or of methodological limitations in testing them empirically.

In the action approach, the reluctance to embrace causal models is based less on considerations of their methodological precision than with the fact that their application is necessarily limited to a highly circumscribed type of explanation. Specifically, the logic of causal explanation is permissible only with respect to clarifying determinate relationships among ideal-typical constructs. But since such constructs, at best, only partially grasp the aspects of the social world they are intended to explain, any "laws" inferred from causal analysis of those constructs can only be hypothetical and abstract.

This limitation of causal models helps explain the action approach's practical, as well as theoretical, bias toward the development and appreciation of ad hoc or unique explanations, as well as the formulation of generalized explanations.

> The range of motives, values, and situational definitions of organizational actors is infinitely variable; that is, each organization and each actor is unique. This imposes a severe handicap on theories which posit a limited number of factors as *universally* explaining the realities of organizational life. . . . Such *a priori* theorizing cannot possibly take account of the unique reality of each and every organization. The quest for universal explanations imports the fundamental bias that the identification of similarities, adherence to or departures from expected norms, or correspondence of organizations with the theorist's preconceived categories is more important than grappling with the uniqueness of any one organization or set of actors. This bias is understandable, since the "scientific" tradition suggests that, the more universal and encompassing the theory, the more important the contribution to knowledge. However, as we have already suggested, the viewpoint of the actor is the starting place for theory (as well as for practice). This therefore dictates a theoretical interest in uniqueness as well as in similarity.[38]

The fuller implications of this statement will not become apparent until the final chapter's discussion of the relationship of theory to administrative practice. It should be mentioned here, however, that the importance of unique explanations has less to do with their possible contribution to general theoretical explanations than with their relevance to the practical concerns of administrators. Indeed, by some definitions of theory, uniqueness would not even qualify as a legitimate theoretical concern. A consideration of the role that theorists may perform in assisting in the improvement of administrative practice marks a departure from the kinds of issues with which Schutz was mainly occupied.

Prediction. A major test of any scientific theory is its predictive ability. The emphasis placed here on motives and meanings rather than causal models, however, alters both the way we may interpret theories that accurately predict behavior as well as our understanding of those whose predictive capacity is relatively low. Since people may decide to act counter to prior conditioning and experience, the degree of optimism with which predictions of actions may be made is substantially less from the action theory viewpoint than that presumed by positivist theories. This tentativeness, moreover, "is borne not out of the theorist's recognition of the primitiveness or inadequacies of his/her methodologies, but from an awareness of the infinite possibilities s/he may discover." [39] If Vickers is correct in saying that "people are predictable because they are concerned to be," [40] then evidence derived from theories that predict action and behavior fairly reliably simply affirms the idea that social life is impossible without some degree of orderliness, regularity, and predictability. Predictable behavior, in short, is a matter of human choice, not of causal laws. More importantly, however, the abandonment of *a priori* causal models permits some attention to the view that the value of prediction is grounded mainly in considerations of social utility and other normative concerns.

A DESCRIPTIVE FRAMEWORK OF ADMINISTRATIVE ACTION

The material presented in the immediately preceding and present chapters provides the basis for a descriptive framework of administrative action (figure 4.1). The framework is not intended as an explanatory model, given the stricter requirements implied by that term, although it does offer a basis on which subsequent explanatory models might be formulated. Such models would include typologies based on ideal-typical constructs of the kind discussed earlier and would, of course, be subject to the previously mentioned limitations inherent in that kind of analysis. In fact, some development in that direction is suggested, although not fully elabo-

FIGURE 4.1   A Framework of Administrative Action

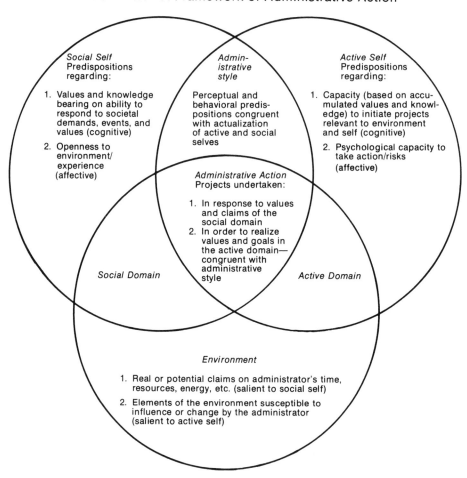

rated, in the next section on administrative environments and in chapter 8's discussion of ideal-typical administrative styles.

One suggestion about the way in which the framework should be viewed is that the area in which all three circles overlap depicts, in a sense, the most "real" aspects of administrative action, whereas areas of less or no overlap are increasingly abstract. Thus the reader is encouraged to imagine the three circles as initially being one circle and that the three are pulled apart only for purposes of theoretical clarification.

The framework is inspired, in part, by Mead's analysis of the subjective meaning that people attach to their experience. This is a reminder that the conceptual boundaries between people and their environments may be overdrawn so as to distort the nature of their interrelationship. In the analysis of action, environments or situations are most usefully conceptualized when account is taken of people's perceptions of them as mediated by their subjective meanings. Moreover, Schutz's notion of the "We-relation," which posits the existence of both a social and an active self, suggests that the relationship between the individual and the environment is one of interdependence. In addition, the sociality of the self means that action taken in response to a perceived demand from the environment or generated in order to realize a desired or possible state of affairs has normative implications beyond the achievement of ends or goals in a purely instrumental sense.

These comments point to the limitations of efforts to explain administrative action solely in terms of its conformity to, or departure from, norms of rationality. The rationalist position holds that (1) values and goals are defined prior to acting, (2) goal *definition* is not itself an action that is subject to rational scrutiny, and (3) goals are fully adequate as criteria from which to measure the effectiveness of action after it has been taken. These three assumptions paint a highly idealized and only partially accurate picture of administrative action. Some of the reasons for this have already been touched upon, while others will be elaborated shortly.

The more encompassing idea of the *project* is employed here and leaves open the range of possible temporal relationships among deciding and acting, goal definition and implementation. The project, as a point of focus of description, also may include a consideration of normative issues beyond simply the instrumental evaluation of behavior through reference to established goals. In contrast to the rationalist position, which holds that values and goals are defined prior to action, in projects value and meanings are created and actualized simultaneously with acting. Additionally, the project encompasses the meaning of action at all levels, from routine and mundane tasks to the most comprehensive level, which is the realization of shared cultural values.

Regarding the administrative action framework's depiction of *administrative style*, it should be pointed out that the use of the term "predisposition" is meant to describe a general tendency or inclination, in contrast to the more determinate ideas of "need" or "drive." Predisposition, as used here, is closely related to "because" motives of which the administrator is aware, but also as they have been influenced by past experience that, to a great extent, may be lost to conscious awareness. Thus, the notion of *choice* implied by our earlier discussion of motives, rather than determinateness, is intended by the framework, but not in an overly rationalistic fashion. Also included in the framework is the common-sense distinction, which has not been addressed in this discussion, between affect (or feelings) and cognition. Feeling and thinking, although interrelated, are understandable in terms of thought processes that are somewhat different from one another. It will simply be assumed here, rather than demonstrated, that both are relevant (albeit each in somewhat different ways) to any description of administrative action.

More important to the meaning of administrative styles are the social and the active natures of the self as they orient our understanding of the predispositions of administrators. The inclusion of the ideas of both the active and the social self stress the *reciprocal* direction of influence between the self and others, between administrators and their environments.

In view of these stipulations, then, administrative style is defined as *an interrelated set of predispositions growing out of the administrator's emotional development, values, knowledge, and experience which inform the manner in which possibilities for choices are perceived and acted upon.*

The dual notions of the social and active *domains* are intended to depict the environment as perceived by the administrator. The two domains comprise the administrator's perceptual field, which informs and constrains projects taken in response to environmental contingencies (the social domain) and enables the initiation of projects (the active domain).

In terms of the various elements of the framework, then, *administrative action* may be defined as *projects undertaken by the administrator* (1) *in response to values, claims, and demands within the social domain and* (2) *in the light of possibilities evident in the active domain, in which such action is mediated and informed, at both conscious and unconscious levels, by the administrator's style.*

ADMINISTRATIVE ENVIRONMENTS

Some cautions are noted here regarding the readiness with which we should accept both theoretical and common-sense distinctions between organization and environment, as well as the relatively passive role often implicitly ascribed to organizational actors in relation to their environments. For example, Weick's preference for the term *enacted* (as opposed to *perceived*) *environment* underscores not only the intentional character of perception but also the truth that people "actively *put* things out there [in the environment] that they then perceive and negotiate about perceiving. It is that initial implanting of reality that is preserved by the word *enactment*." [41] Weick's position, moreover, extends the idea that reality is socially constructed to the formulation of a telling criticism of theoretical approaches that appear to take too literally the distinction between organization and environment.

> Investigators who study organizations often separate environments from organizations and argue that things happen between these distinct entities. This way of carving up the problem of organizational analysis effectively rules out certain kinds of questions. Talk about bounded environments and organizations, for example, compels the investigator to ask questions such as "How does an organization *discover* the *underlying* structure in *the* environment?"

Having separated the "two" entities and given them independent existence, investigators have to make elaborate speculations concerning the ways in which one entity becomes disclosed to and known by the other. But the firm partitioning of the world into the environment and the organization excludes the possibility that people *invent* rather than discover part of what they think they see.

It certainly is the case that organizations bump into things and that their bruises testify to a certain tangibility in the environment, even if that tangibility can be punctuated in numerous ways. The enactment perspective doesn't deny that. But it also does not accept the idea that organizations are most usefully viewed as reactive sensors of those things that happen outside.[42]

While bearing in mind Weick's reservations about the distinction between actors and environment, it is nevertheless both possible and useful, for heuristic purposes, to conceive of environments initially as existing independent of administrators' perceptions of them. To do so avoids the possible charge that the administrative action framework (figure 4.1) is solipsistic and acknowledges the truth in the common-sense observation that certain things in the environment can neither be wished away nor fabricated out of thin air.

Our earlier framework suggested that administrative environments consisted of, first, the real or potential claims on administrators' time, resources, and energy and, second, those features external to administrators that are more or less susceptible to influence or change by them. Taken together, these "parts" suggest the reciprocal nature of influence between administrators (and the organization generally) and the environment. The nature, as well as the variable aspects, of both parts of the environment are clarified by introducing some terminology intended to differentiate among environments in terms of the degree to which they (1) *constrain* or limit the flexibility and discretion of administrators and (2) are amenable to *influence* by them. See figure 4.2.

The discussion of the first dimension begins by borrowing, and quite freely interpreting, two terms used in Emery and Trist's[43] analysis of organizational environments: *turbulence* and *placidity*. A turbulent environment is defined as one in which various groups having claims on the goods or services of an organization change so rapidly and in such unpredictable ways that it is impossible for the organization to develop adequate tactical or strategic responses to cope with the demands made on it. The concepts of turbulence and its opposite—placidity—provide a basis from which distinctions can be made regarding the first dimension of environments noted in the administrative action framework, that is, the claims on the administrator's resources. Specifically, levels of environmental turbulence may be said to vary in terms of the following criteria: the number and magnitude of the claims made on the administrator by environmental actors, the degree of diversity of those claims, the rate at which new claimants enter and old ones exit from the environment, and

FIGURE 4.2 Administrative Environments

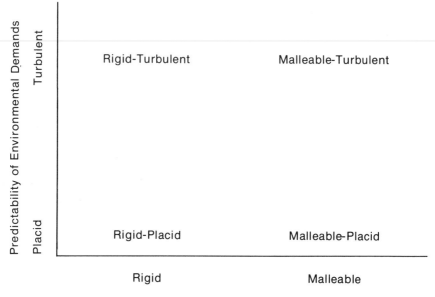

the extent to which multiple claims conflict with or overlap one another.[44]

The notions of turbulence and placidity assist in describing those aspects of the administrator-environment interface in which the cues for action are generated by the environment. This tends to convey the impression, which is relatively common in systems theory, that the administrator occupies a predominantly contingent or reactive posture in relation to the environment, that administrative action is primarily limited to responses to situations or events originating exclusively in the environment. Such descriptions, in other words, may give the impression that the environment ''acts upon'' the administrator but that he or she either does not act upon the environment or that such actions, if they are taken, are limited to those that satisfy imperatives for organizational survival. At an institutional level of analysis, overemphasis of the reactive posture of organizations in relation to their environments illustrates what Perrow has called ''the most significant failure of all organizational theory: the failure to see *society* as adaptive to organizations.''[45]

In order to account for the reciprocal relationship between the administrator and the environment, a parallel concept to turbulence needs to be introduced that depicts the susceptibility of environments to alteration or influence by administrators. Differences in environments implied by this second dimension include the power and resources of actors and groups in the environment relative to those of the administrator; the relative specificity with which environmental and organizational actors define their interests or goals; the amount of slack in the environment (i.e., latent or existing issues to which environmental actors have not or are unlikely to commit significant amounts of resources); predispositions of actors in the environment to engage in bargaining or consensual decision making; and the extent to which the administrator is credible to or trusted by those actors. Collectively, differences with respect to these elements define the relative *rigidity* or *malleability* of administrative environments.

Malleability and rigidity, like turbulence and placidity, should not be viewed as objective qualities of environments but as characteristics imputed to them by actors in the situation as well as by outside observers. For this reason the analysis of environments is closely linked to the idea of administrative style included in the framework of administrative action.

Levels of turbulence or malleability can be fully understood only from the standpoint of the subjective meanings attributed to them by the administrator. Thus, the twin concepts of the social and the active domains are included, which form the nexus of the relationship between actor and environment. Particular administrators, for example, may differ greatly in their tendencies either to perceive environments as relatively malleable or to take actions that "test" their malleability, rather than taking for granted the appearances of rigidity. The assumption here is that environmental rigidity or malleability can more accurately be ascertained through action than through detached observation. While environments constrain action, the extent of those constraints often cannot be accurately defined prior to acting. Administrators, even when they are not conscious of doing so, "construct, rearrange, single out, and demolish many 'objective' features of their surroundings. When people act they unrandomize variables, and literally create their own constraints."[46] By means of action itself, the environment (or situation) is altered, including the stock of information that may inform future action. An important implication for organizational decision making, one that undermines the tenets of the rational decision-making model, is that it may sometimes be more sensible to act, in an "experimental" mode, and *then* observe, than to make decisions about whether to act *after* information is gathered and predictions are made about the likely success of actions based on that information.[47]

SUMMARY OF THE ARGUMENT

To this point, the discussion has dealt mainly with issues pertaining to social science theory in general, with emphasis on beliefs concerning the nature of the self, epistemology, and alternative orientations toward description and explanation. Figure 4.3 summarizes the major elements of the action approach as developed thus far and contrasts them with as-

FIGURE 4.3 Summary of the Assumptive and Descriptive-Explanatory Elements of the Action Theory Paradigm

	Action Paradigm	Alternative Paradigms
1. Major purposes of paradigms	Integration of theoretical categories; clarification of normative concerns; improvement of practice	Explanation and prediction; specification of research agendas
2. Primary unit of analysis	Face-to-face encounter	Individual, group, organization, nation-state, system
3. Assumptions about the "self"	Active-social	Passive-social, passive-atomistic, active-atomistic
4. Epistemology	Intersubjectivist (phenomenology)	Objectivist (positivism)
5. Focus of description	Action, subjective meanings of social actors	Observation of behavior
6. Mode of explanation	Motives of actors expressed in projects	Causes, system functions, goals
7. Sources of motivation	Love, mutual fulfillment	Self-interest, system survival
8. Representative schools of thought	Phenomenology, symbolic interactionism, interpretative sociology, critical theory	Behaviorism, systems theory, public choice

sumptions and orientations of alternative paradigms in social science and public administration. The right-hand column, "Alternative Paradigms," is labeled in the plural inasmuch as the elements listed within it variously apply to behaviorist, positivist, systems, and public choice approaches. For the purpose of this summary, these approaches are not differentiated, although they should not be assumed to be logically consistent with one another in all, or even most, respects.

The normative aspects of administrative action have been frequently alluded to in these first four chapters. It has been suggested that social action is always moral action, in the sense used by Louch,[48] and that explanation and assessment of action inevitably presume a moral frame of reference. Additionally, it has been argued that normative (value) theory logically derives from assumptions about human nature and epistemology that are, in turn, the primary building blocks of social science paradigms. Little has been said about the particular character of the Action paradigm's theory of values. The purpose of chapter 5 is to sketch out the basics of such a theory and, in subsequent chapters, to demonstrate its relevance to issues related to public administration theory and practice.

NOTES

1. Bayard L. Catron and Michael M. Harmon, "Action Theory in Practice: Toward Theory without Conspiracy" (paper presented at the Annual Meeting of the American Society for Public Administration, Phoenix, Arizona, April 1978), pp. 2–3.

2. Fred R. Luthans, *Introduction to Management: A Contingency Approach* (New York, McGraw-Hill, 1976).

3. Catron and Harmon, "Action Theory in Practice," p. 3.

4. Alberto Guerreiro-Ramos, "A Substantive Approach to Organizations: Epistemological Grounds," in *Organizational Theory and the New Public Administration*, ed. Carl J. Bellone (Boston: Allyn and Bacon, 1980), pp. 140–68.

5. Charles W. Morris, ed., *Works of George Herbert Mead*, vol. 1, *Mind, Self, and Society from the Standpoint of a Social Behaviorist* (Chicago: University of Chicago Press, 1934).

6. Manley Thompson, ed., *The Pragmatic Philosophy of C. S. Peirce* (Chicago: University of Chicago Press, Phoenix Books, 1963).

7. Ludwig Wittgenstein, *Philosophical Investigations* (New York: Oxford University Press, 1972); and A. R. Louch, *Explanation and Social Action* (Berkeley: University of California Press, 1969).

8. David Silverman, *The Theory of Organizations* (New York: Basic Books, 1971).

9. Peter L. Berger and Thomas Luckmann, *The Social Construction of Reality* (Garden City, N.Y.: Anchor Books, 1967).

10. Jurgen Habermas, *Theory and Practice* (Boston: Beacon Press, 1974); and Habermas, *Legitimation Crisis* (Boston: Beacon Press, 1975).

11. Alfred Schutz, *Collected Papers*, vols. 1 and 2, ed. Arvid Brodersen (The Hague: Martinus Nijhoff, 1967); Schutz, *The Phenomenology of the Social World* (Evanston: Northwestern University Press, 1967); and Gibson Winter, *Elements for a Social Ethic* (New York: Macmillan, 1966).

12. Max Weber, *The Theory of Social and Economic Organization* (New York: Free Press, 1964), p. 88.

13. Of Husserl's major works, his last, *Phenomenology and the Crisis of Philosophy*, is by far the most understandable as well as the most relevant to the direction of Schutz's writings. The *Crisis*, as it is usually called, was translated into English by Quentin Lauer (New York: Harper Torchbooks, 1963).

14. Guerreiro-Ramos, "Substantive Approach to Organizations," pp. 144–46.

15. Schutz, *Collected Papers*, 2:11.

16. Ibid., p. 14.

17. Berger and Luckmann, *Social Construction of Reality*.

18. Anthony Giddens, *New Rules of Sociological Method: A Positive Critique of Interpretive Sociologies* (New York: Basic Books, 1976), p. 143. Italics in original.

19. Ibid., pp. 160–61.

20. Ibid., p. 162.

21. Charles Hampden-Turner, *Radical Man* (Garden City, N.Y.: Anchor Books, 1971), p. 12.

22. B. F. Skinner, *Beyond Freedom and Dignity* (New York: Bantam/Vantage, 1971), p. 182.

23. Ibid.

24. Skinner, *About Behaviorism* (New York: Knopf, 1974).

25. Skinner, *Beyond Freedom and Dignity.*

26. Skinner, *About Behaviorism*, p. 3.

27. Bayard L. Catron, "Theoretical Aspects of Social Action: Reason, Ethics, and Public Policy" (Ph.D. dissertation, University of California, Berkeley, 1975), p. 88

28. Giddens, *New Rules of Sociological Method*, p. 130.

29. Alfred Schutz, "Concept and Theory Formation in the Social Sciences," in *Philosophy of the Social Sciences*, ed. Maurice Natanson (New York: Random House, 1963), p. 241.

30. Ernest Nagel, "Problems of Concept and Theory Formation in the Social Sciences," in Natanson, *Philosophy of Social Sciences*, p. 209.

31. Schutz, in Natanson, *Philosophy of Social Sciences*, p. 236.

32. Ibid., p. 242.

33. Ibid., p. 246.

34. Ibid., p. 247.

35. Ibid., p. 248.

36. Bronislaw Malinowski, "Anthropology," in *The Encyclopaedia Britannica*, Supplementary vol. 1, pp. 132–33.

37. R. Harré and P. Secord, *The Explanation of Social Behaviour* (New York: Oxford University Press, 1972).

38. Catron and Harmon, "Action Theory in Practice," pp. 8–9.

39. Ibid., pp. 9–10.

40. Sir Geoffrey Vickers, in conversation with Bayard L. Catron.

41. Karl E. Weick, *The Social Psychology of Organizing* (2nd ed.; Reading, Mass.: Addison-Wesley, 1979), p. 165.

42. Ibid.

43. F. E. Emery and E. L. Trist, "The Causal Texture of Organizational Environments," *Human Relations* 18 (1965): 21–32.

44. This discussion has also been informed to some extent by Katz and Kahn's helpful summary of environmental types. See Daniel Katz and Robert L. Kahn, *The Social Psychology of Organizations* (2nd ed.; New York: Wiley, 1978), pp. 124–28.

45. Charles Perrow, *Complex Organizations: A Critical Essay* (Glenview, Ill.: Scott, Foresman, 1972), p. 199.

46. Weick, *Social Psychology of Organizing*, p. 164.

47. Robert P. Biller, "Adaptation Capacity and Organization Development," in *Toward a New Public Administration: The Minnowbrook Perspective*, ed. Frank Marini (Scranton: Chandler, 1971), pp. 93–121.

48. See chapter 3's discussion, and Louch, *Explanation and Social Action*, p. 51.

5

Normative Public Administration Theory: Mutuality, Justice, and Equity

In *Newsweek* magazine, a guest columnist reported on a Georgia woman's experience with a local welfare agency.[1] The woman, who had been self-sufficient throughout her life, was finally forced through financial hardship to request public assistance—for which she thought herself to be eligible—from her local welfare agency. When the case worker asked her what financial assets she had, the woman replied that for many years she had put aside a few dollars a month, which now totaled $2,000, to pay for the cost of her burial, since she did not want the government to have to pay for it. The case worker informed her that in order to receive any public assistance she would have to spend at least $500 (for a color television set or anything else) of what she had saved because only people who had less than $1,500 were eligible for assistance. Rules were rules. Chagrined by what she regarded as an affront to her self-respect, the woman left.

This situation points to two recurring problems experienced by public administrators in their roles as *implementers* of policies and *providers* of services. These problems also underlie parallel conceptual problems for the development of a theory of values for public administration as a self-conscious field of study.

For the case worker described above, the problem was whether to exercise discretion, presuming that some existed, in the application of an administrative rule to the case of a particular client. At a more abstract level, the problem may be seen as making judgments that are fair and just regarding the needs and entitlements of individuals as against, or in conjunction with, the collective entitlements of the population as a whole. The second problem, which is related to and complicates the first, has to do with the extent to which the quality of the interactive process as experienced by both the case worker and the woman influenced the outcome and the perceived fairness of the decision. The problem at a theoretical level, therefore, has to do with the relative priority of, and the conceptual relationship between, substance and process.

Normative theory for public administration need not, and in fact should not, be expected to include precise formulas by which fair and just tradeoffs between individual and collective values may be ascertained. Nor should the theory be expected to specify in any operational and measurable senses the relative priority of substance to process. This is not primarily because such requirements are too demanding but because they are beside the point inasmuch as they suggest that normative theorizing should implicitly regard values as nothing more than instrumental measures of decisional efficacy. When this is done, the two theoretical problems noted above, in effect, are defined out of existence or are prejudged in such a way as to preclude serious attention to them.

The failure of the Classical paradigm's theory of values is not its inability to *solve* these problems at a theoretical level, but that its naiveté about both problems precludes a thoughtful understanding of them. The reason for this is that the primacy of objective accountability in the Classical paradigm prejudges both questions. First, the idea of strict accountability forecloses discretion of any importance or, at most, suggests that its exercise is an extraordinary act requiring compelling justification. Thus, the needs of the collectivity, as represented by the uniform application of a rule, supersede *a priori* the unique needs of clients. Second, given the rationalist decision-making premises of the paradigm, processes are conceived as means that are instrumentally related to ends—with the result that the normative priority of substance over process has already been assumed.

The implicit prejudgment of these issues at a theoretical level has important normative and practical consequences, especially when, in a primarily service-oriented society, "outcomes" involve transactions that are mainly of a symbolic nature intended to *serve,* rather than provide *things* for, clients.[2] The normative theory of the Classical paradigm, then, offers little encouragement to consider how the quality of the transactions between service providers and clients, for example, might bear upon their psychic well-being—which, to one way of thinking, should be prized for its own sake. Nor does the classical view help clarify the manner in which the social processes involved in those transactions affect the quality and reasonableness of decisional outcomes as perceived by the parties involved. These issues of quality have only partly to do with the problem of accountability and are not readily given to empirical determination and measurement. They are, however, intimately related to the meanings and motives of actors in a social context.

It appears, then, that an adequate normative theory of public administration must address the relationship of individual to collective values and of substance to process—and in such a way that does not prejudge the theoretical issues involved. Such a theory should also be prepared to offer guidance for, but not presume to solve in a definitive fashion, the exercise of administrative discretion, both as it is circumscribed by institutional requirements for accountability and informed by personal judgment. As we shall see in the later discussion, the basic elements of the theory of values to be elaborated here are extensions of issues raised in earlier chapters, such as the face-to-face encounter, beliefs about the nature of the self, and epistemology.

PROPOSITION 8. *The primary conceptual issues in the development of a theory of values for public administration are the relation of substance to process and of individual to collective values.*

SUBSTANCE AND PROCESS

As ordinarily conceived in the literature of political science, the normative aspects of so-called substantive issues are reflected in the criteria used in determining the fairness or aptness of *outcomes* resulting from administrative or political decisions. Process approaches, on the other hand, take an agnostic view of the relative desirability of various substantive ends and tend to emphasize, instead, either formal procedures or informal bargaining processes by which individuals and groups seek to enhance their interests. A brief summary of these two positions is followed by a critique of them that points out some reservations about the conventional conceptual distinction between substance and process.

Substantive issues, commonly viewed as those having to do with outcomes or end results, comprise the "what" in Lasswell's famous definition that politics is "who gets what, when, how."[3] Substance is what counts, what is valued. Seen in this light, processes are mainly instrumental, having little or no moral content, except for insistence upon procedural safeguards. But even these safeguards are regarded as important only insofar that everyone who wants to can have a chance of getting his or her fair share of the substantive benefits society has to offer. From a normative standpoint, substantive approaches may include principles that specify certain outcomes as *preferable* to others, such as equitable distribution of benefits or entitlements.

The other side of this conceptual coin is represented by "process" theories of democracy, which suggest that since value judgments about the goodness or badness of substantive outcomes (e.g., political, economic) are unprovable, the more appropriate focus should be on the *processes* by which substantive outcomes are produced. In some cases, for example in Lindblom's[4] theory of "partisan mutual adjustment," existing (mainly Western) political processes are judged to be relatively benign. This assessment, in fact, enables Lindblom to declare that the "public interest," a term ordinarily infused with a high normative content, is instead a term descriptive of *whatever* substantive outcomes emerge from the process at any given time.[5] The end objective is itself procedural, that is, agreement, thus begging the evaluative question: agreement on or for what?

An explicitly normative process theory has been proposed by Thorson[6] who, starting from the same premise of the unprovability of the substantive content of values, contends that only to the extent that individual freedoms are protected and equality of opportunity promoted, both of which he conceives of as *process* values, can a political system be regarded as truly democratic. In other words, the benignity of the political process cannot be taken for granted; it is highly problematic. Judgments about political outcomes can be made only through reference to the process, the fairness of which, Thorson says, is determined by the degree to which it is kept open for change.[7]

The substance and process approaches as summarized here are mainly noteworthy in that their similarities outweigh their differences. Their similarity derives from their initial acceptance of the distinction between substance and process both as self-evident and as synonymous with the common-sense distinction between ends and means. An alternative perspective is available that challenges the substance-process dualism on conceptual grounds by recasting the relationship between these seemingly opposite extremes. The reason why the conceptual distinction is problematic is hinted at in Gregory Bateson's observation that it is an artifact of an epistemology peculiar to contemporary Western culture. Commenting on Margaret Mead's comparative approach to the study of anthropology, Bateson turns upside-down the substance-process dualism. He begins by paraphrasing Mead's position against an "instrumental" view of social science theory.

"Before we apply social science to our own national affairs, we must reexamine and change our habits of thought on the subject of means and ends. We have learnt, in our cultural setting, to classify behavior into 'means' and 'ends' and if we go on defining ends as separate from means *and* apply the social sciences as crudely instrumental means, using the recipes of science to manipulate people, we shall arrive at a totalitarian rather than a democratic system of life." The solution which she offers is that we look for the "direction," and "values" implicit in the means, rather than looking ahead to a blueprinted goal and thinking of this goal as justifying or not justifying manipulative means. We have to find the value of a planned act implicit in and simultaneous with the act itself, not separate from it in the sense that the act would derive its value from reference to a future end or goal. Dr. Mead's paper is, in fact, not a direct preachment about ends and means; she does not say that ends either do or do not justify the means. She is talking not directly about ends and means, but about the way we tend to think about ways and means, and about the dangers inherent in our habit of thought.[8]

Bateson's comment should strike a familiar chord in view of the earlier discussions of both the "project" and the intersubjective process by which knowledge is produced.[9] Bateson affirms the view that *the "value" of human action is found in the action itself,* including its cognitive *and* expressive aspects, in contrast to the view that action is meaningful only as measured against the consequences or outcomes it brings about. Process, in other words, has intrinsic value. Relatedly, the epistemological perspective discussed in chapter 3 suggests that what we usually think of as substance (or ends) is only that which we have individually or collectively decided to *regard* as substance, that is, to objectivate. "Substantive ends" or "outcomes" are fundamentally nothing more than objectivations, in the Berger and Luckmann sense,[10] resulting from intersubjective processes of agreement whether in the form of social facts or normative goals.

This line of argument goes much further than to say simply that the distinction between facts and values is "obscure" or that means and ends are, in a temporal sense, so interrelated that it is difficult to tell one from the other. Instead, it tells us that process radically—which is to say, epistemologically—supersedes substance in the description and normative assessment of social relations. The intrinsically value-laden character of process makes especially salient to a normative theory of public administration the subject of chapter 6, namely, the formal rules used to legitimate and mediate the processes by which public decisions are made and outcomes are attained.

The view suggested here that values are inherent in process is difficult to incorporate into the value theory of the Classical paradigm inasmuch as it contradicts the classical assumption that processes are means that are instrumentally related to ends. That separation has traditionally permitted, in theory at least, the use of values as instrumental tests to measure the degree of correspondence between ends and means, thereby enabling structures of accountability to operate. The quality of decisional processes, on the other hand, is not subject to evaluation and measurement in terms of predefined ends, since the ends themselves are largely a product of the processes. Because substance and process are inextricably bound to one another, evaluations of decisions should take account of both. Moreover, since these decisions cannot be evaluated through reference to an external standard of accountability, determination of the quality of decisions instead must be made through reference to the subjective appraisals of the participants involved in making them. This is not to suggest that structures of accountability are irrelevant; they are simply incomplete contexts for normative appraisal.

From this perspective, our consternation at the plight of the Georgia woman would be based only partially on the seeming unfairness of the *outcome* that derived from the impersonal application of a rule. Our consternation would also stem from disappointment over the psychic violence done to her by the meeting with the case worker, who himself may have experienced psychic damage as well. Equally regrettable is the fact that, for the case worker, the meeting between him and his client was apparently not perceived as a transactional context out of which a decision could evolve.

INDIVIDUAL AND COLLECTIVE VALUES

In the organizational literature, the distinction between individual and collective values is expressed in concerns about conflicts or differences between individual "needs," such as self-actualization, and organizational "needs," such as survival, system maintenance, or productivity. The classical expressions of this conflict in democratic political theory are the tensions between individual rights, conceived in either civil-libertarian or economic terms, and the maintenance of public order. Social theories differ widely in their relative emphasis on one or the other end of the individual-versus-collectivity spectrum, while others seek ways of theoretically "balancing" the two positions.

The manner in which the individual/collective value distinction is dealt with by various social theories can fairly be interpreted to be a consequence both of the primary unit of analysis and the assumptions about the nature of the self those theories employ. These, in turn, influence, if not dictate, the theories' dominant values, even though they may be only implicit owing to frequent disavowals in much of social theory of any normative content. This point is illustrated by the long-standing tensions between "functionalist" and "voluntarist" (or "conflict") social theories. Functionalism, represented by systems theory and structural functionalism, elevates to a position of primary consideration the social system, in which the self is viewed in more or less passive and social terms.

> . . . functionalists take as their concern the relationship of the parts [of the system] to the whole in order to show how what appear to be isolated, if not inexplicable, social phenomena may fulfill some wider purpose related to the stability of society. Thus, their perspective, rather than an ideological bias, generates a concern with the causes and consequences of social equilibrium; problems of change and conflict, while they are considered, are treated as subsidiary phenomena.[11]

Voluntarist theory, by contrast, is critical of the conservatism of functionalist theory owing to its (voluntarism's) use of the individual, conceived as an active-atomistic self, as the primary unit of analysis. To the voluntarists, social collectivities are seen simply as aggregates of individual selves whose interests may and usually do differ from one another, resulting in the view that conflict is a natural state of affairs. The maintenance of the social order, while considered by the voluntarists, is naturally tenuous and is necessary and normatively desirable mainly insofar as it provides the context within which individuals may freely pursue their own interests.

The functionalist/voluntarist debate over order versus freedom is irreconcilable given the ways in which each approach implicitly conceives the nature of the self. Functionalists, who cast their lot with the value of order, implicitly assume that the sociality of the self is necessarily accompanied by the assumption of a passive self, which the voluntarists quite rightly view as anathema to individual freedom. Voluntarists, on the other hand, tend to associate the active nature of the self, which makes plausible the idea of individual freedom, with atomism—which worries the functionalists, for whom the assumption of *sociality* is fundamental to *their* concern with the maintenance of community and the social order. In the discussion of propositions 9 and 10, the possibility of reconciling the freedom-versus-order dualism is demonstrated by showing the logical unity and compatibility of the active and social nature of the self.

Most striking about the controversy over freedom versus order from the standpoint of the voluntarist/functionalist debate is how little relevance it has to an appreciation of the problems of normative theory noted at the beginning of this chapter. Each side of the debate tends implicitly to adopt the theoretical posture that ends are pregiven and that processes may be judged favorably insofar as they lead to the achievement of those ends. The logic of an extreme functionalist position, when extended to a consideration of the issue of administrative discretion, for example, suggests that the uniform application of rules and policies is valued by virtue of its contribution to organizational maintenance and stability. Administrative discretion that leads to departures from such uniform application, although it is occasionally justified by exceptional circumstances, is implicitly discouraged because of its possible threat to the goal of organizational stability. The logic of the voluntarist position, when extended to the same issue, regards the ends (or rights) of individual clients of the organization as being of primary legitimacy. Decisional processes, from this view, are satisfactory insofar as individual rights are protected and a fair balance among individual ends is attained.

From the standpoint of the conncerns discussed earlier, however, normative analysis in terms of the relative merits of these opposing perspectives can, at best, be only partially complete. To choose one side or the other, or to seek a middle ground between them, diverts attention from the qualitative aspects of decisional processes as they affect both the psychic well-being of the participants in the decision and the quality of decisional outcomes as subjectively defined by clients and administrators alike. In the development of normative theory, therefore, the issue of values should be treated in a way that transcends the commonly accepted dichotomies between substance versus process and individual versus collective values.

PROPOSITION 9. *The primary value in the development of a normative theory for public administration is mutuality, which is the normative premise deriving from the face-to-face relation (encounter) between active-social selves.*

The analysis to this point has not addressed the normative criteria by which administrative action may be judged to be responsible or just. The social and active selves have been asserted to be the sources for administrators' responsive and initiative action; yet questions remain unanswered regarding how they ought to decide which environmental claims warrant affirmative response (given limited resources) or how conflicts between or among those claims ought to be resolved. Second, the interdependence of the active self and the social self forces a consideration of the normative criteria by which possible conflicts between projects initiated via the active self and the claims of the social domain ought to be resolved. These issues are especially acute in environments that are highly turbulent, malleable, or both, since environmental turbulence increases the likelihood of conflict among various claims on the administrator's resources, and environmental malleability increases the number of possible projects the administrator may initiate with a reasonable prospect for success.

The normative criteria implied by the framework of administrative action discussed in chapter 4 are derived from the essential relatedness of the self to society as described in the "We-relation." The degree to which the relatedness of self and society is fulfilled in the community and the degree to which possibilities for creativity and freedom exist are the normative criteria by which administrative action may be judged. Winter conveys similar sentiments in suggesting that ". . . the principle of love and mutuality [is] the normative expression of man's relational being; love implies the mutuality of free initiation and free response." [12] It "universalizes the relatedness of man's being as it is experienced in the 'We-relation.' Love in the social world expresses itself as freedom and community." [13]

Mutuality is intended here to depict particular qualitative aspects of the face-to-face relationship. In relationships characterized by mutuality, people act with the knowledge that they are personally responsible for their actions—the recognition of which supersedes considerations of legal accountability. This is not a "should" statement about the preferred priority of personal feelings as opposed to legal requirements. Rather, it is an implied recognition by people of their status as active and social beings. Moreover, mutuality implies that people's actions are taken out of positive regard for others, and each person is also open to the influence of the other. Such relationships are characterized, in other words, by authenticity, rather than acted out on the basis of preestablished role definitions. Mutuality does not mean that people must like or be "nice" to one another, nor does it mean that mutually agreeable solutions to problems will always emerge from their dealings with one another.

When face-to-face relationships take place in contexts bound by formal rules and role definitions, mutuality may be sustained, although usually with some difficulty, when participants are cognizant that personal choice is always involved in their decisions about whether to act in accordance with or depart from those rules and roles. Moreover, mutuality does not mean that people should choose *not* to apply rules in their dealings with others, but merely that rules are not to be confused with moral imperatives. Mutuality is violated when, for example, an administrator says, "I'm sorry, but I have no choice in the matter because the regulations state . . ."; or when clients act in accordance with their preestablished beliefs about administrators by, to use Tom Wolfe's phrase, "Mau-Mauing the flack catchers."

Relationships characterized by mutuality also provide a context in which processes may inform substance. The irony of this is that decisions emerging from relationships of this kind tend to destroy the means-ends distinction on which traditional notions of accountability are based. But it should be recognized that the distinction is artificial (although by no means trivial) to begin with, and that it is often perfectly natural not to know what we want to do until after we have done it.[14]

It should be emphasized that the value of mutuality ought not mainly to be regarded as a preferred virtue, among many that are available, that administrators are exhorted to adopt. Instead, mutuality is inherent in and derived from the basic theoretical assumptions discussed earlier. Its preferred status as a normative principle, in other words, is theoretically grounded. Interpreted as an essential harmony and need for unity with others, the idea of mutuality may be amplified, for example, in terms of the three elements of the "We-relation" discussed in chapter 3. The *gesture,* transmitted by language (symbols), signifies a concern for response from and relationship with the other. The *response* to the gesture by the other denotes an emphathic openness of the other to the gesturer, which is made possible by a shared (but evolving) language and motivated by the other's similar need for harmony. The third element, the *interpretation* of the response, is the unifying link between both the gesture and response, and the self and the other in which each is able to comprehend both his or her own and the other's intentions and meanings.[15]

The idea of mutuality as the normative expression of the "We-relation" may be extended to the normative assessment of administrative action and of the institutional structures in which action is taken. This is because institutions are secondary to, and in a sense "derived from," more elemental forms of human relationships, such as the encounter.[16] From this view, institutions are seen as the means for regulating and making predictable impersonal (non-face-to-face) situations in the pursuit of a common purpose. Institutions, as well as rules and principles, are "substitutes" for the limited number of face-to-face situations in which mutuality is possible. Thus, if institutions are derived from the most elemental unit of human experience (the "We-relation"), it follows that the norms used to determine the efficacy of institutional conduct should themselves be derived from mutuality, the normative expression of the "We-relation."[17]

To assert that mutuality is the overarching normative criterion from which administrative action and structures may be judged does not, of course, provide automatic solutions to the many valuational issues that confront administrators; it simply informs judgments about competing values, claims, and projects.[18] While mutuality may often be a difficult criterion to apply to concrete decisions, however, it reminds us that the denial of freedom to others, and the exploitation of them, is wrong in more than a civil libertarian sense, since it is a denial of the community through which the development of the self, in both its social and creative aspects, is made possible. A concept of justice compatible with the active-social conception of the self, therefore, is one that necessarily assumes the unconditional worth of all persons, rather than viewing them simply as means to ends. The idea of justice involves a consideration of the consequences of action as judged from its effect on the realization of self and society.

MUTUALITY AND THE SUBSTANCE-PROCESS (ENDS-MEANS) DUALISM

From the standpoint of the earlier discussion of substance and process, ends and means, mutuality is qualitatively different as a value or normative criterion from, for example, rational self-interest or utility maximization. These latter values are "substantive" in the positivist sense, which distinguishes between ends (the good) and means (i.e., the correct or most efficient way of achieving them). From the positivist viewpoint, ends and means are linked by the concept of rationality, which emerges as the principal criterion for judging the adequacy of administrative decisions— decisions that presuppose agreement about substantive ends.

By contrast, mutuality is a "process" value, but in a radical, epistemological sense; that is, its preferred status is not primarily contingent upon demonstrations of its instrumental or rational utility.[19] What are usually thought of as substantive ends are intersubjectively created symbols that provide specificity or concreteness to action, but whose value is contingent upon the process by which they are created. *The contingent character of substantive ends or goals (which are infinitely variable) on process renders as logically impossible the task of beginning the development of a theory of values by attempting to identify the grounds for preferring one "substantive" end over another.* This view of the relationship of substance to process undermines not only the rational-instrumental approach to values implied by positivist theory, but erodes as well the *epistemological* foundation of the politics-administration dichotomy and thus the Classical paradigm of public administration. The dichotomy between politics and administration, after all, is simply a "practical" derivation of the substance/process dualism.

MUTUALITY AND THE INDIVIDUAL/COLLECTIVE (FREEDOM-VERSUS-ORDER) DUALISM

Since the idea of mutuality is predicated upon the encounter (or "We-relation") rather than derived from either the individual or a more encompassing unit of analysis, it (mutuality) is uniquely capable of transcending the apparent conflict between individual and collective values implied by the voluntarist-functionalist debate. While people subjectively define their own ends and infuse these ends with meaning through their actions, no inherent nor fundamentally irreconcilable conflict between the individual and the collectivity need be assumed. Indeed, just the opposite is the case. Society or collectivities may constrain freedom, but they also enable it. Individual freedom, which by its nature pertains to a social entity, would be meaningless if not impossible without collectivities—either those bound by formal institutional roles and rules or communities cemented by mutually supportive relationships. The idea of community, which implies more than simply an aggregate of people whose relationships are mediated by instrumental considerations, is made plausible by the notion of mutuality inherent in the "We'relation." Community, moreover, would be equally impossible without individuals acting freely within a social context. Thus the fundamental question is not how to balance the *inherent* conflict between the freedom of individuals and the collective order; rather, it is how to strengthen the natural bonds among people so as to promote a kind of social order that enables more than it constrains through domination acts of individual freedom and social cooperation.

PROPOSITION 10. *Just as descriptive theory about larger collectivities is derivative of the encounter, so too should normative theory about those collectivities be derived from mutuality, the normative expression of the encounter. The idea of social justice is the logical extension of mutuality applied to social collectivities and should therefore be regarded as the normative premise underlying "aggregate" policy decisions made by and implemented through public organizations.*

This proposition grows out of four preceding propositions, namely, that assumptions about the nature of the self and epistemology form the basis for normative as well as descriptive theory (1 and 8); that theory concerning social collectivities logically presumes the encounter as the primary unit of analysis (3); and that mutuality is the normative expression of the encounter (9). Taken together, these propositions suggest that values such as social justice, equity, and indeed any value or normative criterion used to assess the character of, or decisions that apply uniformly to, social collectivities are by their nature *derivative,* rather than primary, and are thus "second-best" values. Put slightly differently, so-called collective values are surrogates, abstractions constructed from empathetic consideration for the well-being of people with whom we ordinarily cannot interact on a face-to-face basis. We can participate immediately in only a limited number of face-to-face situations in which the other person's unique subjective life world may be revealed more or less adequately to us. In the absence of either face-to-face interaction or some other means by which the uniqueness of each individual's situation is knowable, we nevertheless often make judgments, and decisions based on those judgments, about collectivities of people about whom as individuals we have no direct knowledge.

In making decisions affecting collectivities, we are confronted with two possible courses of action that are discussed here in their order of preference as implied by the preceding analysis. The first course of action is to attempt to reduce the scope of the decision, that is, the number of affected parties, so that the situation of each person, as defined by him or her, may be taken into account. Ideally, the prototype for such "disaggregation" [20] strategies is the face-to-face encounter involving two people or a small group. The encounter, in addition to being the epistemological starting point for the action approach, is the normatively preferred decision unit as well. While a discussion of the relationship of decision rules to disaggregated decisions will be deferred until chapter 6, suffice it to say for the present that the smaller the number of actors involved in or affected by a decision, the greater the possibility that it may take account of the unique subjective definitions of the problem by each of the actors. In addition, the smaller the number of actors, the greater the confidence one may have in relying on interactive processes among the actors to bring about a *fair* outcome—as intersubjectively defined by them—rather than relying on an objectivated criterion of fairness or efficacy. Decisions reached as a result of intersubjective agreement are normatively preferable to those based upon "objective" criteria both because the former are epistemologically more correct, and because the interactive processes by which agreements are reached provide the context within which mutuality may be experienced and conflict resolved. The social as well as the active nature of the self find expression primarily through the process of acting and only secondarily through outcomes. Indeed, outcomes may in a general sense be regarded favorably insofar as they enable *subsequent* action that is subjectively defined by the actors as meaningful.

Although disaggregated decisions are normatively preferable to aggregated ones, many categories of issues that beg some sort of public resolution are not easily disaggregated. They include, first, pure public goods whose benefits and costs are not meaningfully divisible; second, cases in which the consequences of a decision made by one person or group may negatively affect so vast a number of others that face-to-face negotiation among all concerned is not feasible; and third, situations in which the population affected by a given problem or issue is highly homogeneous (i.e., in which people define their needs in a similar manner). In these situations potential outcomes of face-to-face deliberations may be so predictable that the deliberations would be regarded as superfluous. In the two latter situations, actors would probably regard the time and energy spent in producing an intersubjectively agreed upon consensus among all those affected as an excessive price to pay when measured against the results it produces. Despite the process bias of the normative theory presented here, people may reasonably conclude that intersubjective processes of agreement are in many cases costly, tedious, or generally not worth the effort.

Under any of these conditions, a normatively second-best approach is preferred. When the uniqueness of individual needs cannot be taken into account in structuring the decisional process, attention must necessarily be shifted to outcomes. Moreover, in evaluating intended outcomes either of social service policies or of policies whose benefits are otherwise divisible among aggregates of people, decision makers are left with the assumption of equality of, or no difference among, those affected by the policies. This is similar to the null hypothesis in statistical theory, which states that no difference between two variables must initially be assumed until or unless adequate evidence can be found to reject that assumption.

The assumption of no difference is made under the conditions noted above, not because all members of a collectivity necessarily define their preferences identically but because the costs involved in discerning and taking into account those differences in preferences are regarded as too great or too time-consuming. In the absence of such known differences, all members of the population (recipients or beneficiaries) are to be treated or affected equally (the same), since unequal treatment would necessarily be the result of arbitrary or capricious decisions. It should be remembered, however, that the "null hypothesis" of equal treatment under the law *is* refutable; that is, "unequal" treatment is normatively preferred when an individual's needs are known or knowable and when their satisfaction does not unduly jeopardize the satisfaction of other people's needs. Equal treatment is defensible as a matter of practical convenience, not as a normative first principle.

The intuitive plausibility of the foregoing argument can be illustrated by returning once again to the case of the woman in the Georgia welfare office. The outrage of the author of the *Newsweek* column apparently stemmed from the fact that an "equality" rule (the $1,500 maximum) was invoked that denied as legitimate the unique manner in which the woman sought to maintain her self-respect. Certainly few would suggest, as a matter of principle, that all citizens should save and set aside a specified amount of money for their burial. Rather, our sympathy for the plight of the Georgia woman derives from an empathic respect, within certain limits, for the projects that others uniquely define for themselves. Disregard for the uniqueness of individual needs or projects when they *could* otherwise be accommodated by alternative decision processes appears to be the key factor in transforming equality into depersonalizing sameness.

The qualification should be added here that the *outcome* of the Georgia welfare example *may,* by some reasonable standard, have been a sensible and fair one. The normative argument developed here does not presume to judge the particular outcome of the case, nor others like it. The normative theory does suggest that the burden of the theoretical argument rests with the position that the "aggregate" value of equal treatment should take precedence over the value of "unique" treatment based on mutual regard among the participants in particular transactions. This is because the value of equality is derived from, and therefore secondary to, the value of mutuality.

THE IDEA OF EQUITY [21]

An intermediate position between extreme aggregation (uniformity) and disaggregation is that of formulating policies that differentiate among intended beneficiaries on the basis of *categories* that reflect differences, either in kind or in degree, in the beneficiaries' needs or preferences. This approach is typically used in redistributive schemes in which equality is not an assumed condition but a normative goal to be at least approximated. Equality, it will be remembered, is a surrogate for intersubjectively arrived at agreements about fairness. Only rough approximations of equality are typically strived for in redistributive policies for the reason that *departures* from completely equalizing benefits for everyone are often regarded as fair or reasonable on other grounds, specifically, for reasons that are explainable in terms of the categories of difference that have been identified.

This is what is meant by the idea of *equity* in a generic sense. Equity is a derivative of the idea of equality, but departs from absolute equality when, as is often the case, sufficient grounds exist for believing that departures from equality are fair or reasonable. Equity provides the basis for making operational the redistributive aspects of theories of social justice, an example of which is John Rawls' discussion of the "difference principle." [22] Rawls claims that decisions regarding redistribution of benefits are just when, after the redistribution is made, no one is worse off (including the most advantaged), and the least advantaged are better off than they were before. A continuous series of these decisions (affecting the same general population) would have the effect of moving more in the direction of equality, but never attaining it completely.

Equity is a subject of enormous complexity both as a philosophical concern and in terms of the various ways in which it is measured and applied (e.g., as a criterion for determining resource input, government provision of services, outcomes for recipients).[23] The intent here is not to defend or refine the concept of equity further, but to clarify its conceptual source and importance as a generic concept. The secondary or derivative status of equity, and that of equality as well, will no doubt be seen as highly arguable given the primary status it is sometimes accorded in other theories.

For many years, the subjects of equity and fairness have occupied the attention of political philosophers. Although their primary focus is typically on the polity as a whole, some have been especially sensitive in recent years to administrative issues as they affect problems of political philosophy. A prominent effort in this regard is Rawls' theory of "justice as fairness," which has influenced to some extent current thinking in public administration.[24] Inasmuch as Rawls treats seriously the subject of administration in democratic government, some of the key elements of his theory are summarized here for purposes of contrast with the normative theory outlined in this chapter. Rawls' theory, while compatible in some respects with the normative position developed here, departs significantly in other respects, owing mainly to implicit differences of opinion about the nature of the self.

JUSTICE AS FAIRNESS

Rawls' intent is to present a theory of justice describing a society in which all benefit and in which the liberties of no one are sacrificed for anyone else's advantage. He begins by defining any theory of justice as the specification of the principles to be used in assigning rights and duties and in defining the appropriate division of social advantages. Further, the principles are subject to initial agreement. In justice as fairness, initial agreement takes place under the veil of ignorance in the "original position" in the state of nature. This original position is not an actual historical state of affairs; rather, it is a hypothetical state in which people make decisions bearing on the social structure without regard to their current and known individual needs and without reference to how social and economic contingencies might affect their own situation relative to that of others. People are *rational* to the extent they can extract themselves from such current and known needs—a kind of moral "bracketing out" in a phenomenological sense. The original position as the basis for the selection of principles assures that no one will be disadvantaged by innate capability or social circumstances in the choice of such principles. This provides the basis for the equality of people as moral persons capable of a sense of both their own good and a sense of justice.[25]

From this Rawls then specifies two principles of justice in their order of priority. The first is that "each person is to have an equal right to the most extensive basic liberty compatible with a similar liberty for others."[26] The second, which follows from the first, stipulates that "social and economic inequalities are to be arranged so that they are both (a) reasonably expected to be to everyone's advantage, and (b) attached to positions and offices open to all."[27]

The first principle establishes the priority of equal liberty and the second pertains to the regulation of the distribution of social and economic advantages. While the first principle is relatively clear, parts *a* and *b* of the second require some elaboration. Rawls says with respect to part *a* that while unequal distribution of wealth is not precluded in justice as fairness, it can be justified only temporarily in order eventually to promote the liberty of all. Rawls calls this the "difference principle," which states that the distribution of goods should be equal unless unequal distribution can be shown to be for the good of all.[28] Moreover, as general economic conditions improve, temporary departures from equal distribution become harder to justify. As the general well-being improves, only less urgent material needs remain unsatisfied. And since equal liberty holds the highest priority, it is irrational from the standpoint of the original position to accept less than equal freedom in order to justify further inequalities intended to bring about added marginal increases in material wealth.[29]

Part *b* of the second principle, which holds that positions and offices should be open to all, is based on Rawls' conception of equality of opportunity. His particular version of equality of opportunity, which is a derivative of the difference principle, is quite different from the long-established meritocratic concept of equality common to American and other civil service systems. The institutions of the just society must evidence the characteristics internally that they seek to create in the society they serve. A just regulation of social and economic advantages requires that those doing the regulating shall have attained their positions without the advantage of social circumstance or natural fortune. Equitable distribution of goods in justice as fairness does not require an external criterion to determine the correctness of the distribution; rather, all that is required is a system of pure procedural justice that assumes the outcome to be correct (whatever it is) so long as the procedure has been followed correctly.

> The principle of open positions also expresses the conviction that if some places were not open on a basis fair to all, those kept out would be right in feeling unjustly treated even though they benefited from the greater efforts of those who were allowed to hold them. They would be justified in their complaint not only because they were excluded from external rewards of office such as wealth and privilege, but because they were debarred from experiencing the realization of self which comes from a skillful and devoted exercise of social duties.[30]

JUSTICE AS FAIRNESS VERSUS UTILITARIANISM

Rawls argues that a rational person would not affirm a societal structure simply because it led to the greatest good for the greatest number, irrespective of his or her own and others' status as free and equal rational beings. Such structures, founded on a utilitarian view of a well-ordered, and therefore just, society, take no fundamental account of how societal goods are distributed so long as the total sum of advantages is maximized. These maximizations are made possible by competition among people for individual advantage. Since individual choices, according to the utilitarian viewpoint, are made on the basis of current and known personal needs, no account is necessarily taken of the possibility that the liberty of the few might be sacrificed in the interests of the many. To the extent that precepts of justice are held, they are either derivatives of the principle of maximization or gratuitous in the light of that principle. Liberty in utilitarianism is construed as a set of rules that allows the maximization of individual needs from limited means. Decisions about the proper distribution of goods are essentially matters of efficient administration.[31]

Rawls argues that in utilitarianism, the good (e.g., pleasure) is defined separately from the right (the most efficient ways in which pleasure may be maximized).[32] The idea of rationality that links the good (ends) with the right (means) thus emerges as the major criterion for judging the wisdom of administrative decisions. Hence, in utilitarianism, it does not matter, except incidentally, how goods are distributed as long as their sum is maximized through the most efficient means available.

In contrast to utilitarianism, justice as fairness is a theory in which the right cannot be defined independent of the good. In this case, the distribution of goods is defined as the good.

> . . . if the distribution of goods is counted as a good and the theory directs us to produce the most goods . . . , the problem of distribution falls under the concept of right as one intuitively understands it, and so the theory lacks an

independent definition of the good. Utilitarianism, in contrast, factors our moral judgments into two classes, the one being characterized separately while the other is then connected with it by the maximizing principle.[33]

In justice as fairness, the idea of equality is tied to Rawls' argument that just decisions are those made by reference to the original position. This means far more than equality simply as impartial, regular, and equal treatment under law and administration; it means that equality should be the guiding principle underlying the structure of social institutions. Social institutions should be so arranged as to reflect a public understanding of the original position.[34]

THE ARISTOTELIAN PRINCIPLE

Rawls contends that for a person to act in accordance with the original position is not only compatible with, but necessary for, the fulfillment of his or her own rational and unique life plan. To show why, he stipulates a basic principle of motivation called the Aristotelian Principle.

> Other things being equal, human beings enjoy the exercise of their capacities (their innate or trained abilities), and this enjoyment increases the more the capacity is realized, or the greater its complexity. The intuitive idea here is that human beings take more pleasure in doing something as they become more proficient at it, and of two activities they do equally well, they prefer the one calling for the larger repertoire of more intricate and subtle discriminations.[35]

Additionally, the presence of other people with similar motivations and capabilities is necessary because, as we see others with compatible capabilities, we take pleasure in experiencing their successes and learn from them how to expand our own capabilities. Moreover, as our own activities become more complex and specialized (because of the Aristotelian Principle), the greater the necessity for others with similar interests and life plans to augment our activities. This is not just because greater specialization and division of labor require greater coordination and cooperation but also because it is necessary in a very basic sense to have our life plans and our identities confirmed by others. Moreover, when those doing the confirming are essentially our equals, rather than subordinates or superiors, their confirmation (or disconfirmation) spares us from either delusions of grandeur or destructive feelings of guilt.[36]

Thus the idea of social union among equals as implied by justice as fairness is trivialized in both a personal and a philosophical sense if it is said to be necessary primarily for cooperation leading to mutual advantage, to meet goals, to get things done. Rather, "we need one another as partners in ways of life that are engaged in for their own sake, and the successes and enjoyment of others are necessary for and complementary to our own good.'' [37] This is because ''the potentialities of each individual are greater than those he can hope to realize. . . . Different persons with similar or complementary capacities may cooperate in realizing their common or matching nature.'' [38] Justice as fairness is not opposed to the idea of the division of labor but suggests that it be regulated by the Aristotelian Principle and the need for social union.

CRITIQUE

In some important respects Rawls' theory is compatible with the normative theory of the Action paradigm. Both are critical of the rational-instrumental relationship between ends and means (substance and process) characteristic of utilitarianism and the bureaucratic model of organization. Each affirms a commitment to the idea of distributive justice, even though that commitment has derivative or second-best status in the Action paradigm. Finally, each stresses the legitimacy of individuals' unique life plans or projects that make personal growth or development possible. That is, both theories explicitly reject the idea that individuals can be regarded as instruments for the fulfillment of the collective good.

Significant differences nevertheless remain, owing primarily to the differing assumptions about the nature of the self that the two approaches employ. Rawls is a contractarian philosopher following in the tradition of Locke, Hobbes, and Rousseau. Contract theory stipulates that rational persons will voluntarily agree to establish governments and other institutions for the maintenance of social relations so that each person may further his or her own interests in a relatively orderly manner. People are assumed to be active rather than passive, and atomistic rather than social. Although Rawls softens the atomistic flavor of justice as fairness somewhat later in his discussion of the Aristotelian Principle, rational self-interest nevertheless remains as the primary motive for the creation of governments. Rawls' position thus contrasts with the action approach, which sees the creation of social institutions, including governments, fundamentally as products of people's natural orientation toward community with others, that is, an expression of their basically *social* nature.

The differences in the two theories' approaches to the idea of justice derive from their differing assumptions about the nature of the self. For Rawls, a commitment to equal basic liberties and distributive justice is plausible only when people temporarily *suspend* their immediate individual or atomistic ends in the longer-term interest of a just and stable political order. The logical device for accomplishing this is the veil of ignorance in the original position in the state of nature. The outcome of a rational person's reflections under the veil of ignorance is equality, whose underlying logic is similar to the null hypothesis discussed earlier in this chapter.

The normative theory preferred here holds that a commitment to equal justice, even though it is logically a derivative concept, is nevertheless a natural outgrowth of people's basically *social* nature and whose expressive or emotive content derives from their experience of and capacity for love or mutuality. The mutually reinforcing interpersonal relationships that promote self-development, which for Rawls assume a position of secondary importance depicted in his discussion of the Aristotelian Principle, are for the action approach the basic source of a commitment to justice. Thus, while people frequently subjectively define their individual goals or projects in diverse and even conflicting ways, such differences can hardly be taken as evidence of an inherent conflict among their natural developmental orientations.

The major arguments of this chapter may be briefly summarized in the following points:

1. Mutuality, the normative expression of the encounter, is the primary value in the normative theory.

2. As a "process" value, mutuality implies a rejection on epistemological grounds of the assumption that means (processes) are mainly instrumentally related to ends (substantive outcomes).

3. "Disaggregated" decisions are *epistemologically* preferable to "aggregated" decisions because they make possible contexts for intersubjective agreements among people, thus accounting more adequately for unique and differing preferences.

4. Disaggregated decisions are *normatively* preferable because they allow more direct involvement in decision processes by those affected, thus facilitating the actualization of people's nature as active and social beings.

5. Equal justice, social equity, or other collective values are logically derived from, and normatively subordinate to, mutuality.

6. Aggregated decisions, that is, those which either apply uniformly to the whole population or differentiate among the population only on the basis of categories, are normatively second-best but are acceptable to the extent that

   a. pure public goods are at issue;

   b. the negative side effects that a disaggregated decision has on other actors are unmanageable through face-to-face negotiation; and

   c. the population affected is relatively homogeneous, that is, when the members of the population subjectively define their needs and preferences in a relatively similar manner.

Some unanswered questions about the fairness or efficacy of decisions still remain and have to do with the organizational/structural context in which they are made. Attention to the normative aspects of decision-making processes is necessarily incomplete when the authority of the state is affected unless attention is given to the means by which the formal legitimacy of decisions is determined. These issues are considered in the next chapter, which conerns formal decision rules employed in public organizations and their relationship to normative theory in public administration.

NOTES

1. Michael Nelson, *Newsweek,* 11 September 1978, p. 17.

2. See Orion White and Bruce L. Gates, "Statistical Theory and Equity in the Delivery of Social Services," *Public Administration Review,* January–February 1974, pp. 43–51.

3. Harold D. Lasswell, *Politics: Who Gets What, When, How* (New York: McGraw-Hill, 1936).

4. Charles E. Lindblom, *The Intelligence of Democracy: Decision Making Through Mutual Adjustment* (New York: Free Press, 1965).

5. Ibid., p. 297.

6. Thomas L. Thorson, *The Logic of Democracy* (New York: Holt, Rinehart and Winston, 1962).

7. Ibid., pp. 138–39.

8. Gregory Bateson, *Toward an Ecology of the Mind* (New York: Ballantine, 1972), pp. 160–61.

9. Alfred Schutz, *Collected Papers* (The Hague: Marinus Nijhoff, 1967), 2:11.

10. Peter L. Berger and Thomas Luckmann, *The Social Construction of Reality* (Garden City, N.Y.: Anchor Books, 1967).

11. David Silverman, *The Theory of Organizations* (New York: Basic Books, 1971), p. 45.

12. Gibson Winter, *Elements for a Social Ethic* (New York: Macmillan, 1966), p. 230.

13. Ibid., p. 250.

14. The idea that we often discover ends and goals by retrospecting on our prior action is a theme that is ingeniously and extensively developed by Karl E. Weick. Moreover, the primary status of process is underscored by the verb "organizing," in contrast to Katz and Kahn's noun "organizations," which appears in the title of Weick's book *The Social Psychology of Organizing* (2nd ed.; Reading, Mass.: Addison-Wesley, 1979).

15. Winter, *Elements for a Social Ethic,* pp. 228–29.

16. Berger and Luckmann, *Social Construction of Reality,* p. 28.

17. The terms "institutional conduct" or "institutional action" should be used with caution. White has argued that all action is *personal* and must be regarded as such in order for people fully to recognize their responsibility for their

actions. See Orion White, "The Concept of Administrative Praxis," *Journal of Comparative Administration*, May 1973, pp. 55–86.

18. Winter, *Elements for a Social Ethic*, p. 223.

19. That the criterion of mutuality is not subject to instrumental tests closely parallels Rawls' argument that a just distribution of benefits need not be defended in terms of independent criteria of utility. See John Rawls, *A Theory of Justice* (Cambridge, Mass.: Harvard University Press, 1971), pp. 27–33.

20. Robert Biller has persuasively argued for a "disaggregated" approach to public decision making in "Toward Public Administrations Rather Than an Administration of Publics: Strategies of Accountable Disaggregation to Achieve Human Scale and Efficacy, and Live within the Natural Limits of Intelligence and other Scarce Resources," in *Agenda for Public Administration*, ed. Ross Clayton and William B. Storm (Los Angeles: University of Southern California, 1979), pp. 151–72.

21. For a discussion of the idea of equity as it pertains to public administration, see articles in H. George Frederickson, ed, "A Symposium: Social Equity and Public Administration," *Public Administration Review*, January–February 1974, pp. 1–51.

22. Rawls, *Theory of Justice*, pp. 75–83.

23. See Astrid E. Merget, "Equity in the Distribution of Municipal Services," in *Revitalizing Cities*, ed. Herrington J. Bryce (Lexington, Mass.: Lexington Books, 1979), pp. 161–92.

24. Some implications of Rawls' theory for public administration are discussed in David K. Hart, "Social Equity, Justice, and the Equitable Administrator," *Public Administration Review*, January–February 1974, pp. 3–11; and Michael M. Harmon, "Social Equity and Organizational Man: Motivation and Organizational Democracy," *PAR*, January–February 1974, pp. 11–18.

25. Rawls, *Theory of Justice*, p. 10.

26. Ibid., p. 60

27. Ibid.

28. Ibid., p. 61.

29. Ibid., pp. 542–43.

30. Ibid., p. 84.

31. Ibid., p. 27.

32. Rawls refers to any theory (such as utilitarianism) in which the good is defined independently from the right as a "teleological" theory. Justice as fairness, in which the good is not specified independently from the right, is a "deontological" theory. "It should be noted that deontological theories are defined as non-teleological ones, not as views that characterize the rightness of institutions and acts independently from their consequences. All ethical doctrines worth our attention take consequences into account in judging their rightness." Ibid., p. 30.

33. Ibid., p. 25.

34. Ibid., p. 504.

35. Ibid., p. 426.

36. Ibid., p. 526.

37. Ibid., p. 522–23.

38. Ibid., p. 523.

6

Decision Rules

As we have seen thus far, the Action paradigm has dealt with theoretical issues pertaining to social science in the broadest sense. The epistemological and normative issues and the action-versus-behavior debate considered in earlier chapters, for example, are subjects of lively debate in all major branches of contemporary social science; only the terminology differs among them. The present chapter links these more general social science concerns with a subject more familiar to the public administration literature: the relationship of decision-making processes in public organizations to various decision rules that constitute the central elements of what is usually termed organizational structure.

A decision rule is defined as a formal specification of authority relationships both within organizations as well as between them and elements of their domains (e.g., legislatures, constituencies, the courts). Decision rules as they apply *within* organizational boundaries specify who makes decisions and the means by which those toward whom the decisions are directed (the "implementors") may be held accountable. Organizational decision rules as they apply to constituencies *external* to organizations both specify the manner in which constituents may voice their preferences effectively as well as clarify the authority of organizations over (and their obligations to) constituents. This definition of decision rule should not be confused with an alternative meaning of the term which defines a decision rule as a *criterion* for determining the normative adequacy of policy or decisional *outcomes,* e.g., efficiency, Pareto optimality, or various criteria of fairness or equity.

The discussion of proposition 11, which sets forth five decision rules, is primarily descriptive and clarifies the relationships between the five rules and various schools of thought in public administration. Proposition 12 proposes the argument that the *consensus* rule is generally preferred by virtue of its compatibility with the epistemology, assumptions about the self, and normative theory of the Action paradigm. The other four rules are criticized on the grounds of their compatibility with alternative epistemological assumptions and normative criteria.

PROPOSITION 11. *Although public administration shares certain assumptions with all other branches of social theory and is bound by common epistemological rules, its uniqueness stems from its primary practical and theoretical concern with the rules and processes used in making and legitimating decisions in public organizations. Decision rules and the institutional processes associated with them are the primary ingredients of what is commonly referred to as organization "structure." Five kinds of rules are or can be employed in public organizations: hierarchy (unilateral decision), bargaining or market rules, voting, contract and consensus.*

HIERARCHY

Hierarchy is the defining element of authority relationships in complex organizations in both the government and business sectors. As visualized in Weber's description of the bureaucratic form of organization, hierarchy is an arrangement of positions into superior-subordinate relationships.[1] In a formal or structural sense, this means that superiors are legally empowered to make decisions and issue orders that, within specified limits, are binding on subordinates in that the former have at their disposal rewards and punishments that induce subordinates' compliance. The most important formal limitations of superiors' authority are twofold. First, the legal-rational nature of the authority means that superiors, whose occupancy of their positions is determined by a combination of technical competence and seniority, are bound by impersonal rules that establish limits on the kinds of rewards or punishments they may mete out. The impersonal nature of rules means that all subordinates are subject to equal treatment; it cannot be arbitrary and/or capricious. The second limitation on superior authority is that subordinates' compliance is voluntary in the sense that, in most bureaucratic organizations, people are not coerced into joining and are free to leave the organization. While employment in bureaucratic organizations is restricted by requirements of technical competence and the availability of positions, employees join the organization of their choosing. The voluntary nature of this membership constitutes an acknowledgment and acceptance of the legitimacy of superior authority.

The underlying norm on which the bureaucratic model of organization is based is that of instrumental rationality. Goals and purposes of the organization are established by hierarchical leaders, legislative bodies, the courts, or elected executives. Regardless of whether goals are established by hierarchical leaders within the organization or imposed on it from without, the function of organizational leadership is to coordinate the efficient attainment of the objectives by employing, when necessary, formal rewards, punishments, and other inducements at their disposal to assure compliance by subordinates. More often than not, subordinates' awareness of the potential threat of such inducements is sufficient incentive to comply.

Under the norm of rationality in bureaucratic organizations, the separation of ends from means is assumed. The separation merges well with the dichotomy in the Classical public administration paradigm between policy (formulation) and administration (implementation) as originally articulated by Wilson.[2] Although Wilson stressed legislatures rather than the hierarchical executives as the legitimate source for the articulation of values and goals, the basic tenets of the Classical paradigm were complemented in most other respects by the bureaucratic model, even though Weber, in contrast to Wilson, did not write as a normative advocate.

BARGAINING AND MARKET RULES

In contrast to the hierarchy rule, which is predicated on formal authority, bargaining and market rules are based on the idea of exchange as the medium both by which coordination is achieved among aggregates and through which individual ends are maximized. Whereas hierarchical rules are presumed to be the means by which collective ends or values may be comprehensively weighed and attained, exchange rules focus on rational self-interest as the dominant motive of actors. Although the conceptual distinction between ends (interests) and means holds for hierarchy and exchange rules alike, the two rules differ with regard to the level of comprehensiveness at which they operate.

As a form of behavior in political systems and organizations, bargaining is typically based on informal rather than formal rules. In political pluralism, perhaps the major school of thought in American political science during the last three decades, informal bargining and other forms of behavior that do not assume central coordination or control are assumed to be the most influential processes for accomplishing political and administrative ends. To the pluralists, interests are generally represented by groups because, in larger systems, single individuals are seldom powerful enough to attain important ends by themselves. Although pluralist political science is avowedly more descriptive than normative in its orientation, much of its important literature attempts to reconcile pluralist bargaining with democratic theory[3] and to demonstrate its preferability to centralized processes of political and administrative control.[4]

While the pluralist literature, by and large, constitutes an implicit defense of existing bargaining processes, public choice theory (or contemporary political economy) is generally, but not exclusively, biased toward altering formal processes of decision making along lines approximating a market. Rational self-interest is assumed as the primary motive of behavior, and the individual rather than the group is assumed both for analytical and decisional purposes to be the primary unit. Public choice has a major concern with devising ways in which individuals may express their unique and differing preferences for government services and at the same time maintain limits on the exercise of individual choices that might otherwise jeopardize public order, exhaust common resources, or engender intolerable negative side effects (externalities).

Public choice theory is less critical of unitary bureaucratic systems of hierarchical control on "humanistic" grounds than because such systems frequently fail to satisfy the dominant norm they are designed to achieve, namely, the rational and efficient attainment of collective goals. Some of the pathologies of large-scale bureaucracies have been summarized by Ostrom.

> The very large bureaucracy will (1) become increasingly indiscriminating in its response to diverse demands, (2) impose increasingly high social costs upon those who are presumed to be the beneficiaries, (3) fail to proportion supply to demand, (4) allow public goods to erode by failing to take actions to prevent one use from impairing other uses, (5) become increasingly error prone and uncontrollable to the point where public actions deviate radically from rhetoric about public purposes and objectives, and (6) eventually lead to a circumstance where remedial actions exacerbate rather than ameliorate problems.[5]

Not all public choice theorists unequivocally oppose the hierarchy rule. Ostrom, for example, takes a fairly eclectic stance about decision rules by arguing both that the choice of rules ought to be based on situational requirements and that the problems of bureaucracies are often associated more with their size than with pathologies intrinsic to the hierarchy rule per se. For this reason, Ostrom advocates the development of self-governing organizations of various kinds, and in cases where such organizations engender negative externalities, he urges the creation of competing and overlapping jurisdictions among organizations as a means for mitigating or adjusting for negative side effects.[6]

Public choice's affinity with marketlike decision rules is most evident in proposals for decision-making arrangements in which a "currency," usually in the form of vouchers, is employed as the medium of exchange either among constituents or between constituents and a public agency. A hypothetical example describing a voucher system as an exhange medium among constituents has been outlined by Buchanan and Tullock.[7] They describe a hypothetical situation in which a local public housing official is confronted with the task of allocating six available housing units among ten families who qualify for public housing assistance. As public choicers, Buchanan and Tullock are skeptical about the ability of bureaucratic decisions to produce outcomes that are regarded as fair and reasonable by the constituents. Any hierarchically made decision, in their example, would be incapable of accounting for the differing preferences of the ten families and would almost certainly leave four of the ten with nothing but a higher position on the waiting list. In addition, a unilateral decision by the housing official would effectively preclude any meaningful participation by the constituents in determining the outcome of the decision.

As an alternative, Buchanan and Tullock suggest the following procedure: A voucher, representing one housing unit and divisible into tenths, is created for each unit. Each of the ten eligible families is given six-tenths of a voucher. Since all ten families presumably have some other resources at their disposal (e.g., money, skills, possessions), the voucher portions, along with the families' current resources, become media of exchange that may be traded with the other families. In other words, families may trade either their voucher portions for other families' resources or trade their own resources for additional voucher portions. The decision process is complete only when six families obtain an entire voucher (ten-tenths), having traded to the remaining four families sufficient resources for them to obtain private housing of comparable quality. The asserted benefits of this approach are threefold. First, differing subjectively defined preferences of the families are accounted for by the "market"; second, all ten families are better off then they were before (there are no losers); and third, all the families have participated in deciding their own fate rather than having it determined for them.

Whereas the vouchers in the example above were the medium of exchange *among* constituents, in other cases they may be used as the currency for transactions *between* constituents and an agency charged with providing a public service. In these cases, vouchers are intended to serve the purpose of holding agencies accountable or responsive to consumer preferences. The best known example of this type is the school voucher system.[8] Under this system, parents are given one voucher for each school-aged child. The voucher, which is equal in value to the average cost of educating a child, constitutes revenue for the school to which the parents send their child and is withdrawn when and if the parents decide to transfer the child to another school. Since schools are dependent on a sufficient number of vouchers for their continued survival, each school will presumably be more responsive to parent requests regarding their children's educational needs, thereby providing a system of accountability through a market, rather than a hierarchical, mechanism. In addition, school voucher systems in an overall sense are intended to provide greater diversity in educational offerings than are typical of bureaucratically structured school systems, which ordinarily demand substantial uniformity among all schools. Market rules and processes permit, at least in theory, effective disaggregation of decisions and can thus account for unique or idiosyncratic consumer demands.

VOTING RULES

Majority rule and other forms of voting, such as plurality rule, are seldom used as formal decision rules *within* public organizations, although voting is, of course, the rule most commonly employed by legislative bodies, higher courts, and the public in making decisions that in one way or another are binding on public agencies. An obvious difficulty of voting as an internal organization decision rule is that the deciding majority within an organization would constitute too large and diffuse a body to be held accountable by superordinate entities such as legislatures and courts. That is to say, while rewards and punishments may be rather easily meted out to individuals on the basis of their performance, it is quite another matter to reprimand, promote, fire, prosecute, or otherwise call to account organization members en masse.

The second difficulty with voting as an internal decision rule in organizations is that it presupposes that a given issue requiring formal resolution is sufficiently unambiguous that its outcome may be determined simply by a vote of yea or nay. This is not often the case since, prior to being voted on, legislation, court cases, and referenda must always be refined, modified, and compromised by other informal and sometimes formal processes and rules. Voting, in other words, is a blunt instrument whose even limited uses presume the effectiveness of prior nonvoting rules and processes on which it (voting) is contingent. For this reason, voting is ineffective as a means both of coordinating disparate parties concerned with a particular issue or of mediating necessary tradeoffs or compromises among interrelated issues.

Finally, voting is subject to the frequent criticism that it cannot take adequate account of the differing intensity of concern or interest about an issue that is held among those who may cast their votes to decide it. Thus, those who are relatively indifferent about an issue have influence that is commensurate to those who feel passionately about it or whose stake in the outcome is substantially greater.

CONTRACT

The contract has a formidable tradition in Western political thought. Social contract theory, which in large measure provides the philosophical grounding for constitutional democratic theory, emphasizes the voluntary nature of cooperation and organization motivated by people's rational consideration of their individual interests. Contracts, which in a formal sense are legally binding agreements (that are voluntarily entered into) between or among two or more parties, are rarely employed as decision rules by individuals or groups internally in public organizations. Contracts are used extensively, however, in public agencies' *external* transactions, for example, with other units of government at various levels (federal, state, regional, local) and with private for-profit and not-for-profit groups. Their purpose is ordinarily to provide services that the contractor agency is unable to provide directly, given limits on its public charter, time, expertise, or other resources. While contract implies voluntary agreement by both (or all) parties, contracts involving public organizations are frequently bound by legal and institutional constraints that limit the range and kinds of permissible agreements.

CONSENSUS

Consensus has several meanings in the literature associated with public administration. As typically defined by political scientists, consensus is a constellation of shared values, usually implicit, which have historically bound and provided coherence, in both cognitive and emotive senses, to political or social systems. These shared values provide a common understanding of the range of goals, policies, and options that political systems may pursue without unduly upsetting their equilibirum. Consensus, by this definition, is not a decision rule, although certain shared values may predispose members of a political system to favor some decision rules and take a skeptical view about the efficacy of others.

Consensus, in the management and organizational literature, has two closely related meanings.[9] The first views consensus as a *process* by which individuals, usually in face-to-face discussions, attempt to reach agreement with one another through synthesizing their initially held and divergent positions on a problem into a qualitatively different (and presumably better) solution than any of those initially proffered. In the process definition, consensus may take place in settings characterized by formal or informal differences in power and status. But, while these differences may influence the character of the interaction by virtue of their being taken into account by the various parties involved, the process is nonetheless a relatively noncoercive one in which the parties attempt in good faith to solve common problems or settle their differences in a mutually agreeable manner. Consensus contrasts with compromise or bargaining in which each person concedes something to others in the hope of outwitting them or otherwise maximizing his or her own interests. Bargaining and compromise, in other words, assume the equivalent of a "zero-sum game," although it should be emphasized that the zero-sum (or alternatively, the "win-win") nature of any situation is necessarily an attribution of meaning or interpretation made by the actors involved in the process. In contrast to bargaining, the process of consensus is facilitated by either the existence or the development of mutual trust among participants. The level of mutual trust is presumed to bear on the extent to which participants' definition of the situation might reasonably be, or evolve into, a win-win, as opposed to a zero-sum, game. The greater the trust, in other words, the greater the possibility that participants will construe their own and others' interests as similar or compatible.

The second meaning of consensus is simply the *outcome* or end result of processes similar to those just described. The difference in the two meanings is one of perspective rather than kind, but it is nevertheless an important difference especially in terms of the normative criteria used to assess the adequacy of consensual decisions. The "process" bias of the Action paradigm suggests that the quality of the process (i.e., the extent to which definitions of the problem are shared and understood, mutual trust is developed, and solutions are arrived at free of coercion or domination) is the principal criterion for determining the goodness of the outcome. This is with the provision that all those who have, or perceive themselves as having, a significant stake in the outcome are included in the process. Additionally, it assumes that adequate means or policies are provided for dealing with any adverse side effects or unintended consequences of consensual solutions.

A primary concern with consensual *outcomes* without reference to the normative adequacy of the process that produced them typically presumes the appropriateness of *a priori* (usually instrumental) criteria specified by observers external to and independent from the situation. For example, the view that "economy-efficiency" measures or various "school solutions" may be assumed to be appropriate tests of the efficacy of consensus or other decision modes is inadmissible because those criteria may not be regarded as important by the parties engaged in resolving a particular problem.

Neither the "process" nor "outcome" definitions directly come to grips with the *rule* implied by consensus decision making. Strictly speaking, the rule consistent with consensual decisions is *unanimity,* whose organizational equivalent is what Thayer calls "structured non-hierarchy." [10] If consensus, viewed in either process or outcome terms, refers to decision making in which coercion or domination is absent, then organizational arrangements consistent with their absence must logically preclude the formal authority of some people unilaterally to impose decisions on others. This means that organization structures must be free of superior-subordinate relationships, both internally and in their relations with clients, in order to assure the genuineness of the consensus.

The requirement of unanimity is a demanding one in which the difficulty of its attainment increases as the number of participants involved in resolving an issue increases. The difficulty in attaining unanimity may often be exaggerated, however, while the practical benefits of reaching unanimity through consensual means may be considerable. If, as the discussion of proposition 12 suggests, consensus is the normatively preferred decision mode, then the issue is not really whether consensus (unanimity) may replace all other rules in all circumstances. Rather, the important tasks are to identify both the means by which consensus may be effectively facilitated and the kinds of circumstances in which it is most likely to be regarded as a plausible alternative to more traditional decision rules and processes. The relative "practicality" or workability of decision rules is probably mainly a function of participants' belief or acceptance of them, rather than a result of causal factors intrinsic to those rules. Whether consensus can or cannot "work," in other words, may largely be a self-fulfilling prophecy based on the level of understanding of and normative commitment to it. In addition, the workability of consensus modes of decision making is likely to be a function of practice and experience.

While the unanimity rule is the least commonly used of the rules discussed here, consensual processes may be far more frequently employed in organizations than we are accustomed to thinking. This is the gist of Thayer's argument in which he states that despite the formal hierarchical structure of the Department of Defense, as an example, decision making in the Pentagon is actually characterized more by consensual processes than by unilateral decisions by bureaucratic superiors.[11] The difficulties in recognizing this, says Thayer, result from the absence of a theory to explain it. Bureaucratic theory, in a formal or Weberian sense as well as informally (the pyramidal organization charts on office walls), may be so deeply imbedded in our ways of thinking that we are oblivious to what would otherwise be the obvious fact that people in organizations voluntarily cooperate with one another far more than they give and take orders or compete with one another. What is needed, he continues, is a better theory to describe, not just prescribe, what actually takes place in formal and complex organizations.

Two conclusions may be drawn from this discussion. The first is that theory, regardless of how explicitly it is articulated, may strongly influence not only how we perceive organizations but may also help *produce* the reality we seek to comprehend.[12] Descriptive theory and social reality are dialectically related. We may be so wedded to particular modes of description and explanation that we fail to see important existing aspects of organizational life while we unintentionally produce others.

The second conclusion is that although the various decision rules discussed are *logically* associated with particular social processes, in practice asymmetries are often present. Within hierarchies (unilateral decision rule), for example, consensual norms and processes may sometimes prevail; under the unanimity (consensus) rule, a dominant leader may control the process or the interaction of group members may be characterized by competition or bargaining rather than cooperation. This should not be surprising in that formal decision rules are only one, albeit an important one, of the many factors that influence collective decision making. While changes in decision rules would not automatically transform processes of organizational decision making, it is nonetheless reasonable to assume that, over time, such rule changes could have an appreciable impact on decisional norms and processes. This, at any rate, is the assumption behind proposition 12, which considers the normative implications of the rules just discussed.

PROPOSITION 12. *The selection of decision rules is the fundamental normative decision in determining the structure of public organizations. The effect of particular decision rules on the quality of the processes by which social meanings are negotiated and the compatibility of various rules with the normative theory of the Action paradigm are the primary criteria for the normative assessment of decision rules. The consensus rule logically satisfies these criteria better than the rules of hierarchy, bargaining, voting, and contract.*

Proposition 12 examines the degree of compatibility of the five decision rules with the normative theory of the Action paradigm. Normative compatibility, it should be stressed, does not imply a categorical endorsement of rules, for many factors should be considered in their selection. The intersubjective epistemology of the Action paradigm dictates that this be the case, but with the caveat that those most immediately involved in or affected by situations requiring decisions should have the primary voice in the selection of rules. The normative assessment of decision rules is a crucial concern for public administration inasmuch as they constitute the central elements of what we ordinarily refer to as organizational "structure." Structure is operationally defined here as a set of formally objectivated meanings that induce more-or-less predictable decisional processes legitimated in large part by decision rules.

The criterion of *efficiency* has traditionally been employed as the standard for judging the normative adequacy of decision rules in public administration. In the Classical paradigm efficiency was presumed to be a logical result of perfection of hierarchical organization along Weberian lines. Simon,[13] and later Ostrom,[14] subsequently challenged this assumption by arguing that empirical evidence showed the relationship of hierarchical organization to efficiency to be highly problematic. Ostrom, whose analysis led to a more fundamental departure from the principle of hierarchy than Simon's, ends up by arguing that efficiency in decision making (i.e., minimizing decision-making costs) may be attained by using a variety of decision rules; the means for empirically determing which rule in a particular situation is most efficient is what he terms a "cost calculus." [15]

Although Simon's and Ostrom's critiques of the principle of hierarchical organization are often cited as radical challenges to the Classical orthodoxy, from the standpoint of the action frame of reference their theoretical postures imply far less than paradigmatic alternatives both in a normative and an epistemological sense. Even though he broadens the meaning of efficiency by linking it to consumer utility,[16] for Ostrom efficiency is still the prime value for public administration. His principal contribution has been to clarify the variable and problematic relationship of decision rules to social efficiency. His normative endorsement of efficiency is understandable in view of his implicit acceptance of the epistemological position that means or processes (induced by various rules) are necessarily *instrumentally* related to ends. In this sense, Ostrom's position affirms the Classical paradigm's insistence on the distinction between ends and means, which constitutes the *epistemological* basis for the dichotomy between policy and administration. Thus, while Ostrom rightly criticizes the dichotomy on *empirical* grounds, his effort to construct an outline for a Public Choice paradigm leaves intact the epistemological, and by extension the normative, foundation of the Classical paradigm. The remainder of this chapter explores the normative character of choices about decision rules based on an epistemological rejection of the ends-means distinction.

Earlier chapters have suggested that, in the normative evaluation of decision rules, attention should be focused on the processes of interaction and decision making that the rules are likely to induce or reinforce. Moreover, the normative concern with process by the action frame of reference should not be confused with (although it may include a consideration of) the idea of "procedural justice," which emphasizes formal or legal rights, privileges, and responsibilities of citizens and public officials. An exclusive preoccupation with procedural justice is subject to the criticism that evaluation of political outcomes may be ignored at the expense of an excessive concern with formal procedural safeguards. The normative process criteria implied by the Action paradigm, on the other hand, suggest that while substantive outcomes are derivative in an epistemological sense from process, those outcomes are integrally a part of that process rather than dissociated from it.

The normative criteria implied by the Action paradigm's epistemology and theory of values are drawn from the major topics discussed in chapters 3 and 5. These criteria include

1. The extent to which the rules are likely to induce decisional processes that affirm or develop the self in its active and social aspects
2. The extent to which the rules and associated processes acknowledge the intersubjective nature of social knowledge
3. The extent to which rules may effectively promote, where possible, the disaggregation of decisions
4. The extent to which decision rules and associated processes affirm the reciprocal relationship between means and ends, and take due account of emotive-expressive, as well as instrumental, considerations in the pursuance of social projects [17]

DECISION RULES AND THE ACTIVE-SOCIAL SELF

Chapter 3 stressed that the active-social nature of the self was intended not as a description of behavior that is most typical of people but as a "natural" orientation whose fulfillment provides a normative standard of health or "goodness." Acting consistent with our nature as active selves is to engage in actions that permit the expression of our creative potential and our need to act as autonomous beings. The social nature of the self is reflected in actions that take into account the actions and preferences of others, not merely as strategies to attain our own ends, but in ways that affirm others' creative potential and needs for social bonds. In assessing the normative adequacy of decision rules, we should be concerned with how processes logically associated with those rules are likely to reinforce or conflict with the orientations toward autonomy and community implied by the active-social nature of the self.

Whatever their practical merit, unilateral decisions hierarchically imposed by one or a few on others logically restrict the exercise of creative potential and autonomous action to those in positions of authority. While people in subordinate positions in hierarchical organizations may find ways of acting relatively autonomously, they do so in spite of hierarchy rather than because of it.

Perhaps the best that can be said about hierarchy with respect to the active nature of the self is that "enlightened" hierarchical decisions may help establish an orderly context that, while constraining in some important ways, also enables "bounded" autonomous action (i.e., action that is cognizant of social consequences). After all, action in the absence of constraints or social context is fundamentally anarchic in a political sense and meaningless in an existential sense. Moreover, insofar as public organizations will no doubt continue to exist in a position subordinate (accountable) to legislative bodies and elective executives, the needs for autonomy, self-realization, and the like, of organization members and their clients must necessarily be circumscribed. This fact probably explains why various "participative management" philosophies have been received less enthusiastically in the public sector than in the private sphere where legal requirements for political accountability are usually less demanding and explicit.

Although the argument here does not imply a rejection of systems of hierarchical accountability, the normative criteria of the action approach suggest that hierarchical systems of accountability are defensible not on the basis of normative "first principles" but because of presumably overwhelming practical difficulties, subject to empirical determination, of administering government organizations without them. The active nature of the self (referring here to organizational subordinates and their clients) is by definition disconfirmed by hierarchical decisional processes. Hierarchical authority may be regarded as necessary, however, on practical grounds, and may even be normatively defensible when decisions cannot reasonably be disaggregared—that is, when (for the reasons noted in chapter 5) decisions cannot take adequate account of the unique individual needs and preferences of organization members and clients. These are the kinds of decisions that superordinate bodies such as legislatures are reasonably called upon to make.

This analysis suggests that representative governments are in the ironic position of requiring that superordinate bodies employ a normatively inferior decision rule—hierarchy—vis-à-vis public agencies; whereas the agencies, whose members deal most directly with clients in the actual provision of services, are often in a better position to employ normatively preferred decision rules that may more adequately account for people's needs for autonomy and self-determination. Recognizing the basic tension between the requirement of accountability of agencies to superordinate bodies and the normative criteria of autonomy and self-determination, governments might profitably focus on the development of what Berger and Neuhaus have called "mediating structures." Although mediating structures are defined as "those institutions standing between the individual in his private life and the large institutions of public life," [18] they are given an additional meaning here. Such structures, whether formally institutionalized or not, would be charged with negotiating or mediating on a continuous basis the tensions between organizations as well as between decision-making levels within organizations. This means more than clarifying legislative intent for the purpose of assuring accountability of agencies to legislatures. For the relationship to be a truly dialectical one, mediating structures would involve the continuous assessment of ways by which decisions could be disaggregated (pushed to lower administrative levels), new decision-making and organizational arrangements experimented with, and legislative intent revised on the basis of experience during implementation, to mention just a few of the possibilities. Although many of these activities already take place informally, it is urged here that such practices be explicitly incorporated into the theory of public administration and assume a prominent position in its institutional framework. A key assumption underlying this suggestion is that there is probably no "ideal" balance that can be identified either empirically or in principle between the general requirement of account-ability, on the one hand, and individual needs for autonomy and discretion in unique contexts, on the other.

The thrust of the discussion thus far is that the practical requirements for hierarchical systems of accountability (which are by no means self-evident in all cases) do not constitute and should not be confused with moral imperatives. Hierarchy exacts a price both in terms of the expression of people's active as well as their social nature. In fact, the normative case against hierarchical rules is even clearer with respect to the social self. Quite simply, hierarchy is a form of domination that obstructs the processes described in the "We-relation" by which our social nature is expressed through mutual commitment and empathic concern for one another as persons. Hierarchy fails the normative test implied by the social nature of the self, first, by replacing the voluntary basis of cooperation implied by the "We-relation" with the threat of domination or coercion. Second, hierarchy substitutes impersonal decisional criteria for the personal and emphathic bases of commitment.

This suggests that an additional task of the mediating structures described earlier would be continuously and self-consciously to assess the tradeoffs between system requirements for accountability and individual needs for mutuality and community. These assessments should be based on a clear understanding that requirements either for accountability or mutuality cannot be objectively determined, but are particular attributions of meaning made by actors. For this reason, *a priori* principles and criteria are unlikely to be helpful in mediating the tensions. The task of mediating structures is fundamentally the continuous negotiation of meaning.

Bargaining, voting, and contract decision rules fare substantially better than hierarchy in their degree of normative adequacy. Each of these rules implicitly grants, consistent with the active nature of the self, that people's orientation toward self-determination is both natural and legitimate. Each of these rules implicitly assumes that people know, or are capable of knowing, what their interests are and are capable of acting sensibly to achieve them. Little if any value is ascribed to the interactive processes by which individual ends are achieved other than to note that no formal power and status differences among participants are necessarily assumed (i.e., everyone is presumed to be equal); and participation is typically voluntary.

Despite the assumption of equality implicit in these rules (which mitigates the problem of domination associated with hierarchy), the decisional processes associated with them do little in the way of affirming social bonds among people. Contract and bargaining are means by which individual interests may be asserted and balanced against the interests of others in a relatively orderly manner. The processes and outcomes generated by contract and bargaining are mediated by law and currency rather than by trust and commitment. The value of those rules and processes is a function solely of the outcomes they produce rather than the quality of the social processes they help to bring about. Voting, especially through secret ballot, is even less satisfactory by virtue of its anonymity (i.e., its asocial nature) and because outcomes of voting result in the domination of the minority by the majority.[19]

The normative argument for the consensus (unanimity) rule is that consensual processes most closely approximate the interpersonal dynamics of the "We-relation." Consensus implies equality among participants in the decisional process and thus the absence of domination intrinsic to hierarchical decisions and voting outcomes. The free expression of points of view through consensus is roughly equivalent to the *gesture* (the first moment of the "We-relation"), which, in addition to expressing individual "interests," may also be taken as signifying concern for a *response* (the second moment) from others. Similarly, the response by others and, in turn, the *interpretation* of the response (the third moment) both affirm a personal concern and empathy among participants that transcends strictly instrumental considerations involved in reaching agreements.[20] The requirement of unanimity implies that agreement is based fundamentally on the presence or development of social bonds and personal commitment and only secondarily, if at all, on the basis of legal obligation, formal authority, currency, or objectivated criteria of correctness. Although the requirement of unanimity as a practical matter is the most demanding of all decision rules, this apparent liability is at the same time its major strength in a normative sense. The rule of unanimity, more than any other rule, biases the process of decision making in directions that permit, and indeed require, modes of action that most fully express our moral nature as active and social selves.

DECISION RULES AND INTERSUBJECTIVITY

The epistemological argument in favor of consensual processes has already been elaborated in chapter 3, which reviewed Thayer's analysis of the relationship between organization theory and epistemology.[21] Briefly summarized, his argument holds that epistemology is a specified decision-making process (bound by rules) employed in the legitimation of knowledge. The intersubjective processes by which knowledge is created are affirmed through consensus in which the criterion of knowledge adequacy is its subjective plausiblity to actors, rather than external standards of correctness or authority. Hierarchy, voting, and other rules are epistemologically suspect because they fail to acknowledge the normative

legitimacy of those intersubjective processes. Rules that permit the imposition of one person or group's view of reality on others (most notably
hierarchy), in effect, constitute acts of domination. Both the epistemological and the normative arguments against such acts of domination, therefore, are identical.

DECISION RULES AND DISAGGREGATION OF DECISIONS

Chapter 5 held that, from a normative standpoint, disaggregated desisions
are preferred over aggregated ones inasmuch as the former may more
adequately take account of the unique needs and preferences of individuals and permit the exploration of a rather extensive range of solutions to
problems. They are preferable, in addition, for the reason that the smaller
the number of people immediately affected by and involved in making
decisions, the less the necessity to resort to rules and processes in which
some people may impose their will or world view on others. For the
reasons noted in chapter 5, there are often practically compelling and
even normatively acceptable reasons for making aggregated decisions that
apply uniformly to everyone. Hierarchy and voting are the rules most
suitable for those situations. Yet, uniformity in the application of decisions and policies exacts a cost, namely, that uniformity is an *imposed,*
rather than a natural, condition. Where disaggregation is feasible, uniformity reflects the pathological side of equality.

Although consensus has been asserted here to be normatively preferred to all other rules on a variety of grounds, bargaining and contract
fare equally well with respect to the disaggregation criterion. All three
rules, although they employ different standards for mediating decisional
processes and legitimating outcomes, permit decisions that reflect the
consideration of unique individual needs and preferences.

DECISION RULES AND PROJECTS

Because the instrumental relationship between ends and means is commonly taken for granted in our everyday thinking, the idea that action
itself has meaning and importance may initially seem puzzling. Without
denying the desirability of knowing in advance what one wants to achieve,
however, the earlier discussion of projects suggests that the relationship
between ends and means is highly fluid and the wisdom of action cannot
be measured solely on the basis of its efficiency or of its compatibility with
preconceived ends. Instead, if action itself is normatively important, we
might do well to view ends and goals as providing a *context* for acting
rather than its purpose. This implies more than just that ends do not
always justify means, but that the quality of the process of acting deserves

serious attention as a normative concern, including the manner in which action is influenced by various decision rules.

Two opposing views about action with respect to the relationship between ends and means have been suggested by Robert Biller. The first summarizes the rational-instrumental view of action, which he says characterizes reform strategies in industrial societies.

> Rationalize action in terms of the *efficacy of goals*. Acceptance of goals implies means. ("If something is worth doing, it's worth doing well.")[22]

His preferred alternative reverses the equation.

> Rationalize goals in terms of the *efficacy of action*. Acceptance of means serves as the basis upon which goals may be inferred. ("If something isn't worth doing well, it certainly isn't worth doing.")[23]

Interpreted from the rational-instrumental perspective on the relation of means to ends, Biller's second statement might appear to suggest that substantive ends are unimportant. Although the context of his statements is not elaborated here, his comments reflect, instead, a broader concern with action itself—in its personal, expressive, moral, as well as its instrumental, aspects. The fluid and dialectical relation between ends and means is in part an acknowledgment that we often learn what we *want* to do by experience, rather than through rational planning, and that ends are naturally modified continually by that experience. The fluidity of means and ends is a product, as well, of the necessity to act—to undertake projects—in the absence of perfect knowledge of consequences and that useful information for subsequent action is *created*, not just made discoverable, by action motivated as much by hunches, commitment, love, and so forth, as by rational calculation.

This perspective on action and its relation to means and ends provides the basis from which an additional criterion may be inferred for assessing the normative adequacy of decision rules. *That criterion is the extent to which various rules encourage decisional processes which induce an appreciation of the dialectical relationship between ends and means in terms of their moral, expressive, and instrumental aspects.* Stated another way, decision rules are normatively satisfactory to the extent that they promote their pursuance of social projects, rather than merely the instrumental attainment of goals.

From this criterion, the case against the rule of hierarchy is quite clear, at least insofar as it is evaluated within the context of the bureaucratic model of organization. The bureaucratic model, as Weber described it, is the institutional embodiment of legal-rational authority and whose day-to-day functioning was governed by the uniform and impersonal application of rules. The legal-rational nature of bureaucratic authority, which assumes that the purpose of action is the efficient attainment of ends in an instrumental sense, fails to acknowledge the dialectical relationship between ends and means that naturally exists in the pursuance of projects; and the norm of impersonality effectively denies the legitimacy of affective or expressive aspects of social action.

Viewed independently from the remaining elements of the bureaucratic model, hierarchy implies that decision makers (superiors) are separate from decision implementors (subordinates). If making and implementing decisions are regarded as two separate functions, as must be assumed because different people are designated to perform the two tasks, then the dialectical means-ends relationship characteristic of projects is muted. This is because those concerned with the development or application of efficient means of implementation (subordinates) are dependent on the good will or receptivity of superiors in order to modify previously defined ends. As many subordinates will no doubt attest, such receptivity is highly problematic.

It may be objected that effective organizations get around this problem by instituting various "environmental scanning" and "participative management" practices, in part, as ways to provide superiors with information enabling them to rethink or adjust ends or goals. In addition, any sophisticated management information system is replete with multiple "feedback loops" so that ends may be continuously adjusted to means, and vice versa. By almost any standard, however, the effectiveness of either of these kinds of feedback mechanisms has been mixed—despite the common-sense and almost self-evident wisdom of using them. It is purely speculative at this point, but it is a reasonable hypothesis that the need for organizations *formally* to institutionalize elaborate feedback and environmental scanning procedures may in part be a function of hierarchical (and perhaps some other) rules and associated processes that prevent or discourage that feedback from *naturally* taking place. A corollary hypothesis holds that much of the ineffectiveness of such formal procedures may result from their violating informal norms commonly associated with hierarchy. At issue here are the rewards and punishments both superiors and subordinates perceive as accruing from their various positions on the hierarchical ladder. Some examples, in the case of superiors, might include (1) the felt need to be "right" in making initial decisions in order to be credible in the eyes of subordinates; and (2) the desire to consolidate or maintain power by limiting the upward flow of information that might alienate current or potential allies. Subordinates, on the other hand, might be reluctant to pass information upward for fear that it might reflect badly on their performance, thus jeopardizing their chances for promotion, or out of the fear of appearing disloyal.

Even if these sorts of problems could be remedied and result in the transmission of complete and accurate information to superiors, there is no assurance that such "feedback" would bring about the kind of continuous adjustment between ends and means discussed earlier. In hierarchies, superiors may still choose to disregard information, effectively preventing such adjustment from taking place. Moreoever, if only superiors define the relevant categories of information, which presupposes that overall values or purposes are firmly set, feedback may be restricted to technical or instrumental categories of information.

Like hierarchy, voting rules also fail the normative test implied by the means-ends dialectic, especially when a secret ballot is employed. Adjustment between ends and means, if it occurs at all, must take place prior to voting. More so than authoritative hierarchical decisions, moreover, voting usually carries with it, at least in Western cultures, such a stamp of normative legitimacy that, subsequent to the balloting, decisions arrived at are typically viewed as less open to revision and change than decisions arrived at by means of other rules. In addition, by reducing choices to two (e.g., yes or no, alternative A or alternative B), emphasis is shifted from continuous negotiation among parties and adjustment of means and ends to the determination of winners and losers. While rule by the many (through majority vote) is by nearly any normative standard preferable to rule by the few (hierarchy), voting nevertheless is ill suited to mediating the creative, evolving, and sometimes murky process of cooperative action.

Contracts, unlike hierarchy and voting, are decisions arrived at by mutual agreement rather than by domination, and are thus normatively preferred over the other two rules. Unlike consensus, however, contractual agreements are bound by mutual obligations rather than by mutual commitment. While it is surely possible to conceive of "flexible" contracts, their legally binding nature suggests that although contracts are freely entered into, compliance can be assured only by the existence of external sanctions rather than commitment to one another as persons. Given the obligatory nature of action taken subsequent to defining and formalizing the terms of the contract, renegotiation of means and ends becomes viewed as an extraordinary act rather than a natural activity conducted continuously.

Substantially the same normative strengths and weaknesses of contracts apply to bargaining rules and processes. Since bargaining is typically seen as motivated by rational considerations of self-interest, the processes of give and take among participants are mainly, if not exclusively, instrumental means for attaining the *end* of rational self-interest. In the absence either of currency or of explicit *quid pro quos* among participants in a decision, bargaining processes are distinguishable from consensual ones mainly by the "mind set" or perceptual lenses that the participants in (or observers of) the decision process bring to it. (Alternative forms of "bargaining," for example, could include bargaining one's willingness to cooperate, good faith, moral support on future projects.) That is, the same process, so long as there are no significant power differences among the participants, could easily be interpreted as either "bargaining" *or* "consensus making," depending on what one is predisposed to observe. The differences would mainly be differences in the meanings attributed to the situation. This is by no means a trivial distinction, given the centrality of the meanings of social actors. Moreover, these differences in meaning are of more than mere theoretical interest since they are likely to influence both the spirit in which people engage in decision-making processes as well as the outcomes produced by thpse processes. A bargaining mind set, one inclined toward compromise rather than synthesis, is likely to be skeptical about the motives of others. The result is that, in the course of protecting one's own interests (ends), little can be learned from decision processes that might lead one fundamentally to reassess one's own "interests" or to develop positive regard for or trust in others.

In the final analysis, the normative argument for the consensus (unanimity) rule is, first, that it eliminates the formal means by which collective decisions may be characterized by domination. Second, by virtue of the face-to-face processes of social interaction in consensual decisions, the likelihood that decisions will be conceived in purely instrumental terms is substantially lessened. Finally, consensus, more than other rules discussed, permits the most comprehensive and continuous negotiation both of shared meanings and the dialectic between ends and means.

Two important qualifications should be added to the argument for consensus. The first, which has already been mentioned, is that practical considerations may frequently and legitimately dictate using normatively less satisfactory rules, although a too ready acceptance of practicality and efficiency criteria over other normative criteria should be cautioned against. The tendency to rely mainly on criteria of practicality and efficiency in the choice of decision rules is itself an acknowledgment of an instrumental attitude toward collective decision making.

The second qualification is that although it removes *formal* obstacles to the pursuance of projects, the consensus rule provides no guarantee of a healthy dialectic between ends and means, nor can it assure that positive regard among decision participants will be fostered. Like other decision rules and processes, consensus may generate its own pathologies, such as the tendency of forceful personalities to be permitted to dominate face-to-face situations, avoidance of affective and interpersonal process issues through exclusive attention to substantive outcomes, and action that tends to assimilate or institutionalize dissenting viewpoints rather than engage them in a forthright fashion. The consensus rule, in other words, eliminates only the source from which some important pathologies of collective decision making are *formally* legitimated; it does not automatically transform (although it may serve to influence) long-standing habits of thought and action typically associated with alternative decision rules.

Making consensus work thus requires of administrators skills, role definitions, and normative and cognitive perspectives that are not ordinarily acknowledged or rewarded in organizational settings in which decision rules other than consensus are used. These subjects are treated in chapters 7 and 8, which consider the moral nature of administrative action and the linkages among the Action paradigm's assumptive, descriptive, and normative elements.

NOTES

1. Max Weber, *Theory of Social and Economic Organization*, trans. A. M. Henderson and Talcott Parsons (New York: Free Press, 1947), esp. pp. 329–40.

2. Woodrow Wilson, "The Study of Administration," *Political Science Quarterly* 56 (December 1941): 481–506.

3. Probably the most widely known of Robert Dahl's works in which this theme is prominent are *Who Governs* (New Haven: Yale University Press, 1961), *Preface to Democratic Theory* (Chicago: Phoenix Books, 1963), and *Modern Political Analysis* (Englewood Cliffs, N.J.: Prentice-Hall, 1963).

4. For two important works that expand on this argument, see David Braybrooke and Charles E. Lindblom, *A Strategy of Decision* (New York: Free Press, 1963); and Lindblom, *The Intelligence of Democracy: Decision Making Through Mutual Adjustment* (New York: Free Press, 1965).

5. Vincent Ostrom, *The Intellectual Crisis in American Public Administration* (University: University of Alabama Press, 1973), p. 64.

6. Ibid.; see especially chapter 3, "The Work of the Contemporary Political Economists," pp. 48–73.

7. James M. Buchanan and Gordon Tullock, *The Calculus of Consent: Logical Foundations of Constitutional Democracy* (Ann Arbor: University of Michigan Press, 1962), pp. 277–79.

8. For a general discussion of the school voucher idea, see Milton Friedman, *Capitalism and Freedom* (Chicago: University of Chicago Press, 1962), chap. 6. For a dissenting view, see Henry M. Levin, "The Failure of the Public Schools and the Free Market Remedy," *Urban Review* 2 (June 1968): 32–37.

9. For a discussion and advocacy of consensual decisions in public administration, see Frederick C. Thayer, *An End to Hierarchy! An End to Competition! Organizing the Politics and Economics of Survival* (New York: Franklin Watts, 1973). Both Thayer's discussion and the idea of management by consensus generally have been strongly influenced by the writings of Mary Parker Follett published half a century ago. See especially her *The New State: Group Organization the Solution to Popular Government* (5th ed.; New York: Longmans, Green, 1926).

10. Thayer, *End to Hierarchy;* see especially chapters 4 and 5.

11. Ibid.

12. Peter L. Berger and Thomas Luckmann, *The Social Construction of Reality* (Garden City, N.Y.: Anchor Books, 1967), p. 178.

13. Herbert A. Simon, *Administrative Behavior: A Study of Decision-Making Processes in Administrative Organization* (New York: Free Press, 1947).

14. Ostrom, *Intellectual Crisis.*

15. Ibid., p. 48.

16. Ostrom is critical of the traditional definition of efficiency conceived as the relation of inputs to outputs. "If public agencies are organized in a way that does not allow for the expression of a diversity of preferences among different communities of people, then producers of public goods and services will be taking action without information as to the changing preferences of the persons they serve. Expenditures will be made with little reference to consumer utility. *Producer efficiency in the absence of consumer utility is without economic meaning.*" Ibid., p. 62.

17. Alfred Schutz, *Collected Papers*, vol. 1, ed. Arvid Brodersen (The Hague: Martinus Nijhoff, 1967).

18. Peter L. Berger and Richard John Neuhaus, *To Empower People: The Role of Mediating Structures in Public Policy* (Washington, D.C.: American Enterprise Institute, 1977), p. 2.

19. This argument is borrowed from Thayer, who says that voting does not constitute a meaningful act of citizenship: ". . . this fundamental act of citizenship [voting], as we now define citizenship—a lonely act performed infrquently and out of sight and sound of all other human beings—is intended to discard or defeat a candidate we have learned to hate or at least thoroughly dislike. Although we often think of voting as a positive step preliminary to our version of the good life, this attractive camouflage cannot conceal its negative meaning. Indeed, the act is kept secret so that those we seek to repress cannot retaliate by repressing us. . . .

"Voting and electoral processes, then, function only as organized systems which determine who *wins* (represses) and who *loses* (is repressed). The larger ceremonies of election symbolize this win-lose drama." Thayer, *End to Hierarchy*, pp. 54–55.

20. The three-moment dialectic involved in Schutz's concept of the "We-relation" (summarized in chapter 3) is more thoroughly presented in Gibson Winter, *Elements for a Social Ethic* (New York: Macmillan, 1966). See especially chapter 4, "The Nature of the Social World," pp. 85–118.

21. Thayer, "Epistemology as Organization Theory," in *Organization Theory and the New Public Administration*, ed. Carl Bellone (Boston: Allyn and Bacon, 1980), pp. 113–39.

22. Robert P. Biller, "Converting Knowedge into Action: Toward a Postindustrial Society," in *Tomorrow's Organizations: Challenges and Strategies*, ed. Jong S. Jun and William B. Storm (Glenview, Illinois: Scott, Foresman, 1973), p. 39.

23. Ibid.

7

Administrative Responsibility and the Problem of Reification

BBC Reporter (*inquiring about the investigation of the "great train rob-bery" in Britain*): Who do you think may have perpetrated this awful crime?

Scotland Yard Inspector: We believe this to be the work of thieves . . . . The whole pattern is extremely reminiscent of past robberies where we have found thieves to be involved—the tell-tale loss of property, the snatching away of the money substance. It all points to thieves.

Reporter: You say you feel that thieves are responsible.

Inspector: Good heavens, no! I feel that thieves are totally irresponsible, ghastly people who go around snatching your money.

"Beyond the Fringe, '64"

Although most discussions of responsibility in public administration are not as funny as the "interview" quoted above, they are often as confusing. Nevertheless, judging from the frequency with which discussions about it appear in the literature, administrative responsibility is probably the most important normative concept in public administration. Its importance is easily matched by the ambiguity of its meaning. The several definitions of responsibility often conflict with one another, resulting both in sharp disagreements in the academic literature about the proper bounds of administrative discretion and in acute moral dilemmas sometimes experienced by practicing administrators when confronted with institutional requirements for action that they cannot square with the dictates of conscience.

Determining the appropriate limits of administrative discretion has been the central question in the long-standing debate about administrative responsibility since before World War II. At issue has been the proper balance point between two sometimes conflicting requirements. The first requirement is that administrators be held accountable to hierarchical and political superiors. The second is that administrators make discretionary judgments in order to deal effectively with unique problems or contexts that are not or cannot be anticipated by statute or hierarchical authority. The debate over the relative importance of these two requirements cannot be theoretically resolved; concrete manifestations of it can only be *managed*. The tension between accountability and discretion is a problem of the negotiation of meaning that should take place continuously within and among institutions of government. Moreover, debate over the accountability versus discretion is cast within an overly restrictive framework that is incapable of appreciating two important and interrelated meanings of responsibility, namely, personal and shared responsibility.

The assumptions about the nature of the self, the epistemology, and the descriptive and normative theory discussed thus far suggest an alteration and expansion of the meaning of responsibility. Subjects of previous chapters such as the project, decision rules, and the disaggregation of decisions will be employed in this analysis in order to demonstrate how requirements for public accountability may be reconciled with specific situational constraints as well as conflicts engendered by crises of conscience. More important, however, is an explanation of why the problem of responsible action is far more ubiquitous, and in a sense more mundane, than commonly depicted. If, as Louch [1] says, all conceptualization has moral content, then all administrative action (which is based on some sort of conceptualization or "appreciation" [2] of situations) involves judgments about what is the responsible thing to do. Responsibility is an issue in both the absence and the presence of "authoritative" standards to determine the correctness of action. While situations involving conflicts between an administrator's conscience and the legal requirements of law or hierarchy are dramatic, they may be less important in an overall sense than situations in which no clear moral standard is discernible and no authoritative command or rule is given.

PROPOSITION 13. *Administrative responsibility is the major concept ordinarily employed in the normative assessment of administrative action. In the Classical public administration paradigm, responsibility implies various mixtures of three conceptually distinct meanings: accountability, causation, and moral obligation. Classical definitions of responsibility are subject to criticisms implied by aspects of the Action paradigm discussed previously: the active-social conception of the self, the norma-*

tive preference for consensual and disaggregated decisions, and the critique of action conceived exclusively in rational-instrumental terms.

ACCOUNTABILITY

Sometimes termed "objective responsibility," accountability is a legalistic notion depicting the rewards and punishments associated with obeying or disobeying legal or otherwise authoritative edicts. Accountability is, in a sense, a factual designation of guilt, which is to say that the standards used to determine whether someone has or has not sufficiently complied with a law or directive imply no necessarily moral content.[3] Although the concept of accountability, in and of itself, has no moral force, powerful social norms may nevertheless develop that lead people to interpret their own and others' actions as immoral if they violate standards and rules of accountability. For this reason, obeying accountability rules is as much a result of internalized beliefs of right and wrong as it is fear of punishment.

Organizationally, accountability is typically conceived as a *hierarchical* concept; directives from superiors to subordinates are the organizational means by which public programs, determined by statute, are implemented. Hierarchically determined administrative procedures are usually more idiosyncratic and of shorter duration than statutes; and the penalties for nonfeasance or malfeasance in their execution are less severe than are those for violating the law.

The idea of accountability is firmly situated within the Classical public administration paradigm. Accountability assumes the separation of, and the instrumental relationship between, means and ends, administration and politics. Herman Finer provided the most explicit and influential treatise on administrative responsibility consistent with the Classical paradigm.[4] Citing in 1941 the tyranny that resulted from unchecked government power in Nazi Germany and the Soviet Union, Finer saw political responsibility as fundamentally a problem of preserving the accountability of governments to the people. Administrative responsibility, in turn, is "an arrangement of correction and punishment even up to dismissal both of politicians and officials."[5] Although he did not categorically reject the "moral" interpretation of responsibility as "a sense of responsibility . . . [based on] deference or loyalty to professional standards,"[6] Finer regarded such a view as subsidiary to political accountability.

> Moral responsibility is likely to operate in direct proportion to the strictness and efficiency of political responsibility, and to fall away into all sorts of perversions when the latter is weakly enforced. While professional standards, duty to the public, and pursuit of technological efficency are factors in sound

administrative operation, they are but ingredients, and not continuously motivating factors, of sound policy, and they require public and political control and direction.[7]

Without minimizing the necessity for accountable government, it bears mention that Finer's certainty regarding the positive force and influence of structures of political accountability may well have been overstated. After all, Hitler, whose tyranny Finer saw as an object lesson in political accountability, ultimately became Chancellor of the Reichstag through constitutional means and had, for more than a decade, nearly overwhelming public support. And whether "responsible" behavior by public officials is more a function of structures of accountability than an "inner sense" of responsibility logically ought to be viewed as an empirical question rather than an ideological issue (as Finer seemed to interpret it).

One additional point that will be considered in some depth later in the discussion is raised here about accountability as a generic concept. The idea of accountability is based on the premise that, in specified social situations, the actions people undertake that may or do affect the actions or entitlements of others should be subject to the consent of the latter. Such consent is necessary in order to assure that these actions are not arbitrary and that they are consistent with, or at least do not violate, the just entitlements of those affected.

All this should be fairly obvious and scarcely arguable in a normative sense. Accountability arrangements (i.e., the mechanisms for assuring consent), however, characteristically assume both a logical separation of ends and means (and an instrumental relationship between them), as well as separation of "deciders" from "doers." Action (or doing) is conceived as occurring after *decisions* are made about what *ought* to be done. *Determination* of the degree of compatibility of the action with the previously made decisions is then made *after* the "implementing" action is taken.

Serious practical difficulties have long been recognized in maintaining the integrity of this "deciding-doing-determining" sequence and are usually cited as evidence of the "breakdown" of the policy-administration (or ends-means) dichotomy.[8] In view of arguments made in previous chapters, however, the problems of assuring accountability are imbedded in the logic and epistemology of the rational-instrumental approach to understanding and evaluating social action. It is not just that the distinctions between policy and administration, deciding and doing, and ends and means are difficult to maintain in practice. Rather, these distinctions are *conceptually artificial* (albeit often useful), as suggested by the previous discussion of "projects" and the overall normative concern with the processes of action.

MORAL OBLIGATION

Finer's essay on administrative responsibility was occasioned by the appearance some months earlier of an essay on the same subject by Carl Friedrich.[9] Noting that the distinction between policy making and policy execution was based on the dubious idea that the "will of the state" was clearly discernible, Friedrich argued that the classical notion of strict political accountability was equally dubious. He sought to discredit the theoretical basis of the policy-administration dichotomy, which many administrators had discovered from hard experience, rather than ideological reflection, was untenable. The practical consequence of the dichotomy's demise was that clear standards of administrative implementation, and therefore of accountability, were frequently unattainable. As a result, administrators were required to exercise substantial amounts of discretion in the implementation of public policy. Implementation, moreover, was a process that Friedrich saw as frequently indistinguishable from and occurring simultaneously with policy making. In those instances where administrators cannot reasonably be held accountable to predefined standards of correctness, they may subsequently be held accountable for their actions insofar as they were taken in accordance with available technical knowledge and prevailing public sentiment. Although these standards are subject to widely divergent interpretations and are sometimes discernible only after the fact, Friedrich was fairly sanguine, at least more so than Finer, about the ability and likelihood of administrators to adhere to them.

Professional standards, codes of ethics, and an appreciation of popular sentiment are some, but not the only, sources of the second meaning of responsibility: moral obligation.[10] Moral obligation is only a general category of meaning, however, and begs questions of the logical defensibility of particular moral standards as well as who has a legitimate voice in determining them. In addition to public sentiments and standards suggested by technical knowledge, sources of moral obligation might also include abstract principles such as distributive justice and equity, due process, self-realization (for either recipients of public services or organizational members), law and order, to mention just a few. Standards of moral obligation, in addition, may refer to substantive outcomes or to "process' criteria such as those discussed in chapter 5. In short, any discussion of responsibility as moral obligation brings us directly back to a consideration of theories of values, a major concern in the creation and defense of paradigms. Although criteria of moral obligation are sometimes described as "inner checks" (because they are often "internalized" in the value system of administrators), they are usually seen as originating from sources *external* to the administrator; only through education and other means of socialization are they "learned" and incorporated into the administrator's set of values.

Accountability and moral obligation, it should be emphasized, are not necessarily mutually exclusive or conflicting views of responsibility. In fact, one could, hypothetically, define as the highest form of moral obligation the obedient and efficient carrying out of the orders of one's superiors, in which case there is no conflict at all. More likely in practice is a more or less subtle tension between the two views that only occasionally reaches dramatic and highly visible proportions. Differences in orientations toward these two meanings of responsibility are likely to be of degree rather than kind, with some people more willing than others to trust the discretion of public officials.

CAUSATION

When the BBC reporter in our example at the opening of this chapter asked the inspector whom he believed to be responsible for the "great train robbery," the reporter was, of course, inquiring about who *caused* the crime to happen. Similarly, ". . . when a Senator claims that Mr. Rusk is responsible for the alleged failure of United States policy in Southeast Asia, he means, among other things, that the Secretary— through action or inaction—helped bring about this failure or was a contributing cause to it." [11]

In "pinpointing" responsibility for actions taken in, or attributable to, organizations, a hierarchical superior is said to be responsible in a causal sense for the actions of his or her subordinates (assuming that they have obediently carried out the superior's policy). The superior's *authority* is assumed to be sufficiently compelling that it is, for all intents and purposes, the equivalent of causal force even though, strictly speaking, that is not the case. Usually, however, more is implied than attribution of causality. Identification of the "causer" is important because it lets us know whom we can blame, that is, who bears the moral brunt (the after-the-fact equivalent of obligation) for a policy's consequences, as well as who may, or should, be held accountable for them. The assumption that hierarchical authority is the equivalent of causal force is implicit in thte ideal-typical bureaucratic model of organization in which authority—the formal power to cause something to happen—is commensurate with "responsibility." Herbert Spiro terms this idea "explicit causal responsibility," which "consists of four elements, present in varying degrees under different circumstances: resources, knowledge, choice, and purpose." [12] "Purpose" means knowing in advance what one wants to achieve, having a goal in mind; "choice" means having reasonable alternative courses of action available from which to choose in order to achieve one's purpose; "knowledge" refers to *fore*knowledge of the consequences that various courses of action will, or are likely to, produce;

and "resources" are people, money, expertise, and material required to get the job done.

Spiro realizes that while, in *fact,* accountability and causal responsibility are seldom proportional, "as a matter of *value,* however, advocacy of a fair balance between causal responsibility and accountability is quite possible" [13] and desirable. This means two things in terms of the four elements of explicit causal responsibility mentioned above. First, when or to the extent that one or more of those elements is missing with respect to a particular action, the "responsible" agent should, to a similar extent, not be held accountable for the result of that action. And second, effort should be made to assure that, insofar as possible, all four elements *are* provided in the future. If purposes are vague, they should be clarified; alternative courses of action should be explored more fully; information should be sought more diligently in order better to predict the likely consequences of particular choices; and if resources are inadequate, efforts should be made to increase them. Balancing causal responsibility with accountability, in other words, entails more adequately approximating the rational-instrumental model of action.

SUMMARY OF CLASSICAL RESPONSIBILITY

Combinations of meanings of causation, moral obligation, and accountability form the basis of definitions of responsible action within the Classical public administration paradigm and the bureaucratic model of organization. Although differences of opinion exist regarding the relative weight or importance of any one of these meanings in relation to another, various classical definitions of administrative responsibility nevertheless share some common assumptions:

1. Insofar as possible, accountability should be maintained by structuring administrative action so that its various elements, arranged sequentially, correspond to the rational-instrumental approach to action. That is, purposes or goals are defined; action is then taken with the intent of achieving them; and mechanisms of accountability are invoked to determine the degree of correspondence between them.

2. The locus of moral obligation rests *outside* the actor (e.g., in law, authoritative edict, or in "learned" moral precepts or principles such as equity and efficiency). Thus, the Finer-Friedrich debate about the proper limits of administrative discretion, for example, took place *within* the Classical paradigm. At issue were empirical questions of how closely, in practice, the rational model of action could be adhered to and how effectively ad-

ministrators could internalize moral/ethical principles, learn and apply technical knowledge, and discern prevailing public sentiment.

3. Hierarchy, division of labor, and the separation of policy making from policy execution are normatively desirable (even though that separation is not always sustained in practice) because they permit the identification or pinpointing of responsibility both empirically (responsibility as cause) and morally (as obligation). Responsibility in the Classical paradigm is thus a highly "individualized" notion. The idea of *shared* responsibility, despite occasional rhetoric to the contrary, is alien to classical interpretations because it is more practical to reward or punish one person than many.

These three assumptions raise questions about administrative responsibility that have an important bearing on the subsequent analysis of the concept of "personal responsibility."

1. If classical interpretations of administrative responsibility are based on a rational-instrumental view of action, then what does it mean to act responsibly in the *absence* of a rational-instrumental context? Does responsibility imply anything more than that ends justify, and give meaning to, means? Does or can responsibility, in other words, have any meaning independent of the Classical paradigm?

2. If the locus of moral obligation rests outside the actor (e.g., in laws, rules, principles), what assumptions about the nature of the self does this imply? Are those assumptions logically tenable and, if not, do we nevertheless wish them to be legitimated by institutional arrangements of administrative responsibility derived from the Classical paradigm? If people, especially those in subordinate roles, view their obligations as being to people or ideas "above" or "outside" them, then does it not follow to that extent that they will perceive themselves as instruments who may shift the moral and legal blame for their actions to someone or something else? If, as the Classical paradigm suggests, legal or hierarchical authority should approximate, and should be *perceived* by organizational actors as approximating, the equivalent of causal force, does it not follow that those actors will, to a similar extent, *not* view themselves as causes? If they do not see themselves as causes, will they not also see themselves as not morally responsible for consequences of their actions?

3. If, as the action approach suggests, people are by nature social rather than atomistic, what is the effect on the values of mutuality and community (that derive from their sociality) by the classical view of responsibility, which, by various institutional

means, *individualizes* the concept? Is it fundamentally more important to parcel out blame or rewards on an individual basis than to induce a sense of shared or communal responsibility for actions? If not, what sorts of institutional arrangements are likely to encourage the latter?

Some of these questions, of course, are rhetorical in their intent. And if the reader, either intuitively or by virtue of being persuaded by the arguments offered in previous chapters, agrees with some of all of the sentiments implied by them, it is likely that a fourth meaning of responsibility lurks somewhere in his or her consciousness. It is a meaning that is termed here *personal responsibility.*

PROPOSITION 14. *Criticisms of classical responsibility implied by the action approach suggest an alternative and normatively preferred meaning of responsible administrative action, namely, personal responsibility. Personal responsibility implies that actors are agents who must bear the moral brunt of their actions, rather than shift the blame or responsibility to other people or external standards of "correctness." While the concept of personal responsibility is derived from and supported by various elements of the action approach, classical meanings of responsibility are nonetheless necessary, but in a normatively subordinate position. The crucial "institutional" task is to manage effectively the tension between personal and classical notions of responsibility.*

Personal responsibility is intended to mean two things simultaneously. First, it implies the existentialist notion that, by the fact of our being, we are the source—the cause, as it were—of our own actions irrespective of the real or imagined constraints within which we act. Second, by virtue of that fact of our existence, we are responsible in a moral sense for the choices we make; the blame cannot be shifted to someone else, nor to any external standard such as a law or even a moral principle. This is not to say that people should not "act on principle," so long as they recognize that principles have no compelling force; they are chosen or "constructed," not forced upon us. To act responsibly, in the personal sense, means that people's actions are taken with due *recognition* that they themselves are the source or cause of their acts, as well as the locus of responsibility in a moral sense. Statements such as "I had no choice in acting as I did; I was only following orders," or this or that "principle compelled me to act as I did," are inadmissible; that is, they are personally irresponsible.

The idea of personal responsibility is a logical extension of the active conception of the self. Under the passive conception, which assumes that behavior is caused, personal responsibility as defined here would be unthinkable. The plausibility of personal responsibility, however, is also contingent upon an additional assumption, that of the *sociality* of the self, without which personally responsible action, when extended to aggregate or social contexts, would result in either chaos or a social order bound together solely by artificial, which is to say externally imposed, means. The sociality of the self explains the source of the motive of responsible personal action in a way that makes plausible a view of the social order produced and maintained through the expression of aspects or motives that are intrinsic to us. If, as chapter 5 suggested, the motive or normative expression of our sociality is mutuality in primary or face-to-face relationships, then the motives underlying responsible action vis-à-vis social collectivities are logically derived from mutuality. Responsible action in the face-to-face situation is a function of the *commitment* of one person to the other—as persons.[14] In larger contexts responsible action is a function of commitments that are *abstracted* from those possible in the face-to-face situation. Thus, acting on principle is permissible when (1) the context of an action is sufficiently large (i.e., impersonal) that face-to-face interaction is not feasible; (2) acting solely on the basis of a moral commitment to another in the face-to-face situation creates negative consequences for others outside that situation; and (3) the principles can plausibly be shown to be derivatives of the moral premises underlying the face-to-face situation.

The active-social conception of the self provides firmer ground for trusting more often the consequences of action taken on the basis of mutual commitment than does any other set of assumptions about the self. Similarly, personal action based on mutual commitment in generally preferable to actions that are removed from direct interaction with those affected because it requires less reliance on abstract principles and external standards. Face-to-face interaction enables decisions to be disaggregated and permits the formulation of unique decisions for unique circumstances. In addition, face-to-face interaction, especially on a more-or-less continuing basis, helps to produce a context less easily reducible to rational-instrumental action. The immediate presence of each person to the other makes it less necessary, and less possible, for either or both of the parties to resort to abstract or external criteria of decision making that almost inevitably transform the mutual formulation of projects, in their richest and fullest sense, into a rational-instrumental stereotype. When action is motivated by mutual commitment, the quality of the *processes* of interaction may be experienced as more than simply instrumentally relevant.

As described here, personal responsibility suggests that administrative action is necessarily *interaction* and, therefore, that personal responsibility is *shared* responsibility.[15] For this reason, the normative defense of personal responsibility is *not* primarily intended as an argument in favor of greater *unilateral* discretion by administrators. Certainly the view of human nature proposed here suggests, by and large, greater reason to trust the discretion of administrators than would other assumptions about the self. But the fact remains that, without the consent and participation of others who are affected by it, the exercise of unilateral discretion runs the risk of being unchecked and arbitrary unless it is bound, if only loosely at times, by decision rules. The trick is to select the rule that is least likely either to violate the preferred values of the normative theory discussed earlier or to reduce action automatically to a rational-instrumental stereotype. As chapter 6 stated, the consensus rule is normatively preferred in these respects. It provides an "institutional" check against arbitrary and capricious action, as does the rule of hierarchy in preserving accountability; but without at the same time reducing the sense of personal responsibility experienced by the parties to a decision, as can happen when action is "institutionalized" by means of hierarchy. In war, for example, "the order to 'kill,' given at the top, is separated from the actual killing done at the bottom. Institutional controls link the two. Neither feel responsible: the bottom because it is only following orders; the top because it had no control over what *actually* happened. Responsibility evaporates: 'The institution did it.' "[16]

Personal responsibility assumes that people's motivation derives from their commitment to one another as persons. Commitment is crucial not only in the interpersonal sense just described but also helps to explain the relative success or failure with which theories of action, strategies, and ideas generally are employed in practical application. Rather than visualizing "practice theories" (e.g., PPBS, MBO, "Theory Y," organizational development) as value-neutral techniques whose merit or practicality is intrinsic, their practicality is instead a function of the relation *between* the actor and the theory. It is the actor who *makes* the theory work (or not work) depending on his or her level of commitment, that is, the extent to which the actor infuses the theory with value.

> No matter how coherent a theory, no matter how appealing the data make it, it cannot be brought into action without a *commitment* to do so. This commitment is acted out through the use of intuition and feeling which we tend to call the assumption of responsibility. . . . Responsibility . . . is the missing link between theory and action. To bring theory to practice, the administrator must be willing to commit himself to bring *values* into a situation—values that can only be communicated and justified in his actions.[17]

Because theory is only a "statement of relative truth," [18] the responsibility for its success or failure in practice ultimately resides with the actors who use the theory and not with the theory itself. Whether theories work when applied in practice is a self-fulfilling (or value-fulfilling) prophecy that may have positive as well as negative value. Whether we should dread the "Hawthorne effect," for example, depends on whether we agree or disagree with the values implicit in the action that brings it about.[19]

MANAGING THE TENSIONS AMONG ACCOUNTABILITY, DISCRETION, AND PERSONAL RESPONSIBILITY

Although various definitions of responsibility are logically associated with particular assumptions about the self and decision rules, the intent here is not to reject as necessary or useful definitions of responsibility and decision rules that do not logically accord with the active-social conception of the self. While the combination of personal responsibility, consensus, and the active-social self has a preferred normative status, numerous occasions arise in which other conceptions of responsibility must for reasons of practicality be "institutionalized."

Although actors may reasonably perceive conflicts between conscience and requirements for institutional accountability, there is nevertheless nothing in the nature of the self to suggest an *inherent* conflict between personal responsibility (integrity) and moral obligation (conscience). Both constitute intrinsic and dialectically related expressions of the nature of the self. If this is the case, then a crucial institutional task is, where possible, either to limit the use of hierarchical structures of accountability and to create mechanisms of accountability that are least likely to diminish the actors' sense of personal responsibility for their actions. The possibility of limiting the use of hierarchical structures increases to the extent that decisions can be disaggregated so that projects undertaken and decisions made reflect an evolution toward intersubjective agreement and interpersonal trust rather than a reliance on externally imposed and impersonal criteria of correctness. However, evil—in the form of exploitation, trickery, domination, or simply the pursuit of narrow self-interest at others' expense—is a fact of life requiring institutional safeguards. The rule of consensus, more than other rules discussed here, helps provide an institutional context in which the preferences and entitlements of all parties to a decision may be heard, negotiated, and accounted for.

Chapters 5 and 6 presented the normative arguments in favor of disaggregated decisions and the rule of consensus, but also stipulated the conditions under which aggregated decisions and the use of alternative decision rules are normatively acceptable: when pure public goods are at issue and when the negative side effects on others of disaggregated/consensual decisions are unmanageable through face-to-face interaction. The larger the number of people affected by a decision, the greater the difficulty both in making the consensual processes work and in effectively disaggregating decisions without *creating* negative side effects (or externalities).[20]

Since many, if not most, policy decisions, especially at higher or more encompassing levels of institutions, necessarily fall into these categories, it follows that normatively second-best decision rules must be employed. And with the use of such rules (most notably hierarchy), of course, comes the requirement for an "institutionalized" mechanism of responsibility: accountability. Here is where, in principle, the clash between personal and "institutional" responsibility becomes theoretically unresolvable but, as will be suggested momentarily, perhaps manageable. Since even the most optimistic view of human nature cannot disguise the existence of venality, selfishness, or even well-intentioned incompetence, the need for legal or hierarchical mechanisms of accountability is evident for the categories of decisions just mentioned. Either government by a technological elite or corruption, if engaged in even by only a small minority of public servants, would by almost any account be intolerable and cannot be justified as an acceptable "cost" for permitting civil servants and their clients to "self-actualize" or engage in consensual decision making at the public's expense. This seems to be Mosher's understandable concern when he states:

> . . . there has already developed a great deal of collegial decision-making in many public agencies, particularly those controlled by single professional groups. But I would point out that *democracy within administration,* if carried to the full, raises a logical dilemma in its relation to *political democracy.* All public organizations are presumed to have been established and to operate for public purposes—i.e., purposes of the people. . . . It is entirely possible that internal administrative democracy might run counter to the principles and objectives of political democracy in which the organizations of government are viewed as instruments of public purpose.[21]

Although Mosher is mainly concerned about the unchecked power of technological elites, his point could apply equally to decisions made by technically unsophisticated members within public agencies as well as between them and their clients. The latter kinds of decisions run the risk of being condemned, often correctly, as collusion. Witness the criticism that regulatory agencies, in particular, are often the captives of the industries they are supposed to regulate.[22]

Although Mosher's criticism is, I think, rightly taken, it tells only half the story. Consider the following statement, which uses some of his phraseology.

> Political democracy, as conceived by the Classical public administration paradigm (i.e., the politics-administration dichotomy), *if carried to the full,* raises a logical dilemma in its relation to organizational actors and their clients as personally responsible actors. It is entirely possible that "political democracy" might run counter to the moral nature of the self, whose development organizations of government should assist or at least not retard.

The juxtaposition of these two statements fairly accurately depicts the basic *tension* between classical democratic and modern organization theory. Yet that tension need not necessarily require that the two positions be viewed in either-or terms; that is, neither position can nor should, as a practical matter, be "carried to the full." Clearly, the action approach suggests a normative bias toward the latter position (i.e., by disaggregating decisions so that they may be consensually made by the parties affected). However, the mechanisms of accountability consistent with the classical view of administrative responsibility are still needed in order to account for the negative side effects (especially of disaggregated decisions) and to assure equitable implementation of aggregated decisions. Moreover, despite the inherent compatibility of moral obligation and personal responsibility implied by the active-social conception of the self, mechanisms of accountability are still required for "worst cases," such as malfeasance and incompetence, in nondisaggregatable decisions. That malfeasance and other "antisocial" actions may be said to be pathological does not obviate the need for institutional mechanisms for recognizing and dealing with them.

No stroke of the theoretical pen is capable of resolving all the logical contradictions and practical difficulties associated with the tension between democratic and organization theory. For this reason, it is difficult, if not impossible, to conceive of definitive arrangements or rules either to institutionalize one theory of values without infringing on the legitimate claims of the other or to guarantee a perfect balance of the two. Therefore, it appears that a crucial task for public organizations, both internally as well as in their relationships with legislative bodies, clients and citizens groups, and other agencies, is to learn how to *manage* on a continuing basis the sometimes conflicting requirements of hierarchical and legal accountability with those of personally responsible actors. This suggests that the "mediating structures" described in the previous chapter for managing the tensions between decision rules are also the devices for mediating between logically conflicting definitions of administrative responsibility. Since public agencies stand in a position subordinate to legislative and executive authority, it is probably unrealistic to suppose that structures designed to mediate the tensions between them would or could be bound by the *rule* of consensus which assumes legally coequal status among the parties involved. As a decision-making *process,* however, consensus seems best suited for managing the tensions between legitimate but conflicting claims. The kinds of recurring questions and issues that could be addressed through such mediating structures might include

1. The extent to which particular decisions could be effectively disaggregated without seriously undermining legislative or executive intent
2. The clarification *and* alteration of legislative intent based on experience during implementation (or, more generally, the intersubjective clarification and negotiation of meaning by the parties)

3. The identification of negative side effects arising from either the excessively uniform administration of some "aggregate" policies or excessive diaggregation of others
4. Frank consideration of how the subjectively defined "interests" of the parties influence their willingness to negotiate and alter their positions.

PROPOSITION 15. *Irresponsible administrative action is rooted in the cognitive processes that lead people to deny or simply not comprehend personal responsibility for their actions. These processes constitute the problem of reification, that is, the tendency to view systems, institutions, roles, and other social artifacts as both existing and having legitimacy independent of the intersubjective processes people actually use in creating, sustaining, and transforming them.*

Responsible administrative action is not merely a matter of following rules—whether explicitly expressed in written procedures and laws or inferred from moral principles or codes of ethical conduct. Because ends and means are dialectically rather than instrumentally related, the conception of responsible action as legally or morally "correct" action is far too limited to encompass adequately the full range of administrators' moral concerns. Responsible action requires an appreciation of rules and standards in terms of their applicability, or lack of it, to contexts and problems each of whose unique character precludes the routine application of standardized solutions. Responsible action presupposes moral *conceptualization,* an ability and willingness to perceive possibilities or choices in situations and in such a manner that they may be *informed* by an appreciation of standards, rules, and situational constraints, but not determined by them. When action is perceived as *determined* by either rules or situational constraints, administrators' sense of personal responsibility for their actions evaporates, and problem definitions are force-fitted into preconceived and often arbitrary categories of meaning.

To conceptualize situations in a personally responsible manner, then, requires a cognitive ability to suspend, temporarily at least, everyday categories of meaning and standards of right and wrong, to view them as often useful, but not compelling, social artifacts. This is no easy task, since institutions exert a powerful socializing influence on the way in which people perceive, from infancy through adulthood, the social world and their relation to it. This problem is magnified by the fact that much of our everyday as well as our theoretical language for describing and comprehending the social world is borrowed from the natural sciences. When used to describe aspects of the social world, natural science metaphors may frequently give the false impression that social institutions, roles, rules, and even situations possess a concrete immutability, a natural existence independent of their intersubjective creation and maintenance by social actors.

This kind of cognitive error has been variously labeled "thingifying," "the fallacy of misplaced concreteness," and Lord Whitehead's tongue-twister, "hypostitization" (which is restricted to *theoretical* thingifying). More typically, however, this mode of thinking is termed *reification*. A concise definition is provided by Postman, who says that reification is "confusing words with things." [23] Berger and Luckmann, quoted here at some length, describe the problem of reification as it pertains to the over-all process by which social institutions are produced, maintained, and legitimated.

Reification is the apprehension of human phenomena as if they were things, that is, in non-human or possibly supra-human terms. Another way of saying this is that reification is the apprehension of the products of human activity *as if* they were something else than human products—such as facts of nature, results of cosmic laws, or a manifestation of divine will. Reification implies that man is capable of forgetting his own authorship of the human world, and further, that the dialectic between man, the producer, and his products is lost to consciousness. The reified world is, by definition, a dehumanized world. It is experienced by man as a strange facticity, an *opus alienum* over which he has no control rather than as the *opus proprium* of his own productive activity.

. . . as soon as an objective social world is established, the possibility of reification is never far away. The objectivity of the social world means that it confronts man as something outside of himself. The decisive question is whether he still retains the awareness that, however objectivated, the social world was made by men—and, therefore, can be remade by them. In other words, reification can be described as an extreme step in the process of objectivation, whereby the objectivated world loses its comprehensibility as a human enterprise and becomes fixated as a non-human, non-humanizable, inert facticity. Typically, the real relationship between man and his world is reversed in consciousness. Man, the producer of a world, is apprehended as its product, and human activity as an epiphenomenon of non-human processes. Human meanings are no longer understood as world-producing but as being, in their turn, products of the "nature of things." It must be emphasized that reification is a modality of consciousness, more precisely, a modality of man's objectification of the human world. Even while apprehending the world in reified terms, man continues to produce it. That is, man is capable paradoxically of producing a reality that denies him.

. . . the basic "recipe" for the reification of institutions is to bestow on them an ontological status independent of human activity and signification. . . . Through reification, the world of institutions appears to merge with the world of nature. It becomes necessity and fate, and is lived through as such, happily or unhappily as the case may be.

Roles may be reified in the same manner as institutions. The sector of self-consciousness that has been objectified in the role is then also apprehended as an inevitable fate, for which the individual may disclaim responsibility. The paradigmatic formula for this kind of reification is the statement "I have no choice in the matter, I have to act this way because of my position"—as husband, father, general, archbishop, chairman of the board, gangster, and hangman, as the case may be. This means that the reification of roles narrows the subjective distance that the individual may establish between himself and his role-playing. The distance implied in all objectification remains, of course, but the distance brought about by disidentification shrinks to the vanishing point.[24]

In their introduction to *The Social Construction of Reality,* Berger and Luckmann stipulate that their intent is to provide a *descriptive* sociological framework while leaving it to philosophers to plumb its moral and metaphysical meaning. Thus, in their analysis, reification is presented as a *cognitive* problem. The *moral* implications of their treatment of it, however, loom so close to the surface that it is difficult to resist speculating about the relationship of reified modes of thinking to personally responsible action.

The relation is fairly obvious because to be personally responsible for one's actions presupposes that choices are available and that the blame or moral responsibility for the consequences of action cannot be shifted to external standards of authority or correctness nor facilely attributed to the "inexorability" of situational forces. In reified thinking, choices are seen as determined by standards or institutional role definitions (which is to say that there are no real choices at all) or effectively eliminated by situational forces. To be sure, *non*reified thinking is not oblivious to situational factors but would tend to regard them as "constraining" or even enabling, rather than determining. The difference is that nonreified thinking appreciates the dialectic between "man, the producer" and the social world. Thus, the notion of reification suggests that the problem of responsible action is less that administrators may make "incorrect" moral choices than that their mode of thinking may preclude the realization that choices are, in fact, available to them.

While the problem of reification has numerous implications for this analysis, four are briefly discussed here. The first has to do with one of the two dimensions of the Administrative Environments Grid (presented in chapter 4), namely, environmental "malleability." Malleability, it will be recalled, characterizes the extent to which environments or situations are relatively susceptible to alteration or influence by administrative action. The degree of malleability is a function of both the "objective" qualities of environments and the cognitive abilities of administrators to perceive possibilities for transforming them. This latter cognitive aspect may fairly be interpreted as the degree to which administrators, by means of various role definitions and institutional arrangements, can and are encouraged to perceive environments and situations in *non*reified terms.

The second aspect of the paradigm bearing on the problem of reification has to do with the normative issue of apprehending and appreciating the *unique* aspects of particular decisional contexts, rather than reducing them to standardized categories of meaning and evaluation. The theoretical and normative implications of uniqueness (in contrast to generality and universality) discussed in previous chapters stressed the importance of elevating an appreciation of uniqueness to a position of intellectual and moral respectability. The context within which uniqueness may be most fully appreciated in practice is the face-to-face encounter in which subtleties of meaning and affect may be more fully explored.

The phenomenon of reification, however, suggests that more is at issue than merely the logic of the argument for uniqueness as a legitimate theoretical and moral concern. Reified thinking is an *unconscious* tendency to *apprehend* aspects of the social world through particular, typically "institutionalized," *categories* of meaning. The categories of meaning are those of the listener (e.g., administrator) rather than the speaker (e.g., client); the result is that the "fit" between the speaker's unique and intended meaning and the listener's categories of meaning is highly problematic.

All this is not to suggest that institutional categories of meaning and interpretation are wrong, unnecessary, or even avoidable (which, of course, they are not). Yet relatively *non*reified thinking implies a cognitive ability to suspend temporarily, to stand apart from, one's usual categories of meaning in order to see and appreciate problems and situations as described by others. Inability to do this depersonalizes the encounter and makes impossible personally responsible action, which is motivated by commitment to one another as persons.

Since reification is an unconscious mode of thinking, the problems generated by it are not solvable by even the most logically persuasive exhortations to public officials *not* to think in reified terms. Solutions must therefore be sought elsewhere—which brings us to the third implication of reification for the Action paradigm: the relation between reification and decision rules. Specifically, to what extent do decision rules variously encourage or discourage tendencies of public officials to reify institutionalized role definitions, procedures, values, and categories of meaning and evaluation? In answering this question, it seems useful to speculate about how various decision rules may make it more or less difficult for people unconsciously to cling to institutional procedures and categories of meaning—in terms of the rules' long-term socializing influence as well as the shorter-term pressures that various decision rules may induce toward the cognitive suspension or dislodgement of those categories.

Of the three decision rules receiving most extensive consideration in chapter 6 (i.e., hierarchy, the market, and consensus), the first two logically appear most likely to encourage cognitive tendencies toward reification. The case against hierarchy is the more obvious of the two; in hierarchies, the authority of some organizational members unilaterally to impose binding decisions on other members (as well as on clients of the organization) also carries with it the tacit authority to define relevant and legitimate categories of knowledge, meaning, interpretation, and evaluation. "He who has the bigger stick," in other words, "has the better chance of imposing his definition." [25]

Decision rules not only influence the way in which clients and consumers may *express* their perferences but also influence the categories of meaning within which they (clients and consumers) are likely to *conceive* of them. The more pervasive a particular decision rule, therefore, the more likely it is that consumers will restrict the defintion of their preferences to categories of meaning logically implied (and therefore legitimated) by that rule. If the decision rule is sufficiently influential, consumers' definitions of their preferences will *not* be matters of conscious choice. Rather, their preferences will be products of reified categories of meaning that determine the bounds of conceivable, as well as permissible, preferences.

This appears to be especially true of market rules in which preferences are expressed through impersonal media of exchange, such as currency or vouchers, instead of through face-to-face interaction. The absence of face-to-face interaction and negotiation of meaning in transactions mediated by market rules means that providers of services or goods must infer consumer preferences indirectly and unilaterally. From an economist's viewpoint, however, this may be seen as a strength rather than a liability. Friedman, for example, argues that market mechanisms avoid "cumbrous political channels" by allowing consumers to express their views and preferences directly.[26] Hirschman, who refers to market arrangements as an "exit" (in contrast to a "voice") function, disputes this contention. ". . . Friedman considers withdrawal or exit as the 'direct' way of expressing one's unfavorable views of an organization. A person less well trained in economics might naively suggest that the direct way of expressing views is to express them." [27] Hirschman is not an advocate of consensus and, in fact, proposes a balance of "exit" and "voice" functions in order to assure the responsiveness of organizations to their clients. Nevertheless, his tongue-in-cheek criticism of Friedman underscores earlier arguments in favor of the consensus rule. Consensus permits the direct expression of "voice" and in a way that allows for an infinite variety of preferences and subjective meanings to be heard and taken into account. While the seeming open-endedness of consensual processes may be "cumbrous," that very open-endess also allows for continual negotiation of what would otherwise be taken-for-granted and hence reified categories of meaning.

The fourth implication of reification noted here is that it clarifies further the linkage between personal responsibility and the theory of justice discussed in chapter 5. The idea of personal responsibility is most clearly relevant in *disaggregated* contexts in which decisions can be made consensually through face-to-face negotiation. In these situations possibilities for relying on reified standards of correctness may be minimized. People's capacity for personally responsible action that does not rely on reified standards has been suggested to be a function of a natural developmental orientation in the direction of affirming the active-social nature of the self.

Similarly, a propensity to employ criteria of justice and equity in *aggregated* decision contexts is, for similar reasons, related to that same developmental orientation toward nonreified thinking. Commenting on the role of reification in the individual's cognitive development, Berger and Luckmann note:

> It would also be a mistake to look at reification as a perversion of an originally non-reified apprehension of the social world, a sort of cognitive fall from grace. On the contrary, the available ethnological and psychological evidence seems to indicate the opposite, namely, that the original apprehension of the social world is highly reified both phylogenetically and ontogenetically. This implies that an apprehension of reification *as* a modality of consciousness is dependent upon an at least relative *de*reification of consciousness, *which is a comparatively late development in history and in any individual biography.*[28]

Dereification involves a conceptual ability to stand apart from existing social and institutional definitions both of "what is" and "what ought to be" in order that *alternative* values and conceptions of the social world may be apprehended and acted on. The cognitive means by which this may be most fully accomplished is through the use of abstract principles. Abstract, principled thought simultaneously permits both the greatest possible distance from current definitions of the social world and at the same time enables the most comprehensive consideration of the rights and just entitlements of others. While the face-to-face encounter allows for the most authentic context for the expression of mutuality, the absence of unlimited possibilities for face-to-face interaction requires that mutuality sometimes be comprehended and expressed indirectly, that is, through abstract principles of justice that appeal to logical comprehensiveness. The crucial point here is that nonreified thought, which enables both personally responsible action and a comprehension of the meaning of justice, is made cognitively possible by an ability to think abstractly. Relative to other conceptual abilities, the capacity for abstract or principled thought is acquired rather late in life, if at all. The development of principled thought, in other words, seems to be explainable as a progressive dereification of consciousness.

The concept of personal responsibility has a normatively preferred, though not exclusive, status insofar as an understanding of responsible administrative action is concerned. In order adequately to comprehend the tension between classical interpretations of administrative responsibility and personal responsibility, the latter notion requires more extensive explication than it ordinarily receives. To attach the rather vague label of "subjective," for example, to personal responsibility tends to trivialize the concept and give the false impression that it is not amenable to reasoned discourse. While it is true that personal responsibility cannot be fairly evaluated on rational-instrumental grounds, it is nevertheless accessible on other, namely, moral-philosophical, terms.

The intent of this chapter has been to link the concept of personal responsibility with the other elements of the action approach; to clarify the tensions between personal and classical concepts of responsibility and to suggest how manifestations of that tension might be managed; and to explain, by means of the concept of reification, personal responsibility as a moral/cognitive issue. From these perspectives responsible administrative action is moral action in the broadest sense of that term and should come to grips with the problem of evaluating administrative action taken in the *absence* as well as the presence of clearly defined goals and objectified standards of correctness. To skirt the question of what responsibility means in the absence of clear-cut goals and standards would constitute tacit admission either that the policy-administration dichotomy adequately depicts the current world or that it is normatively acceptable to pretend that it does.[29]

NOTES

1. A. R. Louch, *Explanation and Social Action* (Berkeley: University of California Press, 1969), p. 54.

2. Sir Geoffrey Vickers develops this idea in his discussion of the "appreciative system" in *The Art of Judgment* (New York: Basic Books, 1965).

3. See Herbert J. Spiro, *Responsibility in Government* (New York: Van Nostrand, 1969), pp. 39–48.

4. Herman Finer, "Administrative Responsibility in Democratic Government," *Public Administration Review* 1 (Summer 1941): 335–50.

5. Ibid., p. 335.

6. Ibid.

7. Ibid., p. 349.

8. Analogous problems are also commonplace in what is usually termed "rational policy analysis." For a vivid commentary, see Aaron Wildavsky, "Rescuing Policy Analysis from PPBS," *Public Administration Review* 29 (March/April 1969): 189–202.

9. Carl J. Friedrich, "Public Policy and the Nature of Administrative Responsibility," in *Public Policy*, ed. Friedrich and Edward S. Mason (Cambridge, Mass.: Harvard University Press, 1940).

10. See Spiro, *Responsibility in Government*, pp. 23–38.

11. Ibid., p. 15.

12. Ibid., p. 16.

13. Ibid., p. 18.

14. Orion White, "The Concept of Administrative Praxis," *Journal of Comparative Administration* 5 (May 1973): 55–86.

15. Ibid., p. 68.

16. Ibid., p. 81.

17. Ibid., pp. 83–84.

18. Ibid., p. 82.

19. For a discussion of the positive aspects of the Hawthorne effect, see Charles Hampden-Turner, *Radical Man* (Garden City, N.Y.: Anchor Books, 1971), pp. 215–22.

20. The possibilities for expanding considerably the domain of the consensus, however, should not be underestimated. Thayer, for example, describes a structure for consensual decision making between or among groups as well as within them. Initial agreements within groups are made tentatively for the purpose of later synthesizing those agreements by representatives of the "primary" groups. See Frederick C. Thayer, *An End to Hierarchy! An End to Competition! Organizing the Politics and Economics of Survival* (New York: Franklin Watts, 1973).

21. Frederick C. Mosher, *Democracy and the Public Service* (New York: Oxford University Press, 1968), pp. 18–19.

22. See Theodore Lowi, *The End of Liberalism* (New York: Norton, 1969).

23. Neil Postman, *Stupid Talk, Crazy Talk* (New York: Delacorte, 1976), p. 135.

24. Peter L. Berger and Thomas Luckmann, *The Social Construction of Reality* (Garden City, N.Y.: Anchor Books, 1967), pp. 89–91.

25. Ibid., p. 101.

26. Milton Friedman, *Capitalism and Freedom* (Chicago: University of Chicago Press, 1962), p. 91.

27. Albert O. Hirschman, *Exit, Voice, and Loyalty* (Cambridge, Mass.: Harvard University Press, 1970), p. 17.

28. Berger and Luckmann, *Social Construction of Reality*, p. 90. Italics added.

29. White, "Concept of Administrative Praxis," pp. 84–85.

8

Administrative Styles and Role Prescriptions

The meanings of administrative responsibility discussed in the previous chapter are reflected, although usually only implicitly, in various role prescriptions for public administrators. In some cases these prescriptions are rather obvious extensions of particular conceptions of responsibility, most notably the idea of the "neutrally competent" civil servant implied by Finer's defense of political accountability. In other instances, role prescriptions must be inferred indirectly from more contemporary descriptions of the political, organizational, and technological contexts within which administrators operate. Also underlying these role prescriptions are varying assumptions regarding the decision rules that, either formally or informally, constrain and enable administrative action.

The present chapter discusses the generic idea of "administrative style" (proposition 16), followed by a typology of five administrative role prescriptions or "ideal-typical" styles (proposition 17) suggested by aspects of the framework of administrative action discussed in chapter 4. Although the range of individual styles is infinitely varied, the five ideal-typical styles will be described and evaluated in terms of their compatibility with the normative theory outline in chapter 5.

Although this chapter concludes with an argument for a normatively preferred administrative role prescription, labeled the "Proactive" style, some pitfalls and limitations are involved in making that argument. First, since the wisdom of any action is in part contingent on the context within which it is taken, the advocacy of any role prescription must be tempered by an appreciation of its "fit," or lack thereof, to the context. Role prescriptions can prescribe general orientations, but cannot supply concrete solutions to specific problems. Second, role prescriptions should not be presented simply as "bags of virtues" (or evils), but instead should be grounded in, and explicitly related to, other aspects of the paradigms or world views from which they derive. Ideal types should, in other words, include a measure of realism so that a normatively preferred style is neither too heroic nor unnecessarily invites charges of "elitism," and those less preferred should not be reduced to cynical or superficial caricatures.

With these qualifications in mind, the following outline of the chapter's argument is presented.

1. The active-social conception of the self, in addition to depicting people's ontological status, also forms the basis for a normative model of psychological health or maturity. Levels of development of both the active and social selves logically differ among people and are reflected in differences in the extent to which they are likely both to *initiate* action and to *respond* to cues for action originating in their environments.

2. Differences in levels and kinds of initiative and responsive action suggest two important and interdependent dimensions from which distinctions among administrative styles may be drawn.

3. These same differences in initiative and responsive action also provide a framework within which five ideal-typical styles (or role prescriptions), inferred from the public administration literature, may be classified, amplified, and evaluated.

PROPOSITION 16. *Administrative action is explainable in terms of the relationship between situations or contexts as perceived by administrators and their predispositions both to initiate projects and to respond to claims and demands originating in their environments. An administrator's "style" is defined as an interrelated set of predispositions toward initiative and responsive action growing out of the administrator's emotional development, values, knowledge, and experience.*

In addition to being a statement of people's fundamental nature, the idea that the self is active and social also has an important normative or aspirational meaning. That is, our maturity as individuals may be viewed in a basic sense as the extent to which we "realize" or act in accordance with that fundamental nature. For this reason, theories of values logically should derive from an understanding of the nature of the self.

Two rather encompassing categories of action may plausibly be inferred from the active-social nature of the self. The active self may be thought of as the source of "initiative" action, while the social self may be seen as the source of "responsive" action. Initiative action is defined as primarily self-generated action (e.g., advocating, creating, asserting), even though it is always constrained and informed by a social context. Responsive action (e.g., adapting, obeying, anticipating) is action taken mainly on the basis of perceptions of cues emanating from outside the person, although such "external" cues do not determine, strictly speaking, the responsive action. Predispositions of individuals to engage in initiative and responsive actions vary not only *within* these two categories (e.g., higher and lower, more and less) but also in terms of the interdependence *between* them (e.g., a cue giving rise to a "responsive" action may itself be made possible by a prior initiative action). In a rough sense, psychological health is indicated by a predisposition to engage in high levels of mutually interrelated initiative and responsive actions.

INITIATION, RESPONSIVENESS, AND ADMINISTRATIVE STYLE

While the framework of administration action (see chapter 4) is intended to be generally descriptive of all action, its several dimensions also provide a basis for drawing distinctions among various administrative styles and environments. Additionally, the active-social conception of the self, together with the related categories of initiative and responsive action, suggest criteria from which normative evaluations of administrative action may be made.

Some possible distinctions among administrative styles are rather immediately apparent from the cognitive and affective dimensions of the social and active selves. With respect to the social self, for example, people vary in the extent to which they are open in an affective sense to others who comprise their environment; at a cognitive level, differences in values and knowledge suggest differing orientations toward perceiving elements in the environment calling for administrative response. Taken together, the affective and cognitive predispositions are important in shaping both the character of the administrator's social domain and his or her capacity to respond effectively to it.[1]

Regarding the active self, differences exist at the affective level regarding administrators' psychological capacity for personal risk taking, and at the cognitive level, differences in values and knowledge affect their abilities and inclinations to initiate projects which transcend the values and claims evident in their social domains. The active domain, in other words, consists of the perceived possibilities for initiating projects consistent with the realization of the active self; and the shape and character of the active domain are influenced by the extent of administrators' risk-taking capabilities and the extent to which their values and knowledge are conducive to the initiation of projects.

For example, an administrator whose capacity for taking risks is high, and whose professional knowledge and sense of purpose are relatively certain and well-articulated, is more likely than others to initiate projects (e.g., policies or programs) that transcend current social definitions of what is possible, prudent, and sometimes wise or ethical. While others might stoically accept existing configurations of power and interests as reflecting the "real world," what is "real" for those whose active self is relatively well developed is visualized as being subject to deliberate alteration through their own actions.

Differences in administrative styles may also be explained as a function of the interrelationship of the social and active selves. For example, the presence of a relatively fully developed social self with a correspondingly undeveloped active self would help explain action that is indiscriminatingly responsive to demands of the environment in which the *immediacy* of the demand or claim would be the effective criterion for determining the nature of the administrator's response. In bureaucratic organizations, responsive action of the kind just suggested would be indistinguishable from mere obedience to higher authority, in which the prevailing norm for the administrator is that of loyalty. From the perspective of an active-social concept of self, this style of character development is pathological since the "I," which would otherwise be the source of initiative action, is dissolved into the "me" (the social self), as depicted by Mead's original formulation.

The reverse instance, in which a relatively undeveloped social self is accompanied by a highly developed active self, is also pathological from the standpoint of the active-social theory since the absence of a more fully developed social self would presumably lead to the initiation of projects and activities that disregard the essential interdependence between self and society. Projects initiated by such an administrator would logically be motivated out of narrowly defined self-interest, and the mode of his or her relationships with others would be governed by norms of power and control. Or, alternatively, these projects would be simply irrelevant to the environment.

Whereas the two preceding paragraphs describe two inadequately developed styles, an administrative style reflecting healthy self-development is characterized by the interdependence of a highly developed active and social self. Their interdependence is evident when the initiation of projects is informed, as well as constrained, by an awareness of prevailing social values. With respect to issues that involve or affect others, an awareness of the interdependence between self and society is reflected in a predisposition to employ collaborative or consensual modes of decision making. The dominant norm implicit in responsive and initiative action governed by an appreciation of such interdependence is that of mutual fulfillment. The underlying assumption here closely resembles Abraham Maslow's concept of *synergy*, which states that the realization of healthy human needs is ultimately compatible with a corresponding realization of the needs of others.[2]

PROPOSITION 17. *Prominent role prescriptions (or "ideal-typical" styles) in the public administration literature may usefully be differentiated according to their orientations toward initiative and responsive action.*

The categories of initiative and responsive action are sufficiently encompassing that they offer a general context within which dominant role prescriptions in the public administration literature may be conceptually situated and amplified. Using a "grid" format similar to that employed by Blake and Mouton,[3] responsiveness, depicted on the grid's vertical (or X) axis, represents actions, decisions, or projects taken in response to requests, demands, or cues from sources external to the administrator. These sources include, for example, hierarchical superiors, legislative bodies, clients, pressure groups, and professional peers. Initiative action, depicted on the grid's horizontal (Y) axis, includes actions such as planning, advocacy, and decisions, which are mainly generated and made possible by motives or resources intrinsic to the administrators, such as professional or technical expertise, moral commitment, principles of personal conduct, and personal needs for power and control.

By any overall measure, a relatively high position on either axis is not necessarily preferred because some of the examples of both responsive and initiative action just mentioned could easily reflect behavior that is normatively questionable. A dialectical relationship *between* the two categories of action, however, mediated either by principles (for aggregated decisions) or by authentic face-to-face interaction (for disaggregated decisions), is likely to satisfy crucial tests of responsible administrative action.

Both initiative and responsive action seem to fit the "public" aspects of administrative action inasmuch as they are capable of depicting its *relational* character, especially insofar as action taken in the name of public organizations is intended to affect the just entitlements of persons and collectivities ordinarily regarded to be "outside" the organization's boundaries. Similarly, as a matter of both democratic ideology and practice, such persons outside the confines of public organizations are presumed, at least, to possess both legal and practical means for influencing those organizations. Initiation and responsiveness, in other words, are intended to depict action that transcends the boundaries between public organizations and their environments. This differs, for example, from the two dimensions on Blake and Mouton's Managerial Grid—"concern for people" and "concern for production"—which deal primarily with "internal" organizational matters.

FIGURE 8.1 Administrative Styles Grid

High	*Rationalist:* Implements public policy outlined by legislative bodies; responds effectively to—and sees self as primarily responsible to—elected representatives and/or hierarchical superiors. The administrative process is seen as highly rational by virtue of the separation of means from ends.	*Proactive:* Institutionalizes and facilitates consensual decision processes both within organization and with clientele or publics served. Initiative and responsive actions are dialectically related and are motivated by personal commitment (for disaggregated decisions) and by principles of social justice and equity (for aggregated decisions). Orientation is toward personal responsibility and development of conditions for shared responsibility.
Responsiveness	*Reactive:* Out of tactical and strategic necessity participates in the formulation of public policy and programs. Responsive and initiative actions vary depending on current requirements for the maintenance and incremental improvement of organization's effectiveness and the political and social systems that ensure the organization's continued existence.	
	Passive: Attempts to limit the intrusion of external forces seen as a threat either to the existence of organization or to the efficiency of existing programs. Primary loyalty is to immediate organizational unit.	*Professional-Technocratic:* Uses professional expertise as source of influence in the definition and solution of public problems. By virtue of being the exclusive source of knowledge, can effectively control, rather than respond to, environmental demands. Primary loyalty is to profession and/or organization.
Low		

Low   *Initiation*   High

PASSIVE STYLE

The Passive style is the only style on the Administrative Styles Grid[4] that has no normative support in contemporary administrative theory and practice. For this reason, the Passive style, while constituing an "ideal type" in the Weberian sense, is not literally a role prescription, as are the other four ideal-typical styles. The Passive style seems to capture an unfortunately pervasive negative stereotype of narrowly focused government bureaucrats mired in red tape and whose actions are motivated primarily out of concern for their organizational survival or the parochial interests of their organizational units. Perhaps the best face that can be put on the style is that it is not necessarily inappropriate in organizations whose tasks are legitimately largely routine and generally approved of by those outside the organization who benefit or are otherwise affected by their performance. In the terminology of chapter 4's discussion of administrative environments, the Passive style is likely to be rewarded, or at any rate not seriously questioned, by environments characterized by high "placidity" and/or "rigidity." Actors in placid environments, by definition, seldom alter their demands for an organization's services, making unnecessary a high capacity for responsiveness; and rigid environments resist or impede initiative actions.

RATIONALIST STYLE

Much has already been suggested in previous chapters about the preferred role for administrators implied by the Classical public administration paradigm. The policy-administration dichotomy, the rational-instrumental relation of means to ends, the dominance of the rule of hierarchy, and Finer's[5] interpretation of responsibility as accountability clearly imply a preferred style or role for public administrators. The responsible administrator, according to this view, is governed by norms of loyalty to higher authority and to the efficient implementation of politically determined goals. The competence or expertise of the administrator for the Rationalist style is politically and value neutral, which is to say that it is logically separate from and indifferent to the political values it is intended to help realize. In the Rationalist style, responsiveness is virtually synonymous with obedience to hierarchical authority, which constitutes, in Scott and Hart's term an "organizational imperative."[6] Initiation is limited to actions directly related to the development of more efficient means for the attainment of political ends as defined by those in positions of superior authority.

This brief summary of the Rationalist style is no doubt oversimplified and probably has never accurately characterized the dominant mode of behavior of public officials even during the era of administrative orthodoxy. While the abandonment of the politics-administration dichotomy has been usually attributed to the increasing complexity and uncertainty surrounding bureaucratic decision making and political events, its demise was helped along by the failure of the obedience ethic to assure the consistent and uniform application of rules in the performance of administrative tasks. Rules of conduct are both mediated and transformed by the person's own set of rules and cognitive orientation. The result is a highly varied array of subjective interpretations of presumably the same set of externally prescribed rules, and these interpretations may vary greatly in their substantive content. Moreover, when considering the appropriateness of any set of externally imposed rules, people naturally assess to a degree at least the effect the application of those rules will have, rather than following them exclusively for their own sake. The consequence of this for the Rationalist prescription of administrative responsibility growing out of the politics-administration dichotomy is that it could not account for the manner in which the highly complex nature of human cognition affects the translation of the superficially unambiguous obedience ethic into action.

The Rationalist style was and still is important, however, because it provided an easily grasped set of principles on the basis of which normative judgments about the action of administrators could be made. As the political and technological contexts of administrative action began to be more fully appreciated (beginning roughly in the later 1930s), the normative as well as the descriptive adequacy of the Rationalist role prescription was undermined. In its place emerged two alternative prescriptions, referred to here as the Professional-Technocratic and Reactive styles, which provided a greater degree of realism and sophistication to descriptions of administrative behavior. Neither of these two more contemporary styles could claim as coherent and explicit a normative theory to support them as could the earlier Rationalist prescription. Even more importantly, these two more contemporary styles are *implicitly* based on the same theory of values as the Rationalist style.

PROFESSIONAL-TECHNOCRATIC STYLE

The Professional-Technocratic style depicts an orientation toward conceptualizing administrative problems and situations in primarily technical and instrumental, rather than moral or political, terms. Accordingly, the solution to these problems involves the application of technology, the legitimacy of which derives from "objective" scientific standards (in the positivist sense), rather than by reference to standards implied by moral or political discourse. As might be expected, criticisms of the Professional-Technocratic style are mainly based on the liabilities of employing the natural science metaphor and the "objectivist" epistemology in the description and evaluation of the social world.

Given the Classical paradigm's separation of administration from politics and its enchantment with science, the idea of a science of administration staffed by professionals acquired rapid currency early in this century and has more or less sustained its appeal until the present. While most of the advocates of professionalism soon discarded their pretensions to immunity from "political" or "value" questions, their later defenders have continued to maintain that professionals acting on the basis of scientific knowledge promised better solutions to administrative problems than did the early Rationalists, who continued to insist on the sanctity of Wilson's dichotomy. It was around this issue, in fact, that the debate about the question of administrative responsibility began to revolve immediately prior to World War II.

In his landmark essay on the subject, Finer had reaffirmed the orthodox view of the politically neutral administrator who, Finer said, should be held in check by a vigilant Congress enforcing a strict separation between politics and administration.[7] Friedrich, with whose argument Finer had earlier taken issue, insisted on the inevitability of administrative involvement in policy matters. Friedrich asserted, however, that the "inner check" of professional knowledge and ethics was usually sufficient to ensure responsible administrative action in situations where the "public will" was ambiguous or where unique situational requirements could not be anticipated by, nor easily inferred from, legislative enactments.[8]

Friedrich's optimism about the salutary influence of professionalism in administration has more recently received an updated expression by Warren Bennis.[9] Because of increased professionalization in large organizations, Bennis argued that bureaucratic authority was rapidly being supplanted by the authority of expertise in making key decisions. That Bennis was sanguine about this trend is evident from his assessment (which he later acknowledged to be premature) that it represented an inevitable *democratization* of modern organizations and, correspondingly, the death of bureaucracy.

Although the Friedrich and Bennis positions differ from one another in important respects, they are subject to similar criticisms, the most important of which is their failure to explore the moral and political ramifications of professional expertise. The political character of professional knowledge is emphasized, for example, in Sayre and Kaufman's study of New York City government, in which they found that city administrators made essentially political decisions under the guise of technical expertise in order to enhance their political power.[10] While the impression is given that these actions were deliberate and callous (and perhaps they were), even in the *absence* of political motives, bureaucratic expertise is nonetheless political in nature. This assertion parallels the argument made by Thomas Kuhn about the political character of scientific knowledge.

In *The Structure of Scientific Revolutions,* Kuhn challenged three myths about scientific knowledge that pertain to the issues considered here: (1) that scientific progress is necessarily directed toward some final end, (2) that sensory experience is fixed and neutral, and (3) that the standards used to determine the validity of scientific knowledge are free of value or political considerations.[11] Regarding the first of the myths, Kuhn states:

> We are all deeply accustomed to seeing science as the one enterprise that draws nearer to some goal set by nature in advance.
>
> But need there be any such goal? Can we not account for science's existence and its success in terms of evolution from the community's state of knowledge at any given time? Does it really help to imagine that there is some one full, objective, true account of nature and that the proper measure of scientific achievement is the extent to which it brings us closer to that ultimate goal?[12]

For Kuhn, such a view of scientific progress is not only unnecessary but also wrong, since it mistakenly assumes that there exists an objective standard of truth, as yet to be discovered, on which knowledge may be validated. He rejects this assumption because the sensory data from which scientific knowledge is derived is itself neither fixed nor neutral. Rather, scientific knowledge, like any other, is not so much "discovered" as it is "constructed" by means of a transaction between the perceiver and the phenomena being studied. "What a man sees depends both upon what he looks at and also upon what his previous visual-conceptual experience has taught him to see."[13]

Not only is scientific knowledge a product of what scientists have been trained to see, but their methods of observation and standards for validating knowledge are developed and reinforced through professional socialization and institutionalized in the form of a paradigm. The acquisition of new knowledge *within* a paradigm, which Kuhn calls "normal science," is cumulative and incremental. However, knowledge derived from newer emergent paradigms, since they do not adhere to the same set of rules, is regarded by adherents to the dominant paradigm as unacceptable. Moreover, conflicts between paradigms cannot be resolved by testing both against the same set of standards, since it is the standards themselves that are in question. As a result, the conflict among paradigms is in a sense political; and new paradigms usually triumph only when adherents to the old paradigm die off.[14] Further, established paradigms tend to persist because they usually have sufficient autonomy to select only those puzzles to solve that are amenable to solution by the current set of standards.

Kuhn's analysis suggests several criticisms of the Professional-Technocratic style by revealing important similarities to the Rationalist style. First, the "inner check" of professional values and knowledge to which Friedrich refers is not an *inner* check but an *external* one subject to political determination. Decisions to solve certain puzzles, as well as the standards used to validate knowledge, have both normative and political elements. Thus administrative action justified on the ground that it adheres to scientific or professional knowledge and standards is correctly viewed as both political and normative. Kuhn's analysis, especially as it deals with the political character of scientific paradigms, suggests a certain naiveté in Bennis' claim that organizational decisions are necessarily democratic because they are based on professional knowledge. It is at least possible that bureaucratic authority, even if Bennis' prediction were to prove correct, would merely be replaced by the authority of professional and scientific knowledge.

The belief that policies and administrative action may be justified by science and technology is probably more subtle and implicit than the previous discussion may seem to suggest. Science and technology not only condition our perceptions of alternative solutions to social and political problems but influence as well the very definition of those problems.[15] The basis for this assertion is twofold: first, technology fosters modes of consciousness that render rationality and objectivity as the only acceptable thought processes for evaluating social questions. Second, "objective consciousness" finds crucial support in the dominant contemporary social institution—bureaucracy—whose *raison d'etre* is the rational and efficient attainment of objectives through authoritative control. Our sophisticated technological capacity for "solving" problems outstrips aesthetic and other extrarational resources so that technology takes on a potent aura of legitimacy.

An important consequence of technology has emerged that elevates the *Professional-Technocratic* style to a position of profound influence. As Benveniste says, ". . . the call for planners and the corresponding demand for increased rationality in policy-making do not arise from the emergence of a more profound or better scientific understanding of society. They are the result of the excessive social dislocations and uncertainty fostered by science and teechnology."[16] Thus, the early premises of administrative rationality, in which science and technology are thought to be employed in solving predefined problems, are actually reversed. The social uncertainty fostered by technology requires more technology and a redefinition of social values to coincide with existing or future technological capabilities. Invention, it seems, becomes the mother of necessity, rather than the other way about.

This subtle, but profoundly important, reversal of sequence has lent credibility and potency to the Professional-Technocratic style, while it has rendered as archaic its Rationalist forebear. An important consequence for public administration orthodoxy has been what White calls "one-dimensional scientism or 'technology' as the model for policy analysis; . . . the transition has been a move from politics to administration as the paradigm of government." [17] What is to be most feared of this new paradigm, he continues, "is that public policy will be set purely in terms of the capabilities which unfold mechanically as various technologies are elaborated. Questions of purpose may well be lost, and because scientific policy analysis carries such a strong propensity to act, we may fall into a pattern of development and utilization for the sake of development and utilization. . . ." [18]

REACTIVE STYLE

The realization that public administration is inevitably political has long been regarded as one of the major turning points in the history of its academic study. The new era in the discipline was accompanied by a markedly diminished concern about the issue of administrative responsibility and normative questions generally, especially as they had been construed during the Finer-Friedrich debate. It made little sense to quarrel about whether administrators *should* be political actors if nothing could be done about it. To the extent the "ethical administrator" was considered at all, she or he was thought to be someone who prudently balanced the dictates of professional knowledge against political reality and reflected upon the verities of the Scout Oath from time to time. But, by and large, the imperatives for survival in a kind of Hobbesian world of bureaucratic politics relegated normative considerations to a position of secondary importance.

Although a number of reasons may be cited for the absence of normative argument over the emergence of the Reactive style, the main reason is that there was simply no normative argument to be made. Just as there are basic similarities between the Rationalist and Professional-Technocratic styles, so also is there no fundamental normative difference between the Rationalist and Reactive styles. Both styles assume an instrumental relationship between ends and means in which the good is defined independently from the right. In the case of the Rationalist, the good (the specification of ends by political actors) is held to be distinct from the right (efficient implementation by neutral and competent administrators) through the enforcement of the policy-administration dichotomy. Similarly, the milieu of political pluralism, which effectively encompassed the Reactive style, did not seriously question the normative foundations of the dichotomy. The pluralists in political science simply sought to describe, and implicitly to justify, a more efficient and realistic mechanism from which the greatest political satisfaction for the greatest number could be derived.

To illustrate, Charles Lindblom's theory of political pluralism, which he calls "partisan mutual adjustment" (PMA), purports to explain how political decisions or outcomes are arrived at through negotiation, bargaining, discussion, reciprocity, and other such means. While his description of the process seems reasonable enough, he goes a bit further by christening the outcomes of the process the "public interest."

> . . . one's general evaluation of partisan mutual adjustment may lead one to endorse, for some category of decisions, any decision reached through the process. For such a category we will not ask whether partisan mutual adjustment serves the public interest, but will declare that whatever emerges from partisan mutual adjustment . . . is in the public interest.[19]

Lest there by any doubt about Lindblom's normative stance toward PMA, the book in which he elaborates the theory is entitled *The Intelligence of Democracy*.

Two variations on the Reactive style can be inferred from partisan mutual adjustment. The first is the administrator as an active partisan in the political process who participates prudently and according to the rules of the game. The second is the neutral mediator or broker who referees the game in which others participate actively. Performance of the latter role may be judged by how efficiently the game is run and whether the sum of all possible advantages of the participants is maximized, irrespective (in theory) of the particular way in which they are distributed. For the Reactive style, as for the Rationalist, efficiency is still the principal objective; the mechanisms by which efficiency is achieved differ only in their complexity.

Partisan Mutual Adjustment, and political pluralism generally, suggest that the preferred role prescription (one that is compatible in most respects with the Reactive style) is one of providing access for various interests to centers of decision making and preserving an orderly balance or equilibrium among those interests. Rather than assume that equilibrium is virtually automatic, owing to a rough equivalent of Adam Smith's unseen hand of competition (as some defenders of pluralist political science do), maintaining "fair" access for, and a reasonable balance among, competing interests requires deliberate and skillful effort by the administrator. In *The Public Interest,* Schubert appears to support this conception of the administrator's role.[20] After describing and criticizing three schools of thought in public interest theory—Rationalist, Idealist, and Realist—Schubert ends up by giving a qualified endorsement to a subset of the third school, which he labels the "Due-Process Equilibrium Realist" (DPER) position. In this theory,

> . . . people accept democratic decision-making processes because these provide the maximum opportunity of diverse interests to seek to influence gov-

ernmental decisions at all levels. A plurality of decison-making points afford
access to a plurality of interests, which can seek to change or provoke particular decisions. The job of official decision-makers . . . is to maximize con-
tinuity and stability in public policy; or, in other words, to minimize disrup-
tion in existing patterns of accommodation among affected interests. The
extent to which agitation continues . . . provides a rough measure of the
extent to which adjustment has, in terms of the equilibrium standard, been
successful or "satisfactory."

> . . . Due-Process theorists . . . claim . . . that decisions reached as the
result of such full consideration [of competing claims], are *more likely* to meet
the test of equilibrium theory, i.e., "satisfaction," acceptance, etc., and . . .
do so *most of the time,* than are decisions arrived at as a necessary consequence . . . of processes that assure less than full consideration.[21]

While Schubert sees the process just described as conservatively
biased toward the status quo, DPER does not necessarily imply that decision makers who endorse the process need be content with things as they
are, nor concerned only with equilibrium and stability. Presumably, institutions can be altered in ways that permit more equal opportunities for
access; and decision makers—including administrators—who accept
DPER as descriptive of the processes by which the social order is maintained and altered are bound by certain ethical principles derived from it.
Namely, ". . . a consistent Due-Process Realist believes that the principal consideration in the group struggle is the obligation of official
mediators to maximize opportunities for access and consideration of all
relevant interests." [22]

Numerous criticisms may be leveled against this conception of the
administrator's role, some of which are only distantly related to the arguments previously developed in this book. First, even granting for the sake
of argument the presence of both of a plurality of "access points" in
public institutions and of decision makers acting in good faith, the DPER
theory merely suggests a highly "public" version of the rational model of
decision making assumed in the Classical paradigm. If one decision maker
is left with the responsibility of sifting through the points of view of "all
relevant interests," he or she is not likely to be successful in weighing and
deciding among them for precisely the same reasons why Simon,[23]
Lindblom,[24] and others have commented on the impossibility of meeting
the requirements of "synoptic" or comprehensive rationality. Add to this
the much more explicitily political nature of decision making in DPER
than in the rather enclosed and protected milieu that the conventional
rational model ordinarily assumes. Second, although the meaning of "access" is not very clear, any definition of it that does not include formal
and real involvement in decision making by those granted access necessarily means that access falls far short of real power or influence.

In addition to leaving ultimate authority for decision making in the
hands of one person, the DPER theory can also accommodate decision

processes in which one decision maker is not responsible for final determination of the outcomes of competing interests. Instead, policies, rather than thought of as products of conscious deliberation, are viewed as outcomes of the process of mutual adjustment among interests such as described by Lindblom.[25] Fairness or equity, from this perspective, would require that, in addition to equal access for various competing interests, political resources (however defined) should be distributed fairly and equitably among competing interests prior to the beginning of the mutual adjustment process. Such distribution could be justified on the ground that cooperation and the pursuance of individual ends presuppose that everyone has a fair share of resources with which to engage in these endeavors.

There is reason to question whether attempts either to facilitate equal access of interests to decision centers or to distribute political resources equitably among them will result in relatively fair opportunities for all citizens to pursue successfully their individual ends. For some pluralists this is not especially troublesome because they seem to be more concerned with equilibrium and gradual change than with normative issues such as fairness or equity. For many Due-Process Realists, however, this question should be of some concern since fair access and full consideration of all interests are valued on the assumption that they would lead to the most satisfactory results for the most people.

This assumption has been challenged by Olson, who notes that what is rational behavior for individuals is not necessarily rational for collectivities or groups.[26] Since most political activity of any consequence requires the resources of more than one or a few people, the notion of "interest" almost invariably connotes the existence of a group whose leaders or representatives act to further the common ends of group members. However, if membership and participation in groups is voluntary (as is most often the case in political activity), it is *not* individually rational for potential members to pay the costs of membership and participation unless they can perceive a direct benefit deriving from that payment, a benefit they would not receive if they were not "paying members." In other words, if one can receive the benefits of the group's activity without paying for them, it is more rational from the standpoint of the individual not to join. Ironically, the more widespread the (potential) group interest, the *less* rational it is for the person to join, since any individual contribution or effort will have a less appreciable effect on the success of the group's activities and on the benefits the person will get back in return. This is the reason why smaller groups in which social pressures are greater and individual "return" on investment much more direct tend to dominate larger (usually latent) groups in which potential members rationally perceive a correspondingly lesser payoff deriving from their participation. Therefore, the contention that pluralistic activity among multiple-interest groups can most satisfactorily reflect the totality of individual wants and interests is untenable even if "fair" access were provided. The appearance of stability and equilibrium, from Olson's analysis, simply means that large latent interests lack the requisite incentives for organizing in order to express their collective displeasure with things as they are.

Two criticisms of pluralist bargaining and, by extension, of the Reactive style are suggested by issues raised in earlier chapters. The first is that the notion of "interest" is implicitly conceived as a self-evident, if not reified, entity that either exists independent of people's conceptualization of it or is a more or less automatic expression of their wants, which are determined by their particular situation, station in life, occupation, socioeconomic class, and so on. This view appears to ignore that people's perceptions about what their interests are result from actively perceiving, creating, and synthesizing information and values that they may then designate as reflecting their interests.

Second, the notion of rational self-interest is skewed implicitly toward an atomistic conception of the self, thus ignoring the importance of social interaction in the process by which interests are formulated. This is an important liability for the concept of "equilibrium" sometimes embraced by both pluralism and systems theory, since equilibrium necessarily assumes an atomistic conception of interest. A social conception of interest, on the other hand, permits an analysis of the means by which individual conceptualization of wants, needs, and interests may be synthesized with those of other people, rather than balanced against them by means of a kind of market process.

The "real world" of administrative politics. Much of the appeal of the Reactive (as opposed to the Rationalist) style is attributable to its apparent compatibility with the "real world" of politics and administration. The study of public administration during the decades of the 1940s, '50s, and '60s reflected a growing emphasis on empirical investigations of administrative politics at the expense, according to some critics of this trend, of its earlier concern with normative issues such as administrative responsibility. The methodological movement—behavioralism—which underlay these investigations was a product of the positivist model of science (or objectivist epistemology) criticized in chapters 3 and 4. Behavioralist methodology incorporated the positivist biases of rigorous quantification, the value of predictive accuracy, and a concern with the observation and measurement of behavior of political actors and groups.

Leading pluralists and practitioners of behavioralist methodology defended the merits of being attuned to the real world of politics while attempting to dispel some of the romantic illusions that characterized much of the earlier study of democratic politics.[27] The methodology of behavioralism, which professed to adhere to a strict separation of value from fact, was intended to reveal the empirical reality of the political world so that "what is" would not be confused with "what we would like to see."

Political and administrative "realism" as revealed by behavioralist methods, however, is suspect on both methodological and normative grounds. Peter Euben, for example, has interpreted the arguments of Kuhn in order to expose the implicit normative and political biases of behavioralism.

> ... Kuhn's analysis suggests that the real world of behavioralism is a paradigm which like all paradigms is simultaneously prescriptive and descriptive, normative and empirical, a partially (in two senses) articulated framework for analysis, a set of mutually reinforcing images of man and politics supported, as are scientific paradigms, by those authorities who are given or assume responsibility for maintaining the (politically) scientific community, and who are thus able to define in broad terms what constitutes appropriate and inappropriate behavior for "professionals" and to punish deviancy.[28]

Just as the scientific and professional knowledge of the Professional-Technocratic style seems to carry with it its own implicit justification for action, so too does the real world of politics and administration imply a convenient rationale for inaction and silence. What is obscured by behavioralist methodology is that the "real world" is nevertheless humanly created and therefore humanly changeable. What appear superficially to be simply descriptions, if they are compelling enough, become self-fulfilling prophecies by helping to sustain the reality they are intended to describe.[29] While it is not as dependent as the two previous styles on the imperatives of formal bureaucratic authority and professional knowledge, the Reactive style's "real world" seems to acquire a certain inevitability through the sheer force of its existence. The real world, in other words, is a reified world reinforcing the tendency to view events and decisions as predetermined and for which persons bear no responsibility. The reified world of administrative politics is one in which choices are perceived, not only as justified, but as determined, by the situation.

PROACTIVE STYLE

The descriptions of the Rationalist, Professional-Technocratic, and Reactive styles suggest that what have appeared to be fundamental changes in prescriptions and descriptions of administrative roles are really variations on a common theme. They all reflect an instrumental orientation toward the relation of means to ends; each is based on a common epistemology; and each is subject to tendencies to reify either bureaucratic authority, scientific and technical knowledge, or the real world of administrative politics.

The description of a preferred orientation situated on the Administrative Styles Grid must logically begin by coming to terms with the relationship between the grid's two axes—responsive and initiative action. The Proactive style embodies the idea that these two categories of action are dialectically related, that is, each informs and influences the other. But since this is also true of the Reactive style in which responsiveness and initiation are "balanced" against one another in the interests of survival or political expediency, the notion of proactivity should characterize that dialectic quite differently and in a manner generally more compatible with the Action paradigm's theory of values. The task, then, is to describe a general orientation toward responsive and initiative action that is likely to satisfy the paradigm's normative preferences for personally responsible action and consensual and disaggregated decision processes.

To comprehend adequately what is meant by the dialectic between responsive and initiative action (especially as it differs between the Reactive and Proactive styles) it is necessary to appreciate the various motives and values that administrators bring to bear in deciding how to act. A request from a particular client group for a new range of services, for example, may evoke a remarkably diverse array of questions that, depending on their *relative* importance in the mind of the administrator, are likely to be important in influencing his or her subsequent actions:

- Is the provision of such a service consistent with the legal charter of the agency?
- What political liabilities or benefits are likely to accrue to the agency if the service were provided?
- What effect would providing the service have on my own career?
- Does the agency have the technical and financial resources to provide the service?
- What other services requested by other client groups will likely go unmet as a result of providing this service?
- What principles of equity or fairness are involved in deciding whether to provide the service?
- Can the needs of the client group be better satisfied by providing a different kind of service?
- Since I don't have the authority to approve or deny unilaterally the request for the service, to what extent should I attempt to influence the decision?
- Who should make the decision and how should it be made?

That administrators act on the basis of their answers to such questions underscores the idea that action is predicated on the subjective understandings that people have of situations. While consideration of any one of the above questions does not necessarily preclude consideration of any of the others, it is probably also true that some of the questions may not be asked at all or that the relative weight or importance of one or two questions will be sufficiently high that others will be allotted little time for serious thought. Differences in behavior can be explained both in terms of objectivated differences among situations or environments (e.g., placid or turbulent, rigid or malleable) and in terms of differing predispositions among administrators regarding the manner in which they perceive, and ask particuar questions about, those situations. The relative importance of the various questions noted above, in other words, reflect differing conceptual priorities, differing approaches to mediating between one's own existential need to act, to "make a difference," to initiate, and one's needs for community with others, and to respond to their needs or wishes.

The Proactive style suggests two general orientations by which the dialectic between responsive and initiative action may be mediated, the first in the context of disaggregated decisions and the second in situations calling for aggregated or generalized decisions. For disaggregated decisions in which the face-to-face situation forms the decisional context, consensual processes are preferred. In these situations, two alternative roles for the administrator are suggested. The first, described by Thayer,[30] is strictly limited to a decision "facilitator" role (or "professional citizen" as he calls it) in which the administrator takes no part in urging the acceptance or rejection of a particular substantive solution but instead manages the interpersonal and intergroup processes so that others may authentically interact in reaching consensual decisions. In part, the plausibility of the facilitator role derives from what Thayer regards as the crucial liability of the traditional authoritative functions of managers. *"The effectiveness of group processes is inversely proportional to the amount of formal decision authority assigned to chairmen; the less authority assigned an individual chairman, the more likely an effective outcome."* [31] Most significant about the "professional citizen" role is that it affirms the Action paradigm's central normative and epistemological concern with the quality of interpersonal processes—whose effectiveness cannot ultimately be measured against objectivated standards of correctness more appropriate for aggregated decisions. Interpersonal consensus, after all, is preferred precisely for the reason that the *unique* needs and preferences of individuals and small collectivities differ from one another and thus cannot be evaluated against "average" needs or preferences of larger collectivities. Face-to-face interaction among interested parties is the context in which all may simultaneously initiate proposals for cooperative action and hear and respond to the initiatives of others. The dialectic between initiative and responsive action is facilitated by the interactive processes that administrators *assist* rather than dominate or control. Responsibility for decision outcomes, as a result, is shared rather than individualized.

For other disaggregated decisions, the administrator must necessarily play an active role in determining "substantive" solutions to problems (in addition to facilitating the process), for example, in situations in which he or she possesses technical expertise relevant to the issue in question and/or when he or she must interact face-to-face with a client in need of the services provided by the administrator. In such cases, the task of solving the client's problem effectively is one in which possible solutions initiated by the administrator consistent with the agency charter and available professsional knowledge must fit with, and be seen as responsive to, the problem or sitution as defined by the client. Since, in a consensus of this kind, the solution must be agreed to by both parties (not simply imposed by the administrator), the interaction between administrator and client must be characterized by a high degree of empathic understanding. The primary motive underlying the administrator's dealings with the client is that of commitment to the client as a person whose unique perception of his or her situation determines the applicability of the administrator's solutions and available resources. The motive of personal commitment, roughly speaking a derivative of the motive of mutuality in the "We-relation," maintains the dialectic between initiative action (in the form of expertise-based solutions) and responsive action (solutions congruent with the problem or situation as experienced by the client).[32]

The "consensus facilitator" function of the Proactive style sheds light on some additional normative concerns discussed earlier, namely, the *social* (as opposed to atomistic) character of "interests," the rejection of the view that means are only instrumentally related to ends, and the quality of decisional *processes* as well as their outcomes.

An administrative role prescription that affirms the social nature of the self is one that effectively promotes cooperative rather than competitive means of decision making. If "interests" are created, rather than assumed as given, and if interests that we ordinarily assume to be "individual" are in fact socially created, then cooperative or consensual modes of decision making appear logically to be the clearest institutional acknowledgment of that fact. This suggests that the biases in pluralist theory toward an atomistic conception of self-interest may in large part be a reflection of the competitive and hierarchical models of decision making that have been firmly institutionalized at most levels of society.

Since the process of self-development is inherently a cooperative social process, the means by which the administrator may best promote that development is to engage in and institutionalize decision-making processes in which people affected by decisions participate actively in making them. This requires a recognition that politics and administration are inseparable from the process of self-development. Neither is something that we do in our spare time before or after engaging in the other. Rather, cooperative decision making in matters of politics and administration is important because it provides the opportunity for resolving tensions between the social and active selves with the assistance of others who themselves are simultaneously engaged in the same process. One implication of this is that means and ends, usually assumed to be conceptually distinct, actually converge. Instead of viewing ends solely as outcomes, the "end" of self-development is itself a spinoff of the process of mutual participation in decision making. In some cases, such as those described in chapter 5, outcomes may be evaluated from a frame of reference external to the process which led to them; but usually the standards by which we judge ends are themselves influenced and altered by our participation in making decisions.

This view of the relationship between ends and means provides a striking contrast, for example, with Buchanan and Tullocks' analysis of the "costs" to citizens and decision makers associated with various decision rules. The major premise of their important work, *The Calculus of Consent*, is explicitly derived from the "methodological individualism" of contract theory, economic theory, and utilitarianism.[33] It is a premise based on an atomistic conception of the self. In making their case for decision rules based on "market" assumptions, Buchanan and Tullock assert that rational persons would prefer to maximize utility (conceived as *ends*) through modes of decision making (*means*) that are least costly in terms of time and other resources. Marketlike structures, which the authors see as appropriate to many of what have heretofore been regarded as public issues, have the asserted advantage of reducing in many cases the costs of decision making and at the same time either maintaining as constant or increasing the sum of individual benefits. Resources employed in market decisions are conceived as *means;* and means are, by definition, costs.

The relationship between ends and means implied by the active-social conception of the self suggests two criticisms of Buchanan and Tullock's thesis. The first is that it cannot be assumed *a priori* that the time and effort people spend with one another in making decisions *is* a cost, for that is a matter of subjective definition by decision makers themselves. Some people enjoy politics for its own sake, for example, which is to say that they more than occasionally subjectively define the "costs" of decision making as *benefits*. Moreover, it is a reasonable hypothesis that people's propensities to define political and other kinds of collective decision making as a benefit would increase as opportunities for growth and development (which are influenced by decision rules) become more apparent.

To rejoin that Buchanan and Tullock's position is intended to apply only to situations in which people act rationally to maximize their individual interests (the implication being that those who define participation as a benefit are nonrational) is to misunderstand the issue. This leads directly to the second criticism, which is that, because of its dependence on an atomistic conception of the self, the concept of rational self-interest's legitimacy as a central theoretical premise evaporates if the atomistic conception is rejected. (It should be made clear that the rejection of theories based on rational self-interest does not necessarily mean, as Buchanan and Tullock suggest, an acceptance of either "conflict" theories or "organic" theories, which they hold to be the only alternatives to their own. Conflict theories presuppose an active-atomistic, and organic theories a passive-social, conception of the self.) The active-social conception offers the basis for a theory of collective decision making fundamentally different from the other conceptions, especially with respect to the relationship between ends and means. The *end* of self-development is part and parcel of (indistinguishable from) the *means* through which people engage with one another in making collective decisions. The *quality* of this social process, rather than utility maximization, is the principal criterion for deciding among various decision rules.

Consensus, from the standpoint of the active-social conception of the self, is not only the mode of decision making most compatible with healthy self-development but by extension is the way in which "natural" processes for maintaining a relatively stable social order are institutionalized. The social order, however, while always requiring some sort of institutionalized modes of decision making so that it can run smoothly and relatively efficiently, is maintained more fundamentally as a natural consequence of the interaction among active-social selves from which the social order is initially derived. The maintenance of the social order, in other words, is a natural phenomenon voluntarily based, rather than held together through external control (usually in the form of hierarchy). Institutions play a supporting instead of a dominant role when it is recognized that they are humanly created (and thus changeable), rather than independent entities to which people must accommodate their actions.

The rule of consensus also provides the possibility for moving beyond the pluralist conception of access of interests to decision centers toward a greater equalization and sharing of power. Access is commensurate with power only when agreement is required in *making* decisions by those who are affected by them. Decision by hierarchy, the market, and through voting all run counter to the social processes of sharing power through consensus. In its place they substitute either the domination of one person or group over others or a parceling out of political benefits on the basis of individual might, wealth, or status.

The dialectic between responsive and initiative action in making *aggregated* decisions requires of the administrator more abstract thought processes in the sense that personal or idiosyncratic knowledge of public and client needs is unavailable. Because face-to-face interaction with all parties affected is precluded and consensual decision processes more difficult to sustain in making decisions for larger aggregates of people, the Proactive style must be altered in two ways. First, the motive of personal commitment must be generalized to a more abstract level. That is, the motive of personal commitment or mutuality applicable in face-to-face disaggregated contexts must be set aside in favor of disinterested or uniformly applicable standards. Those standards are acceptable to the extent they can be shown logically to derive from the primary motive of mutuality implied by the "We-relation." As discussed in chapter 5, justice is the logical derivation of mutuality when extended to larger collectivities; and equity modifies the generic notion of justice to permit differences in treatment of clients baseed on commonly accepted categories of differences among them.

Second, in aggregated situations, since the scope of decisions is too great to permit active participation by all those affected, the probability is higher that the administrator will be required, either by force of statute or practical circumstance, to decide or attempt to influence the outcome unilaterally (i.e., hierarchically). For this reason, normative concern with the quality of the decision *process* is more or less moot, necessitating the use of the impersonal or objectivated outcomes of the decision.

Thus, for aggregated decisions, the tension between possible alternatives suggested by the administrator's knowledge, resources, and the like, and the external demands to which she or he is obliged to respond, are mediated by abstract principles of reasoning. Principles, according to this view, are seldom, if ever, "applied" in a deterministic sense. Instead, they are the cognitive/moral devices available for weighing and balancing between and among conflicting external pressures and alternative possibilities for initiation made possible by one's understanding of the situation and one's professional and organizational resources.

SUMMARY

The bases for distinguishing among administrative styles, including the five ideal-typical styles on the grid, are the kinds (and levels) of action *initiated* by the administrator in order to realize possibilities for altering the environment or improving the lot of his or her relevant public, and actions taken in *response* to claims, needs, or demands emanating from the environment. Styles also differ, as suggested earlier, in the extent to which and manner in which initiative and responsive action are interrelated. In the passive style, both kinds of actions are minimal and are limited exclusively to short-term accommodations to situational factors bearing on the maintenance of the administrator's current position and status. For Rationalist, responsiveness is high, but in the narrow sense of obedience to higher authority. Initiation is minimal and is limited mainly to the development of methods for more efficiently implementing policies and programs enunciated by organizational superiors. The Professional-Technocratic style is characterized by high levels of initiation of technical or expertise-based solutions but with minimal effort to ascertain the fit of such knowledge with needs as subjectively defined by the parties affected. The Reactive style may engage in varying levels and kinds of initiative and responsive action depending on tactical requirements for enhancing his or

FIGURE 8.2 Characteristics of Ideal-Typical Styles

Style	Passive	Rationalist
1. Responsive action	Limited to short-term requirements for administrator's survival in the organization	Efficient implementation of hierarchical orders
2. Initiative action	Limited to short-term requirements for survival	Recommendations to hierarchical superiors; limited to implementation issues
3. Loyalty (source of legitimacy of actions)	Organizational subunit	Political and hierarchical superiors
4. Motivating values	Survival	Loyalty; obedience
5. Administrative responsibility	Adjustment to imperative of survival	Political accountability; "objective" responsibility
6. Preferred decision mode	Isolation from environment and other organizational units	Implementation of authoritatively determined goals (hierarchical decision rule)
7. Power and control	Power is used to prevent change from occurring	Administrator's power is minimal and is used only to check intolerable abuses of it by others; control is an internal function to assure efficiency of program implementation
8. Conflict a. causes b. strategies	a. No explanation required because . . . b. Conflict is avoided, not perceived, or not acknowledged	Conflict is not an immediate issue because it is absorbed by other (policy-making) units
9. Function in relation to environmental groups	None	Provides information; enforces existing standards and regulations
10. Function of professional knowledge and technical expertise	Useful as a means of making marginal improvements in efficiency; threatening when it forces changes in basic modes of operation	Neutral force that is or can be utilized in the accomplishment of organizational goals

FIGURE 8.2 (Continued)

Professional-Technocratic	Reactive	Proactive
Minimal because of perception of environment and other organization members as uninformed	Tactically oriented to respond to elements inside and outside organization having influence on administrator's position and status in the organization	Motivated by personal commitment to clients and orientation toward consensual decision processes
Initiates substantive proposals and solutions based on professional expertise	Motivated by tactical considerations related to enhancement of power in the organization	Institutionalizes consensual decision processes; expertise-based solutions fitted to client definition of problem
Professional codes of ethics	Organization	Clientele or public served
Professional integrity	Self-interest	Love, mutual fulfillment (disaggregated decisions); justice, equity (aggregated decisions)
Accountability to professional standards and codes of ethics	Adjustment to situational imperatives; requirements of the "real world"	Personal responsibility; development of conditions for shared responsibility
Unilateral prescriptions based on professional knowledge (hierarchical decision rule)	Partisan adjustment and advocacy (within bargaining context)	Interpersonal collaboration and confrontation (consensus decision rule)
Power is characterized by dominance-submission mode; control is prescriptive	Power is restrained by competition among competing political actors and environmental groups	Power is socialized, i.e., used to increase power of others; control is contextuating, self-restraining, and consistent with responsive action
a. Environment is uninformed b. Inform, repress or manipulate	a. Under conditions of scarcity, groups compete for social goods b. Compromise and mutual adjustment	a. Absence of "shared subjective reality definitions" between administrator and environment or among environmental groups b. Confrontation; consensus building
Adviser (offers solutions to clients' problems)	Acts either as self-interested partisan or neutral arbitrator among conflicting groups	Catalyst for community or client participation in decision making; facilitates consensus
Viewed positively as a major source for the discovery and articulation of social values	Viewed as an independent force for which accommodations and adjustments are made; adjustments in long-range social objectives are made possible by technological forecasting	Viewed as important positive and negative influence on the development of social values; necessary to understand its relationship to values underlying social choices

her political position. The dialectic between initiative and responsive action is mediated by the motive of political self- or organizational interest. In the Proactive style, distinction is made between disaggregated and aggregated decisions with respect to the relationship between responsive and initiative action. In the former instances, the dialectic is produced collectively through consensual decisional processes in which the administrator either performs a facilitative role or, when he or she plays a part in determining the *substantive* outcome, the dialectic is mediated by the personal commitment of the administrator to the client. In aggregated decisions in which the administrator is required to decide on (or advocate) outcomes nonconsensually, the tension between client demands and professionally informed opinion is mediated by abstract (i.e., impersonal) principles appealing to logical comprehensiveness (e.g., justice, equity, social utility).

Figure 8.2 summarizes much of what has been said in the present chapter about the five ideal-typical role prescriptions on the Administrative Styles Grid. Additionally, some other dimensions are included in the table that draw from issues discussed in previous chapters, such as administrative responsibility and preferred decision rules.

Role prescriptions and decision rules, even those that are normatively preferred, cannot prescribe, much less guarantee, correct administrative action. A central theme of this book has been that, to the extent that it is confused with "correct" action, responsible action is fundamentally misrepresented. Role prescriptions may suggest preferred orientations but cannot be expected to offer solutions to problems. Only people can do that—through reflective appreciation of the possibilities and constraints peculiar to unique circumstances and contexts as they present themselves. This qualification notwithstanding, the Proactive orientation as described in the preceding pages may still appear more heroic than is generally thought realistic or possible in contemporary administrative contexts. Hierarchy, the prevailing decision rule in public organizations, still profoundly influences decisional processes in ways that seriously impede the development of consensual processes. In addition, political pressures from both within and without the organization may frequently make a concern with justice, equity, or any other normative principle seem to be an unaffordable luxury, especially when the survival of one's position or program is at stake.

Chapter 9 offers a measure of optimism by suggesting that organizational, technological, and political "imperatives" are not as imperative as they might appear. Possibilities for effecting organizational change and engaging in administrative action in a manner generally consistent with the normative theory of the Action paradigm may be inferred from previous chapters. That is to say, the Action paradigm is relevant for dealing with and attempting to solve practical problems of administration, as well as to an improved normative and theoretical understanding of them.

NOTES

1. No special meaning is intended here for "cognitive" and "affective" other than the everyday definitions that state that *cognitive* refers to knowledge acquired through intellectual processes and *affective* to emotions or feelings.

2. Abraham H. Maslow, *Eupsychian Management* (Homewood, Ill.: Irwin, 1965), p. 88.

3. Robert Blake and Jane S. Mouton, *The Managerial Grid* (Houston: Gulf Publishing, 1964).

4. The Administrative Styles Grid is a modification of the Policy Formulation Grid in Michael M. Harmon, "Administrative Policy Formulation and the Public Interest," *Public Administration Review*, September/October 1969, pp. 483–91.

5. Herman Finer, "Administrative Responsibility in a Democratic Government," *Public Administration Review* 1 (Summer 1941): 335–50.

6. William Scott and David K. Hart, "The Organizational Imperative," *Journal of Administration and Society* 7 (November 1975): 259–85.

7. Finer, "Administrative Responsibility."

8. Carl J. Friedrich, "Public Policy and the Nature of Administrative Responsibility," in *Public Policy,* ed. Friedrich and Edward S. Mason (Cambridge, Mass.: Harvard University Press, 1940), pp. 3–24.

9. Warren Bennis, *Changing Organizations* (New York: McGraw-Hill, 1966).

10. Wallace Sayre and Herbert Kaufman, *Governing New York City* (New York: Russell Sage Foundation, 1960), p. 404.

11. Thomas Kuhn, *The Structure of Scientific Revolutions* (Chicago: University of Chicago Press, 1970).

12. Ibid., p. 171.

13. Ibid., p. 113.

14. Ibid., p. 151.

15. See Charles Hampden-Turner, *Radical Man* (Garden City, N.Y.: Anchor Books, 1971); and Theodore Roszak, *The Making of the Counter Culture* (Garden City, N.Y.: Anchor Books, 1969).

16. Guy Benveniste, *The Politics of Expertise* (Berkeley, Calif.: Glendessary Press, 1971).

17. Orion F. White, Jr., "Organization and Administration for New Technological and Social Imperatives," in *Public Administration in a Time of Turbulence,* ed. Dwight Waldo (Scranton: Chandler, 1971), p. 159.

18. Ibid.

19. Charles Lindblom, *The Intelligence of Democracy* (New York: Free Press, 1966), p. 297.

20. Glendon Schubert, *The Public Interest: A Critique of the Theory of a Political Concept* (Glencoe, Ill.: Free Press of Glencoe, 1960).

21. Ibid., pp. 204–15.

22. Ibid., p. 216.

23. Herbert A. Simon, *Administrative Behavior: A Study of Decision-Making Processes in Administrative Organizations* (New York: Macmillan, 1957).

24. Charles E. Lindblom, *The Intelligence of Democracy* (New York: Free Press, 1965); and David Braybrooke and Charles E. Lindblom, *A Strategy of Decision* (New York: Free Press, 1963).

25. Lindblom, *Intelligence of Democracy*.

26. Mancur Olson, *The Logic of Collective Action* (Cambridge, Mass.: Harvard University Press, 1965).

27. See especially two important works of Dahl, *A Preface to Democratic Theory* (Chicago: Phoenix, 1963), and *Modern Political Analysis* (Englewood Cliffs, N.J.: Prentice-Hall, 1963).

28. J. Peter Euben, "Political Science and Political Silence," in *Power and Community: Dissenting Essays in Political Science*, ed. Philip Green and Sanford Levinson (New York: Pantheon, 1969), pp. 21–22.

29. Ibid., p. 17.

30. Frederick C. Thayer, *An End to Hierarchy! An End to Competition! Organizing the Politics and Economics of Survival* (New York: Franklin Watts, 1973).

31. Ibid., p. 19; Italics are Thayer's.

32. Orion White, "The Dialectical Organization: an Alternative to Bureaucracy," *Public Administration Review*, January/February 1969, pp. 32–42.

33. James M. Buchanan and Gordon Tullock, *The Calculus of Consent: Logical Foundations of Constitutional Democracy* (Ann Arbor, Michigan: The University of Michigan Press, 1962).

9

Action Theory and Administrative Practice

Since its inception as a field of academic study, public administration has typically been regarded as a professional or "applied" field, meaning that its primary purpose is to improve the *practice* of administration in organizations of government. Its designation as a professional field is usually intended to differentiate public administration from academic "disciplines" such as political science, sociology, and economics, whose functions are to formulate testable theories and hypotheses providing general explanations of their various domains of social activity. These general and disinterested explanations, unencumbered by the expectation that their immediate practical relevance can or need be demonstrated, are the fundamental building blocks from which public administration academics as well as practitioners may then derive practical and specific applications. According to this admittedly oversimplified view, the role of the public administration academic is a sort of intermediary between the theoretical and the practical, the general and the specific.

While many academics in public administration have been more or less content with this role, others have been less satisfied with it, and even defensive about it, since they regard the intellectual respectability of their enterprise as tied to the field's attainment of disciplinary status.[1] Because of this book's theoretical orientation, it may appear upon casual analysis to represent an attempt to "elevate" public administration to the status of a discipline commensurate with those to which it has heretofore been subordinate. Given the nature of academic politics, this would not as a practical matter be a bad idea if it were shown to be the only avenue available for attaining the respectability to which, presumably, most academics in the field aspire.

As the attentive reader will probably have concluded, however, the action approach disputes on intellectual and normative grounds the wisdom of proceeding along such lines, for to do so fundamentally distorts the relation of theory to practice and fails to comprehend the moral purposes of social theory. The relationship of theory to practice, as argued throughout, is a primary practical *and* theoretical issue for public administration—and thus of doubtless intellectual respectability. That is, the relation of theory to practice involves the practical as well as moral problem faced by all administrators of *understanding in order to act*. This is a problem of profound and pervasive importance that would appear to *diminish* in its salience to public administration to the extent the field were successful in moving in the direction of disciplinary status as traditionally conceived.

The improvement of administrative practice is a fundamental purpose of the Action paradigm. The relevance of the paradigm, however, extends beyond those fields of study that are self-consciously regarded as professional or applied in their intent. Chapters 3 and 4, in particular, stressed reasons why the action approach offers a preferred epistemology for *social science* and that the purpose of social science, properly understood, is the improvement of social practice. Thus the *improvement of practice* as a normative criterion of evaluation applies to the more traditional social science disciplines as well as to professional or applied fields. The usual distinction between academic disciplines and applied fields, therefore, is highly dubious because it assumes a logical dichotomy between theory and practice. If that dichotomy is rejected (i.e., by conceptualizing theory ultimately as theory *for* practice), the traditional distinction between academic and applied fields collapses. It may nevertheless be useful, as a matter of convenience, to maintain some sort of rough distinction among disciplines or fields based on the *kind or immediacy* of the applicability of the knowledge they generate to practical contexts. But since all social theory is, in one manner or another, moral theory, it must in the final analysis be judged in terms of its contribution to human betterment.

The purposes of this final chapter (and proposition 18) are, first, to determine whether the action approach as outlined here satisfies the three criteria of paradigm adequacy outlined in chapter 2. The second is to explore the implications of the action approach's assumptive, descriptive, and normative aspects for the improvement of administrative practice. Special attention will be devoted to showing why administrative practice is a moral issue rather than simply an instrumental one as is often assumed. The practical relevance of the paradigm will be illustrated by some examples of how "nonconspiratorial" theory, discussed in chapter 3, may result in nonconspiratorial practical application.

PROPOSITION 18. *The preceding seventeen propositions constitute an outline for an Action Theory paradigm for public administration. The integration of its assumptive, explanatory, and normative elements satisfies the criteria of paradigm status and adequacy stated in the first proposition. It provides a framework within which "applied" theory and administrative practices may be developed and critically evaluated.*

CRITERIA OF PARADIGM ADEQUACY

In chapter 2, the idea of paradigm was redefined in a manner appropriate for public administration conceived as both a branch of social science and an area of applied knowledge and practice. A public administration paradigm was defined as an interrelated theory of values and set of ground rules for the formulation of knowledge whose primary purposes are to describe, inform, and evaluate the practice of administration in public organizations. In addition, a paradigm may be evaluated according to (1) the defensibility of its theory of values, (2) the extent to which it successfully integrates various kinds of theory, and (3) the ability of the paradigm to assist in improving administrative practice in a manner consistent with its theory of values.

DEFENSIBILITY OF VALUE THEORY

Showing how the Action paradigm satisfies the first criterion was the main subject of chapters 3 and 5. Chapter 5's presentation of the paradigm's theory of values was based on the earlier chapter's defense of the active-social conception of the self. The argument was made that the defensibility of values depended on assumptions about human nature, since the former are derived from the latter. Thus, the value theory of the paradigm stands or falls on the basis of the argument in chapter 3 regarding the active-social nature of the self and the extent to which chapter 5 was successful in demonstrating the logical derivation of the values of mutuality, justice, and equity from that conception of self. To the degree that argument was successful, the first criterion of paradigm adequacy has been satisfied.

INTEGRATION OF CATEGORIES OF THEORY

The second criterion of paradigm adequacy, that is, the extent to which the paradigm integrates or demonstrates the logical interrelationship among various categories of theory, has been a recurring theme throughout the book. Chapter 2 summarized four categories of theory for public administration—assumptive, descriptive-explanatory, normative, and

instrumental—and suggested that they are useful for clarifying some crucial interdependencies among various theoretical concerns as well as the
relation of theory to practice.[2] Summarized below are three kinds of
linkages among the categories discussed thus far; a fourth linkage, the
relationship between normative and what Bailey calls instrumental
theory, deals with the main substantive concern of the book's final proposition.

Assumptive and normative theory. Assumptions about human nature and
epistemology constitute what I understand Bailey to mean by "assumptive" theory. Assumptions about the nature of the self constitute the most
plausible basis for the development of value or normative theory that is
not unduly relativistic nor simply an apology for the status quo. Failure to
ground value theory in a theory of the self (i.e., to clarify the dependence
of value theory on assumptive theory) inevitably results in either an arbitrary selection of values or a naive reliance on a "majoritarian" approach
to determining their legitimacy (e.g., "If most people believe in freedom
of speech, it should be regarded as a correct or legitimate value").

In addition to assumptions about the self, epistemology has also been
included in the general category of assumptive theory. The relationship of
epistemology to normative theory was discussed in chapter 3's review of
the relationship between epistemology and organization theory. Epistemology, it was argued, is a set of rules for determining who shall legitimately decide what is to be regarded as "valid" knowledge.[3] The relationship of various epistemologies or models of the scientific method to
administrative action will be taken up later in this chapter.

Epistemology and descriptive-explanatory theory. This linkage, the subject of chapters 3 and 4, should be fairly clear by now, but requires some
amplification. Stripped of its "paradigmatic" aspirations, the action approach as formulated by other authors, such as Silverman, is really
nothing more than an epistemology.[4] At the heart of that epistemology are
the related notions of intentionality and intersubjectivity (corresponding,
respectively, to the active and social nature of the self), which provide the
bases for acceptable descriptions of social phenomena, that is, those
based on the situational definitions, the lived experience, of the actors
being studied. In a like manner, explanatory theory, which draws inferences about cause and effect or, more accurately, the relationships between motives and actions, is also bound by those same epistemological
rules.

In this regard, it would be well to acknowledge that empirically
minded readers may be troubled by the relative neglect of the category of
descriptive-explanatory theory in this book. Only one chapter (number 4)
has been devoted substantially to it, while three chapters (numbers 5, 7,
and 8) have dealt mainly with *normative* theory and related concerns. Any
paradigm worthy of the name, it might seem, should also offer generalized

descriptions and explanations of the domains of social activity it purports to study.

The action approach is not biased exclusively against general descriptive and explanatory theory, although its aspirations in this area are limited by its epistemology. The kind of general descriptive-explanatory theories that are permissible within the paradigm are those that depict "ideal types" [5] (e.g., ideal-typical actors acting according to ideal-typical motives in ideal-typical contexts or institutional settings). In this category, for example, may be placed Weber's theory of the bases of social authority and the bureaucratic model of organization, the Administrative Styles Grid, and numerous others not discussed here.

Important limitations of general (which is to say, theoretical) description and explanation based even on ideal types, however, are evident from the action frame of reference. First, the validity of ideal types depends on their correspondence or match with the actual motives, actions, and contexts as seen by real actors. The likelihood of the match diminishes greatly in highly heterogeneous populations. To the extent general theory, ideal-typical or not, is incapable of comprehending the vast range of motives, actors, and contexts, it necessarily fails to account for the phenomenon of *uniqueness,* a prominent practical and theoretical concern of earlier chapters. This is not so much an argument against general theory based on ideal types, for there is much of it in this book, as it is a reminder that too great a preoccupation with general theory, especially for purposes of explanation, may as often obscure as illuminate the purposes of social theory. The essential point here is that the complexity and range of motives and contexts are so great that attention is probably better given to spelling out the *ground rules* for describing, explaining, and comprehending the *unique and problematic* contexts as experienced by social actors.

In addition to the argument that general descriptive-explanatory theory may obscure or view as trivial unique problems and contexts, there is another and perhaps more compelling argument for the Action paradigm's relative bias in favor of normative, as opposed to descriptive-explanatory, theory. It has to do with the inherently moral and practical character of public administration conceived simultaneously as social science and social practice. Sir Geoffrey Vickers, directing his remarks specifically to decision theory, puts the argument as follows:

> As usual, in this field [decision theory in public administration], my first query is—"Why this emphasis on theory? What do you want a theory for? Are you still stuck in the natural scientist's belief that you can't understand anything particular unless you have a general theory?" . . .
>
> But wait—there is one sense in which I warmly agree that one needs a theory of decision making. Somewhere, I think in the *Art of Judgment,* I say that the process of decision is directed to learning what to want rather than learning how to get. If that is a theory then surely we need it. The criterion of

method is that it would present as fully as may be the alternative mixes of value which are in fact available. And the result is that we finish up not merely decided on what to do but changed in our norms of what is worth doing. So we start from a different place next time. But I hoped everyone knew by now that merely instrumental decisions (how "best" to get what you want) are an unimportant class of decision making unless the criteria of "best" are themselves open to evaluation. And if they are, the ends-means model disappears and is replaced by a model of "seeking right action," which is, of course, an ethical model.[6]

In a literal sense, social theory cannot explain; only people can. This means that what is usually referred to in social science as explanatory theory can reasonably (in a manner that is epistemologically acceptable) only approximate and summarize the explanations of social actors about their motives and projects. Since such motives and projects are highly varied, too great an emphasis on general explanatory theory runs the risk both of oversimplifying the phenomena it purports to describe (being "reductionist" in the pejorative sense of the term) or suggesting, if only implicitly, *a priori* causal explanations of those phenomena. While simplification is an appropriate and indeed indispensable purpose of theory, it almost invariably invites the difficulties just mentioned.

Descriptive and normative theory. The logical-positivist tradition in Western social science in this century holds, among other things, that values and facts are and should explicitly be recognized as being separate and distinct. From this perspective, the "integration" of description (matters of fact) with normative evaluation (matters of value) is pointless, if not contrary to the canons of the scientific method. While there is doubtless much wisdom in the common-sense admonition to distinguish between "is" and "ought" statements, we should not forget that *descriptive* appraisals of social phenomena implicitly deal with the moral purposes of, as well as the consequences for, the actors involved. Thus, the success with which social science paradigms enable us to comprehend the manner in which descriptive and normative theory are interrelated is a crucial measure of their adequacy.

In the action approach, the integration of descriptive and normative theory derives from their common assumptions about the nature of the self and epistemology. Descriptive-explanatory theory is based on the definitions of situations and motives of those whose actions are being described (or explained). The situational definitions and motives, as well as other aspects of the social world, are particular attributions of meaning *intentionally* constructed and *intersubjectively* agreed upon (and sometimes disagreed upon) by actors. Description may be considered valid to the extent that it accurately depicts, it only in summary or ideal-typical form, the understanding of the actors themselves. The notions of intentionality and intersubjectivity, which form the dual foundation for epistemologically sound description and explanation, are in turn correlates to the active and social nature of the self. That is, intentionality presupposes an active, rather than a passive, self; and the fundamental motive toward subjective agreement among people derives from their sociality. Completion of the link between descriptive-explanatory and normative theory, then, is chapter 5's argument that value theory derives directly from the active-social nature of the self. The creation of shared meanings among people, as well as the depiction of them by social scientists, not only involves attempting to understand one another *accurately* but is also a *moral* act since the creation of those meanings is a principal way of expressing our sociality, our need for harmony or unity with others.

THEORY FOR ADMINISTRATIVE PRACTICE

The most puzzling of Bailey's categories of theory for public administration is what he terms "instrumental" theory.[7] In contrast to assumptive, descriptive-explanatory, and normative theory, which, according to his definitions of them, are categories of theory dealing with concerns somewhat removed from the day-to-day activities of administrators, instrumental theory is intended to include those theories having the most immediate relevance for administrative practice. Some objections may be offered, however, both to Bailey's label of "instrumental" theory and its conceptual separation from the other three categories.

To regard as "instrumental" those theories having most immediate practical relevance is misleading for two related reasons. First, "instrumental" connotes a rigid conceptual separation of value from fact, thus providing implicit support for the view that action, especially *administrative* action, can be conceived only in rational-instrumental terms. This incorrectly assumes, of course, that value issues can and should be resolved prior to acting. Rational-instrumental action is merely one particular kind of action deriving from and supported by the Classical paradigm's dichotomy between policy and administration. While the Classical paradigm's bias toward rational-instrumental action makes somewhat easier the task of deciding and pinpointing who is accountable for what in bureaucratic organizations, it also raises a host of other problems. The most important of these is that it gives the false impression that obedience and efficiency are the sole normative issues with which administrators need to be concerned. And to the extent obedience and accountability are maintained, the sense of personal responsibility for one's acts evaporates; *others* are perceived as morally responsible. This, at any rate, is the mind set that naturally grows out of viewing administrative practice purely as instrumental. The consequence of Bailey's equating "instrumental" with "practical" is that normative questions are someone else's department.

Just as equating "instrumental" with "practical" tends to obscure the normative or moral aspects of administrative practice, the conceptual separation of instrumental theory from *other* kinds of theory obscures the latters' potentially practical character. The conceptual distinctions among Bailey's categories perpetuate the frequently observed distance of academic theorists from the "real world" (i.e., the intersubjectively created world) of administrative life. While at times this distance may result from the personal proclivity of the theorist, it is reinforced as well by a too literal acceptance of the distinctions among theoretical categories.

The categories may still be useful, however, as long as their interrelationships are recognized and taken into account. That is, the relationship of epistemology, description, and normative evaluation to *practical* (in the broadest sense of the word) problems and contexts seems crucial in the assessment of a paradigm's adequacy. The suitability of the action approach in this regard is evident in at least three respects.

1. The *epistemology* of intersubjectivity provides a basis for understanding the sources of cooperation and conflict among individuals and groups in organizational contexts. As almost anyone who has labored in large organizations can attest, there is immense practical value in understanding the diverse world views held by organizational members and those outside the organization who are in some measure affected by it. Practical action requires an appreciation, and an understanding of the appreciation by others, of shared meanings that appear to encourage or constrain the successful initiation of actions and projects.

2. *Descriptions* that take account of contexts as they are seen by organization members are likely to have greater practical salience to practicing administrators than those that impose an external frame of reference. This is not to suggest that the action theorist simply accepts at face value all he or she is told; the action theorist can play an important role as critic both *of* and *for* organizations. Nevertheless, "theoretical" descriptions will likely have practical value if they reflect the concerns and perceptions as expressed by organization members.

3. Despite the presence in this book of a general framework of *normative* theory, specific prescriptions for how administrators should act in order to be morally or ethically correct have been deliberately omitted. While normative theory and ethical principles can provide bases for moral reflection, they cannot offer concrete solutions or provide an unarguable moral defense for a particular action. Normative theory deals in generalities, while administrators deal with specifics; the relationship of one to the other, although important, is always subject to redefinition and negotiation. The closest the argument of this book has come to moral absolutism is its admonition to assure that the *processes* for redefinition and negotiation should be carefully maintained. This dictum, moreover, is a logical outgrowth of an epistemology that emphasizes that action be

understood from the unique perspectives of the actors being studied. In order to be practical, normative theory must reflect an appreciation of this. Thus, in avoiding both the moral simplicity of the Classical public administration paradigm and the implicit ethical relativism of much contemporary management theory, the action approach balances out as a sort of situational theory with a built-in moral sensibility.

THE ROLE OF THE ADMINISTRATIVE THEORIST

The Classical paradigm's implied stance regarding the theorist's or scientist's role in the improvement of administrative practices derives from the paradigm's compatibility with the bureaucratic model of organization and rational-instrumental action. Two prominent characteristics of this role are, first, the value of disinterestedness of scientists personally with respect to those who may eventually benefit from their knowledge; and, second, the presumed value-neutral and technical nature of the solutions or practices they might develop or that might be inferred from the knowledge they create.

The value of disinterestedness is central to the positivist model of science (roughly speaking, "objectivist" epistemology as described in chapter 4), which is often conceived as synonymous with the "scientific method." The compatibility of the positivist model of science with the Classical public administration paradigm's endorsement of the bureaucratic form of organization is far from coincidental, as Blankenship states:

> We see here a remarkable resemblance between such positivist norms of behavior and "ideal" bureaucratic values. Scientific inquiry, like bureaucracy, is presumably governed by certain universalistic criteria and abstract laws. In the case of science, recognition and prestige in the scientific community comes from performance according to certain objective criteria; promotion up the bureaucratic hierarchy is a result of achievement as measured by certain objective standards related, ultimately, to the ends of efficiency and effectiveness. In neither case does the scientist or bureaucrat legally "own" his position or status or the "tools of production," and the behavior of both is supposed to be conducted *sine ire et studio*. Each is expected to be impersonal, fair, objective, committed only to abstract, altruistic, rational ends: the law and justice in one case, science and its particular empirical "truth" in the other.
>
> Clearly the "ideal" values underpinning the positivist model have a significance for much more than a style of inquiry. They capture, as well, much of the bureaucratic-professional ethic which underlies public administration both as a field (to be learned) and as an occupation (to be practiced).[8]

The value of personal disinterestedness of scientists regarding the results of their research, in turn, supports the second assumption of the

Classical paradigm that scientific findings, and most especially the "expertise" or "applied" knowledge that derives from them, are value-neutral. That is, even though expertise may be used for evil purposes, the evil (or good) lies in the ends, not in the expertise itself, which is conceived as a "means" or instrument. From the Classical view, ends are politically determined; administrators, especially if they are "generalists" who must rely on the expertise of others, seek to determine the fit or practicality of that expertise to the achievement of ends.

To be sure, these *are* useful and reasonable assumptions in cases, for example, when goals are clear and unambiguous, when those charged with implementing the goals are committed to their attainment, when the fit of available expertise with the goals is clearly understood and generally agreed upon, and when the expertise is genuinely morally and politically innocuous. When all these conditions pertain, rational-instrumental action *is* practical, and the positivist model of science may be of great assistance in the improvement of administrative practice.

The catch, of course, is that as administrative environments and society in general become increasingly turbulent, and technical expertise becomes more arcane, these conditions apply with far less frequency. The ease with which shared agreements among actors (including politicians, administrators, experts, and clients) may be arrived at vastly diminishes regarding the definition of problems, the desirability of particular ends, and the likely social and political consequences of various technologies. Increasingly, problems of improving administrative practice are shifted from the search for technological fixes to the more generic problem of comprehending problems and acting sensibly to deal with them.

As our conception of improving administrative practice is fundamentally changed and expanded, the role of the theorist or expert is dramatically altered as well, as is the model of scientific inquiry on which it is based. Leaving aside for the moment the question of how an alternative model of science might help to *improve* administrative practice, it is instructive to note how a key aspect of the action frame of reference—the subjective viewpoint of the actor—changes the relationship between theorists and their subjects. In order for theorists to understand the motives and viewpoints of their subjects, the latter must first be willing to reveal what those motives and viewpoints are. Their willingness is largely a matter of mutual trust, which is jeopardized by the values of disinterestedness, unobtrusiveness, and detachment—the hallmarks of the positivist model of science. Blankenship outlines an alternative model of inquiry, the "humanist" model, in which the relationship between researchers and subjects is almost the reverse of the positivist model.

> The relation between observer and observed in the humanist model is characterized by closeness and intimacy, at least during a major portion of the research. This intimacy occurs because the concern of the observer is to gain

an understanding of the world through the "eyes" of the subject. The observer wants to comprehend the inner, subjective reality of the observed, the moral and ethical meaning they attach to their own acts, the way in which they make decisions, the way in which they confront and deal with their environment, the pressures they feel, the aspirations they have. Such intimate, private knowledge requires a series of interactions between observer and observed in which both learn about each other. The scientist abandons his "impersonal" stance to become a partisan in events, since this is a way of creating within himself the same feelings which move his subjects and give meaning to their world. *They* rather than *he* are the experts. He may argue with them, point up inconsistencies in their values and behavior, inject himself into conflicts. By participating he "learns" from his mistakes, since his subjects react to them; at the same time, his behavior may force them to become reflective about their own orientations and values.[9]

Closeness, trust, and intimacy, then, are crucial not so much because they increase the prospects of the researcher's obtaining "hard facts" about the subjects' *behavior,* but because they permit a fuller exploration, interpretation, and even criticism by both the researcher and the subjects of the values and the subjective (and sometimes hidden) meaning of the subjects' actions.

In the humanist model the theorist-researcher's role is a difficult and complicated one. Since intimate involvement with subjects runs the risk of diminishing the theorist's capacity for independent judgment and criticism, she or he must be able effectively "to move back and forth between involvement and withdrawal."[10] Moreover, the humanist model's version of the relationship between theorist and subject suggests that the theorist has two sometimes opposing obligations. The first is to the larger scientific community concerned with general or universal principles and explanations; the other is to the unique or particular concerns of the research subjects with whom she or he may have formed an almost therapeutic relationship.[11]

While the latter obligation may sometimes create tension with the former, the trust and intimacy strived for in the humanist model are also the basis for its relevance to the improvement of administrative practice. This holds both in those instances in which the theorist possesses *technical* expertise that is potentially useful for the administrator (e.g., software for a new management information system), and in those cases where the theorist's role is mainly diagnostic, critical, and therapeutic. For both roles, an understanding of the administrator's subjective understanding of the situation, as well as of the relevance of outside expertise to it, is crucial.

When the theorist's role is one of creating and disseminating technical ("substantive") expertise, a major task is to assist the client (administrator) in determining whether and to what extent that expertise fits the client's perception of the problem or context. In addition to its technical merit, the workability or practicality of the new MIS software, for example, will depend on whether the client sees it as a sufficiently *plausible* solution for his or her information needs that he or she will be *committed* to make it work.[12] Joint determination of this by the theorist and client entails a rather thorough and intimate understanding by both parties of the subjective meaning that each has of the situation. At issue is not only the plausibility of the expertise in terms of its technical match with the client's problem but its possible match or conflict with interpersonal, ethical, and political norms in the organization that might impinge on its eventual effectiveness.

THE ACTION THEORIST AS THERAPIST

In the Classical paradigm the role of "applied" organizational theorists ("theorist" is used broadly here to depict an expert from outside the client organization) is typically prescriptive and instrumental. It is prescriptive in the sense that the theorists have knowledge, not otherwise readily available to the organization, that provides the source for the advice they offer. The theorists' credibility derives both from their knowledge of complex subject matter (for which the client has little need on a permanent basis) and from the "objectivity" that accrues from their status as outsiders. (To be sure, these sources of "credibility" may be depicted unflatteringly, e.g., "An expert is anyone who lives more than fifty miles away from the office and carries a briefcase.") Their advice, from the classical view, is instrumental in that the client, presumably, knows *what* to do but not *how* to do it.

The action approach, by contrast, requires that we view as highly problematic such questions as the clarity and specificity of organizational goals, the nature of their relationship to instrumental means (technology) and organizational processes, and the bearing that the organization's cultural and political history has on how its members decide both what to do and how to do it. In client organizations in which these questions are problematic, a different role for the applied theorist is suggested.

For want of a better label, the term "action therapist," roughly an amalgam of sympathetic critic, therapist, and "process" consultant, will be used to designate the prototype of the applied theorist's role suggested by the Action paradigm. Before describing the basic elements of the role, however, some examples of the kinds of situations for which it might be relevant are listed here:

- A group charged with writing regulations for a new social program agonizes over the "intent of Congress" in passing the legislation.
- A briefing paper containing program options is passed from a

bureau to the secretary. Both the senders and the receivers are ambivalent about the several options, and the normative premises of each are not clarified.

- The commissioners of a regulatory agency feel powerless, since they depend on agency staff for the facts of a given issue. Agency staff feel powerless, since they are at the beck and call of the commissioners.
- A lower-level division director stews over what the Assistant Secretary *really meant* in her last directive.
- A service provider, convinced of the greater effectiveness of the mode of service he has decided on, contemplates the resistance he will encounter from clients.
- An agency director, about to adopt a scheme that will alter both the incentives and the distribution of benefits of a particular service, contemplates the political costs in his primary constituency, the possibilities for misunderstanding among the ultimate consumers, and possible loss of credibility in the eyes of his hierarchical superiors.
- A fire chief is concerned about the repercussions of closing certain firehouses on a rotating basis.
- A contractor and contract officer reach an impasse about what the contract requires.
- A new agency director attempts to calculate the effects on staff morale of her announced reorganization of priorities.
- The operational definition of "health and safety" used by the agency has been challenged by an influential constituency.
- A diplomatic move has been countered by the other side. A group meets to interpret it, and discussion ensues as to whether the other side interpreted our move in the way we intended.
- The White House has requested a statement of agency policy on a certain issue. The agency directorate is convened to discuss the implications of the request for the agency. Most of the meeting is spent speculating on the intent and on the assumed use to which the policy statement will be put after it is submitted.[13]

Obviously these are situations that are amenable neither to purely technical nor, in most of the examples, strictly hierarchical solutions. They are instead political and managerial contexts characterized by either conflict, misunderstanding, or vagueness about actors' meaning, intentions, and motives. The examples reveal:

> Various interpretations of what is warranted and what is required by the situation are generated: individual perceptions are not easily verified or falsified; the issuing of formal requests of instructions from superordinates to subordinates is part of the problem, not part of the solution; the forwarding of information from subordinates to superordinates does not satisfy the re-

quirements of the situation. Most importantly, norms or other effective mechanisms are not available to assist in determining the intentions of individual actors or the meaning of the overall situation.[14]

Generally speaking, the function of the action therapist in situations such as those mentioned above is to assist the client organization in the *negotiation of meaning in order to make possible cooperative action.* At the risk of oversimplifying or seeming to trivialize this function, it involves primarily an effort by the action therapist to help the members of the client organization have better conversations. This means initially that people be enabled to hear one another as they intend to be heard and understood. The action therapist's role is substantially more complex, however, than that of a communications or "human relations" expert, for it also deals with helping clients to assess such fundamental but seldom discussed concerns as shared or conflicting values and organizational processes. Illustrative of the kinds of activities in which the therapist might assist the client are

- Determining the extent to which the exercise of formal (hierarchical) authority helps or hinders the creation and transmittal of shared meanings that enable cooperative, responsible, and accountable action.
- Developing and surfacing alternative "world views" of the organization held by its members and exploring the effect of these differences on past organizational successes and failures, as well as on the effectiveness of current projects.
- Clarifying the effect of dominant but implicit organizational norms and processes of social interaction upon both the *specification* and the effective achievement of organizational ends.
- Exploring the effect of individual members' motives and feelings (e.g., self-interest, altruism, fear, ambition) on interpersonal and intergroup cooperation.
- Engaging, both internally and with relevant parties in its environment, in an ongoing assessment of the organization's overall goals, its methods of dealing with environmental groups, and even its reason for being.
- Determining the compatibility of relatively specific or discrete projects undertaken in the organization with its general stated purposes; and bringing about changes in *either,* the specific *or* the general, based on fresh insights about the other. (The idea here is that organizations can learn from successes and failures in specific projects that may suggest changes in the organization's overall sense of purpose. This contrasts with the bias in the Classical paradigm that specific projects and activities should necessarily be derived from and reconciled with explicit overall goals.)
- Conducting research and gathering data, both within and outside

the organization, useful in identifying possibilities for and constraints on the successful initiation of projects.[15]

This list is by no means exhaustive; the examples serve merely to characterize the kinds of activities in which the action therapist may be helpful. These activities share some common elements, three of which deserve special mention. First, they focus mainly on organizationsl *processes* and the *relationship* of those processes to so-called substantive policy and management goals, rather than to the wisdom or efficacy of the substantive goals themselves. This is not to say that the latter are unimportant; only that the action therapist's role primarily requires expertise about process issues, albeit broadly conceived. As an ethical matter, however, action therapists are obliged, when deciding whether to begin or continue a relationship with a client, to determine for themselves the degree to which the overall purposes of the client organization are compatible with their own personal values. The degree of their compatibility would determine whether a professional association with the client would involve an intolerable violation of personal conscience.

The second characteristic of the action therapist's role is that *moral-ethical* aspects of the client organization's processes (which are usually only implicit or even hidden in the minds of its members) are surfaced and negotiated. This is quite different from the rational-instrumental role of the expert or theorist implied by the Classical paradigm. While the action therapist seeks not to impose values on the client, the therapist seeks to create a climate in which moral-ethical issues may be critically evaluated and may even play an active part in that criticism.

The third characteristic of the role is that it is "nonconspiratorial." In chapter 4, positivist theory was criticized for its reliance on assumptions, values, and theoretical constructs that disregard the subjective understanding of situations and motives of research subjects. As *applied* theorists, the action therapists' role is similarly constrained. That is, they must begin their involvement by developing a grasp of the clients' own unique subjective appreciation of the organization, despite whatever critical posture the therapists may subsequently take toward it. In addition, action therapists must be frank in revealing what their own values and assumptions are and, more generally, say what they are "up to." Although the therapist's role avoids being prescriptive in the instrumental sense, it is nevertheless one that involves the therapist as a moral actor.

Being nonconspiratorial requires that action therapists appreciate the *unique,* as well as the common or universal, aspects of the client organization. Their "interventions," therefore, should be tailored to fit those unique aspects. While more will be said about this in the subsequent section on critical organization development, unique treatment by the therapist of the client organization may have a salutary effect on the organization's treatment of *its* clients. The similarity of the relationship of the therapist to the (client) organization, on the one hand, and the organization to *its* clients, on the other, is strikingly illustrated by a "creative" editing of Robert Biller's remarks favoring a disaggregated approach to the delivery of social services.[16] The disaggregated approach, according to Biller, differs from the more common, typically bureaucratic, approach, which treats clients uniformly or only differentiates among them on the basis of general and often inflexible categories. His position is similar in some interesting respects to the "theory-as-conspiracy" argument presented in chapter 4, in that people (the organization's clients) stand in generally the same relationship to public administrators, in Biller's account, as administrators are to theorists. The similarity of the two conspiracies is illustrated by inserting, in brackets, substitute terms from the theory-as-conspiracy argument into the following excerpt from Biller's paper.

Recognizing that policies [general theories] on complex aggregated information are always "wrong" with respect to the preferences [definitons of the situation] of every person [administrator] to whom they are applied, . . . you would expect that we would concentrate on *limiting* the force of such policies [theories] to the specification of minima or "floors" made necessary by our joint action [understanding]. Rather than trying for "better" aggregated policies [general theories], we would try for "fewer" or more limited aggregated policies [general theories]. Such limitations would be as spare and minimal as possible, for the resources not consumed in their operation [development] would then be usable in non-aggregated [nongeneralized] and personspecific [administrator-specific] ways—that is, in a disaggregated fashion . . . (p. 154)

Professionalization [theorizing] provides that means by which we establish a common language, a vocabulary, a set of expectations and metaphors, an agreement on the standards of performance [valid knowledge], and other such matters that permit "quality" performances [theorizing] that are in some measure predictable precisely because they transcend particular persons [administrators] and circumstances. To become a professional [theorist] is to become comfortable with that set of things which one's colleagues and you can agree are to be taken seriously, and what is to be done about them when they are encountered. . . . (p. 156)

What must be remembered is that professionals [theorists] always have knowledge about "answers" derived from that aggregation of knowledge which the profession has [other theorists have] codified. Persons [administrators], in this sense, are quite opposite from professionals [theorists]. Persons [administrators] tend to experience increasingly unique problems and opportunities that produced for them the need to seek out the specialized services of professionals [theorists]. At the interface between persons [administrators] and professionals [theorists], each brings quite opposite though symmetrical definitions. The professional [theorist] brings *answers* codified from knowledge developed from the common experiences of many persons [administrators]. The person [administrator] brings *questions* that are uniquely contextuated in a lifetime's increasingly particularized experiences. . . . Persons [administrators] are different with respect to their unique biological and social histories. To be human [an administrator] is to be unique. . . . (p. 158)

Instead of trying to increase the quality of aggregated policies and organizations [general theories], we might ask how individualization [administrator-centered theory] might be increased while retaining the advantages that professionalization [theorizing] offers. *Basically this involves a process of disaggregation by which policies and organizations* [theories] *became smaller in scale, less comprehensive in aspiration, and thereby less homogeneous* [universal] *in how they carry forward their still fully professional* [theoretical] *orientations. Persons* [administrators] *become increasingly empowered to elicit performances* [from theorists] *relevant to their own unique situations and contexts.* (pp. 161–62)

To readers acquainted with the work of Carl Rogers,[17] an additional parallel should be evident between his "client-centered" approach to psychotherapy and the "disaggregated" strategy proposed by Biller. For each, the preferred approach is to discover the unique manner in which clients define their needs, feelings, and situations as the basis for a healthy professional-client relationship. This contrasts, for both therapeutic and administrative contexts, with approaches in which the professional imposes a common theory (policy) of how clients should behave or what kind of services or assistance they should receive.

CRITICAL ORGANIZATION DEVELOPMENT

Several features of action therapy are not altogether foreign to contemporary theory and practice concerning the role of organizational consultants. Some of the recent literature on organization development (OD), in particular, is cognizant of the crucial importance of the subjective meanings of organization members to improving organizational performance. The OD literature has traditionally reflected a strong concern with "process" issues,[18] although, with some exceptions, it has not stressed as heavily the critical and moral aspects of the consultant's role as does action therapy. In addition, some OD approaches, especially "grid" OD programs,[19] give evidence of perpetuating rather than eliminating the conspiracy of theory over practice.

The preceding discussion of the action therapist's role and, indeed, virtually all aspects of the Action paradigm that bear on the improvement of administrative practice suggest what might be called a "critical approach to organization development. Critical OD is not really a new approach to organization development, since most of its features may be found in, or readily inferred from, the current literature. Nor does it constitute a program or an explicitly formulated OD strategy. Critical OD, instead, constitutes a set of criteria or ground rules for judging the extent to which current OD practices are nonconspiratorial (i.e., consistent with the key assumptions about administrative theory and practice of the Action paradigm). Some contemporary OD theory and practice *is* conspiratorial and some is not.

The first criterion is that OD activities not be regarded *a priori,* either by the consultant or the client, as purely instrumental, that is, as a series of techniques for the attainment of ends such as increased productivity, job satisfaction, or improved morale. These ends may certainly *turn out* to be significant, depending on problem and situational definitions of the actors in the client organization; but this should not be assumed in advance. In addition to whatever instrumental or technical problems organization members may identify, the OD activities should also involve critical assessment of moral-ethical issues confronting the organization—as defined by its members as well as by its constituents.

Second, critical OD resembles what Kirkhart and White term the "situational-emergent" approach, as opposed to "grid OD." [20] Consultant strategies and interventions in the S-E approach are jointly determined (by the consultant and the client, including members of the client organization at varying levels of influence and authority) to fit the unique problems and contexts confronted by the client. Grid OD efforts, on the other hand, tend to enhance the theorist-client conspiracy by permitting the theorist to formulate unilaterally both the strategies to be used and the theory or assumptions on which the strategies are based.

Third, apart from its general theoretical assumption of the importance of clarifying and negotiating subjective meanings regarding organizational values and processes, critical OD relies mainly on the usually implicit "theories" extant within the client organization. Examples of such theories include prevailing beliefs about *power and influence* (e.g., who has it and how does one get it?), assumptions about *cause and effect* (e.g., what does it take to get ahead or to get things done in the organization?), and norms and values (e.g., what styles of personal behavior are perceived as legitimate and what does or should the organization stand for?).[21]

Taken together, these three criteria suggest a fourth criterion for critical OD, namely, that organizational development be viewed generically as all activities and technologies, related to both "substance" and "process," affecting the improvement of administrative practice. This is not proposed in the hope of elevating to a loftier status the role of OD consultants, but to emphasize the vital interdependence among organizational processes, values, and technology. Recognition of such interdependence would serve the dual purpose of broadening the conception of OD beyond that of a "human relations" activity or "applied sensitivity training." In addition, it might force a fuller consideration of normative, cultural, and political constraints in organizations on the effectiveness of proposed technological and instrumental solutions to problems.

In fairness, it should be noted that, despite the "human relations" flavor, still, of much OD theory and practice, similar suggestions are appearing with increasing frequency in the literature of both organization development and applied organizational technology. Some crucial tasks, it seems, are to examine ways in which process and technical consultants might be encouraged to collaborate with one another in their consulting roles; and also to explore strategies for gaining acceptance by their clients of the necessity to view organization development in this expanded context.

In Kuhn's description of scientific progress, paradigms provide the ground rules for the conduct of "normal science"—the solving of puzzles using methods and assumptions implied by the paradigm.[22] Paradigms, in the natural sciences, establish not only the proper methods of inquiry but also the standards for determining the *correctness* of solutions to problems. Classical public administration is similar to Kuhn's analysis of natural science paradigms in two important respects. First, the basic assumptions and ground rules of scientific paradigms correspond roughly to the Classical paradigm's belief that normative issues, both about "substantive" ends and about the institutional processes for deciding them, should be resolved prior to the conduct of administrative practice. Later defenders of the Classical paradigm often concede that this premise is complicated in the real world by the intrusion of political, cultural, and interpersonal "variables." But these are regarded as regrettable, although to some extent manageable, impediments to effective policy formulation and administration. Second, the improvement of administrative practice in the Classical paradigm is seen roughly as the equivalent to normal science; that is, practice is an instrumental function whose correctness is determined by criteria of efficiency and obedience (accountability).

The Action paradigm disputes the appropriateness of the natural science metaphor for understanding public administration both as a branch of social science and, most especially, as a category of social practice. Paradigms dealing with social science, theory, and practice cannot reasonably be expected to reduce the practice of administration to such normatively uncomplicated terms; nor can they promise answers or set standards of correctness, in any definitive sense, for judging *particular* administrative acts.

Instead, the construction of a paradigm should be seen as a search for a *moral context,* one that may help to clarify possibilities for and constraints upon cooperative action. It should be emphasized, however, that this apparently more modest requirement for public administration paradigms is evidence neither of the inherent inadequacy of social science theory nor of the intractability of problems related to administrative practice. The denial of lawlike explanations of administrative behavior serves, instead, to illustrate that administrators, as all social actors, freely choose, in an existential sense, to act as they do based on their subjective appreciation of unique and problematic contexts. Moreover, the rejection of the possibility, as well as the desirability, of ultimate or definitve standards of correctness for administrative acts has the virtue of reminding us that administrators, and members of organizations generally, bear personal responsibility for their actions. Instead of proposing utopian visions of the future, which would be boring and oppressive in any event, the arguments offered here have emphasized the importance of creating and institutionalizing processes of social interaction in which the search for meaning and community may take place in a more humane manner.

NOTES

1. Dwight Waldo, "Scope of the Theory of Public Administration," in *Theory and Practice of Public Administration*, ed. James C. Charlesworth (Philadelphia: *Annals of the American Society of Political and Social Science*, 1968), pp. 6–22.

2. Stephen K. Bailey, "Objectives of the Theory of Public Administration," in Charlesworth, *Theory and Practice*, pp. 128–39.

3. Frederick C. Thayer, "Epistemology as Organization Theory," in *Organization Theory and the New Public Administration*, ed. Carl Bellone (Boston: Allyn and Bacon, 1980), pp. 113–39.

4. David Silverman, *The Theory of Organizations* (New York: Basic Books, 1971).

5. Max Weber, *The Methodology of the Social Sciences*, trans. and ed. Edward Shils and Henry A. Finch (New York: Free Press, 1949), p. 90.

6. Geoffrey Vickers, *Dialogue, The Newsletter of the Public Administration Theory Network* 1, no. 3 (January/February 1979): 3–4.

7. Bailey, "Objectives of the Theory," p. 135.

8. Vaughan Blankenship, "Public Administration and the Challenge to Reason," in *Public Administration in a Time of Turbulence*, ed. Dwight Waldo (Scranton, Pa.: Chandler, 1971), p. 193.

9. Ibid., pp. 197–98.

10. Ibid., p. 199.

11. Ibid.

12. Orion White, "The Concept of Administrative Praxis," *Journal of Comparative Administration* 5 (May 1973): 55–86.

13. Bayard L. Catron and Michael M. Harmon, "Action Theory in Practice: Toward Theory without Conspiracy" (paper presented at the Annual Meeting of the Americal Society for Public Administration, Phoenix, Arizona, April 1978), pp. 13–16.

14. Ibid., p. 16.

15. This activity is very similar to what is commonly referred to as "action research." For a helpful discussion, see Neely Gardner, "Action Training and Research: Something Old and Something New," *Public Administration Review* 34 (March/April 1974): 106–15.

16. Robert P. Biller, "Toward Public Administration Rather Than an Administration of Publics: Strategies of Accountable Disaggregation to Achieve Human Scale and Efficacy, and Live within the Natural Limits of Intelligence and other Scarce Resources," in *Agenda for Public Administration,* ed. Ross Clayton and William B. Storm (Los Angeles: University of Southern California Press, 1979), pp. 151–72.

17. Carl R. Rogers, *Client-Centered Therapy* (Boston: Houghton Mifflin, 1951).

18. See Edgar Schein, *Process Consultation* (Reading, Mass.: Addison-Wesley, 1969).

19. Robert Blake and Jane Mouton, *Building a Dynamic Corporation Through Grid Organization Development* (Reading, Mass.: Addison-Wesley, 1969).

20. Larry Kirkhart and Orion F. White, Jr., "The Future of Organization Development," *Public Administration Review* 34 (March/April 1974): 129–40.

21. Chris Argyris and Donald Schon, *Theory in Practice* (San Francisco: Jossey Bass, 1974).

22. Thomas S. Kuhn, *The Structure of Scientific Revolutions* (2nd ed.; Chicago: University of Chicago Press, 1970).

Index